Pathways
to Cultural
Awareness

Editors
George and Louise Spindler

Pathways to Cultural Awareness

Cultural Therapy With Teachers and Students

CORWIN PRESS, INC.
A Sage Publications Company
Thousand Oaks, California

For information address:

Corwin Press, Inc.
A Sage Publications Company
2455 Teller Road
Thousand Oaks, California 91320

SAGE Publications Ltd.
6 Bonhill Street
London EC2A 4PU
United Kingdom

SAGE Publications India Pvt. Ltd.
M-32 Market
Greater Kailash I
New Delhi 110 048 India

Printed in the United States of America

Library of Congress Cataloging-in-Publication Data

Spindler, George Dearborn.
    Pathways to cultural awareness: cultural therapy with teachers
and students / George and Louise Spindler.
        p. cm.
    Includes bibliographical references and index.
    ISBN 0-8039-6108-1.—ISBN 0-8039-6109-X (pbk.)
    1. Multicultural education—United States. 2. Educational
anthropology—United States. 3. Cross-cultural counseling—United
States. I. Spindler, Louise S. II. Title.
LC1099.3.S68 1994
370.19'6'0973—dc20   93-6440
                                                                                    CIP

94 95 96 97 10 9 8 7 6 5 4 3 2 1

Sage Production Editor: Rebecca Holland

Contents

Foreword

I wonder what of the contemporary anthropological work will be recorded by future generations as the most significant in the history of the social sciences. Will, for example, they know that George and Louise Spindler edited several hundred case studies? Will they read the books written in honor of the Spindlers? Will they ever know that George and Louise established on solid grounds the new field of educational anthropology? It is likely that the Spindler name will be associated with the Council on Anthropology and Education because of the scholarship award named after George and Louise. But will tomorrow's educational anthropologists ever know that a number of organizations, such as the American Educational Research Association, bestowed upon the Spindlers excellence awards for their research? Perhaps there is no way to know for sure. But I believe that the Spindlers' *Pathways to Cultural Awareness* is a contribution that the next generations will never forget. Cultural therapy is visionary and intuitive in its focus on the need to heal. Yes, the entirety of humankind needs to heal from its multiple wounds, conflicts, and contradictions, and the way to get some healing is through a better understanding of the nature of local cultures and interethnic relations. This volume represents a significant, eloquent, and timely statement on the universal need to heal and is a testimony to the Spindlers' keen sense of the role that the social sciences should play in the healing of all humankind.

Could anybody really question the universal need for healing? The daily stories about hatred, cruelty, war, and conflict dividing nations, regions, states, cities, and neighborhoods reveal clearly

the open wounds and hurts of many. We all carry profound emotional injuries that affect another deeper sense of self and the
ability to recognize who we are individually and collectively. George
advanced the notions of the "enduring self" and the "situated self"
in an effort to explain the complexity of modern life facing individuals who undergo rapid social and cultural change; people strive
to arrive at an integrated self-concept through the process of social
identification. Everyone asks the questions, "Who really am I? Am
I an American?" or "What does it mean to be an American?" As
we go through a series of changes and fundamental adaptations
to new living environments, we depart further and further from
our initial "enduring self," the identity we acquired during the
early years of socialization at home. The traumatic path that we
follow from infancy to present adult life results in confusion,
insecurity, and marginalization. Many Americans lack self-confidence and hope and feel a profound bitterness about their present
situations. These feelings, a desire to know more about their cultural
background, and their efforts to resolve problems of social and
cultural identification suggest the need for cultural therapy.

The assumptions at the heart of cultural therapy as a healing
process are that for healing to take place there has to be an
acceptance of the self based on reflective knowledge, a profound
historical and cultural sense of one's own family, of its roots, its
ethnicity, and social, linguistic, and religious background. Theo-
retically, cultural therapy does not assume that each member of
humankind needs psychotherapy; it does assume that much of the
sad state of affairs in the world today is related to social and
cultural conflicts and assumptions not examined reflectively. Cultural reflective analysis is based on the premise that the personal and
collective empowerment of many individuals (especially those from
low-income, racial, and ethnic backgrounds) depends on their ability
to reflect on, and to act within, the appropriate sociohistorical context that surrounds critical life events, particularly those that have
the potential for hurting us the most.

The condition sine qua non for healing from hurts caused by
racism, prejudice, and bigotry, for example, is possession of cultural knowledge and understanding of the nature of human be-

havior and the mediating role of language and culture in the acquisition of all knowledge. Cultural therapy helps to see the ethnocentrism of individuals and groups who learn to hate and to dehumanize others as a means to exploit the powerless and move up the socioeconomic ladder. Cultural therapy can also help in understanding the role of religion in people's lives, the possible misinterpretation of people's religious behavior, and the frequent neglect of people's rights and even dehumanization linked to religious beliefs. We can follow, for example, the history of Europeans in the New World during the sixteenth, seventeenth, and nineteenth centuries, or we can read about recent historical events (such as the Holocaust), or we can just read the daily newspapers or watch TV coverage of atrocities that members of the human species commit against other fellow members. Academic disciplines have mirrored the colonial mentality of Western societies and have contributed to the stereotyping and degradation of some ethnic groups. Some nineteenth-century anthropologists, for example, postulated unilineal cultural evolution, which exalted the genetic/biological superiority of white European groups over others. Some psychologists, both from the last and this century, defended principles of eugenics and the need to assess the mental deficiencies attributed to persons of color or some European immigrants. It was in the context of both unconscious and conscious racism, in the 1950s, that the Spindlers began to ask questions about cultural assumptions, about interactional patterns, perceptual frames in the interpretation of people's behavior, interethnic interactions, and the role of schools in the disempowerment of the underclass.

Cultural therapy represents the fruit of historical analysis of American culture and is a bold statement on the dangers of the ethnocentrism that is embedded in the dominance of a single cultural and subcultural group. The Spindlers kept reminding us with their writings and their lives that, regardless of the color of our skin and "accents," we all belong to a single human species and that America is quintessentially heterogeneous—culturally and linguistically diverse. The hurt of any member of the human species is the hurt of all of us, and the healing of those who are hurt requires a recognition of their cultural histories and our solidarity on this planet. George and Louise Spindler, as did Paulo Freire and others, suggest that, to come to terms with the meaning of being human and free and to share our cultural diversity in schools and society, we all must first understand better our ethnic cultures and personal histories.

As human life becomes increasingly complex and tense in modern times, with high technology, rapid communication, the split-second transfer of massive amounts of data, unimagined military power for destruction, and most of all, the contrast between the rich and poor becoming so conspicuous and overwhelming, George and Louise point out, with candor and courage, that in America and many other countries social institutions are neglecting children and their home and school learning environments for selfish and myopic reasons. Children are true victims of continued slavery and oppression in many countries, and victims of our public ignorance and silence. Children have no voice; many are born and die young without ever knowing the meaning of being human or having the right to live their lives free of fear and enjoying the excitement of learning. Rather than writing technical books and displaying their massive ethnographic knowledge of peoples around the world, George and Louise have preferred to make us reflect on our humanity by looking at each other's cultural values. With a keen sense of historical criticism, George and Louise Spindler analyzed the low achievement of minorities in the context of cultural discontinuities and change and showed us that children often have to engage in a major cognitive and cultural reorganization of their learning modes. Indeed, the Spindlers have done a lot more; they have modeled for us the practice of cultural therapy by giving themselves to us, with generosity, openness, care for all of us, total honesty about their feelings and an uncanny ability to help us understand difficult ideas without patronizing us. They mentored many of us and encouraged our intellectual growth without demanding acceptance of their ideas or compliance with academic codes of appropriate behavior. Their genuine love for all of us, a truly human experience of cultural therapy, has helped heal other wounds and opened up for us the opportunity to find a home in academia. George and Louise have demonstrated in their writing and lives the art of living in a multicultural society, pursuing systematic and rigorous cross-cultural studies, and using it to find who we really are and to accept ourselves individually and collectively.

This book is a major effort by the Spindlers and 12 others (most of them former students of theirs at Stanford, Wisconsin, or the University of California at Santa Barbara) who have explored the application of cultural therapy in their culturally diverse institutions. It will long be recognized as a landmark in the continuing development of cultural interpretations and application to educational processes. My colleagues around the world will appreciate it as a significant contribution to the anthropology of education and to the improvement of relations among ethnic groups and between the dominant culture and the diverse constituents of school populations.

Henry T. Trueba
Dean of the School of Education,
University of Wisconsin

Preface

What this book is *not* about is the remediation of minority cultures and persons to fit mainstream concepts of rightness. Rather, what it *is* about is ways of increasing awareness among teachers, and among students, of the ways the culture of the school and classroom, the culture of teaching, peer culture, and personal culture, influence perceptions of self and others, particularly in culturally diverse schools. Teachers carry into the classroom their personal cultural background. They perceive students, all of whom are cultural agents, with inevitable prejudice and preconception. Students likewise come to school with personal cultural backgrounds that influence their perception of teachers, other students, and the school itself. Together students and teachers construct, mostly without being conscious of doing it, an environment of meanings enacted in individual and group behaviors, of conflict and accommodation, rejection and acceptance, alienation and withdrawal.

Cultural therapy, in its manifold forms, increases awareness of this constructed cultural environment and one's position in it. Our underlying assumption is that this awareness makes possible informed choice that will lead to less tension and a more productive environment for social behavior and learning.

It is important to understand that we are not fabricating a new way of making students conform to the school, to the classroom, or to the teacher. In the politically charged atmosphere of today, such a preconception would be fatal to understanding the complex and subtle issues and processes that the contributors to this volume are discussing.

Acknowledgments

The idea for this book emerged from a 2-day conference on schools and cultural diversity held at Stanford in October 1991 under the auspices of the Center for Research on the Context of Secondary Teaching (CRC), School of Education, Stanford University. Patricia Phelan, an associate of the CRC, organized and directed the conference. Those invited to attend and participate included eight academic personnel, four from Stanford and four from the University of Wisconsin and the University of California at San Diego, at Davis, and at Riverside. Other sectors of the community represented were the superintendency, high school staff, counseling, and special services. We thank all of the people who participated in the conference. Every one of them contributed to our understanding of what we are trying to do with cultural therapy. The balance of theorists and practitioners guaranteed that theory and praxis would be joined at the conference, and this orientation has persisted in our development of this book.

Certain individuals made special contributions to this book through their counsel and support as well as their criticism. There are many, but we think particularly of Patricia Phelan, Henry Trueba, Pete Mesa, Reba Page, Ray McDermott, Shelley Goldman, Christine Finnan, Ann Davidson, Concha Delgado-Gaitan, and Harry Wolcott.

At Corwin Press, we are indebted to Gracia Alkema, who was receptive to the idea of the book from the start, and the Production Editor, Rebecca Holland.

We deeply appreciate all the help we have received from everyone.

Introduction

This book is dedicated to the hope that if we can achieve better understanding of ourselves as teachers we can teach others better, especially those unlike ourselves in ethnicity, social class, and culture. It is also dedicated to the hope that, if students understand themselves and their situations better, they can learn with less rancor and resistance.

As anthropologists, we regard teachers and students, both, as cultural agents. They bring to school, and schooling, preoccupations, preconceptions, assumptions, and habits that have been acquired by experience in culturally framed encounters with parents, peers, and the myriad "others" in contemporary society, including the mass media. In the school and during the schooling process, they assign meanings and consciously as well as unconsciously create cultures. They create school culture, classroom culture, peer and clique culture, and a pervasive culture of teacher-student relationships.

This book is devoted to an attempt to understand these complex processes. Our colleagues have written nine chapters, each focused on certain aspects of cultural therapy, as drawn from Chapter 1, where we set forth a framework for the process. We start with Phelan and Davidson's "Looking Across Borders: Students' Investigations of Family, Peer, and School Worlds as Cultural Therapy." They detail student reactions to "cases" drawn from their peers' negotiation of discontinuities and conflicts between their experiential worlds, in the context of group discussions. How this process may be seen as cultural therapy is clear. We end the book with Frank Logan's chapter on a 10-day program of intensive cultural therapy with youths who have experienced the worst that our culture has to inflict on children and young people.

Cultural therapy, for us, has been directed primarily at teachers or teachers-to-be. It started with Roger Harker, a young fifth-grade teacher in a California school in the early 1950s. Roger volunteered as a "case" to be studied, as most teachers, administrators, and counselors did who were contacted by the "Stanford Consultation Service" headed by Dr. Robert Nelson Bush of the School of Education at Stanford University during that period. The project was a combination of research and consultation to improve professional competence, by a team composed of Dr. Bush, a psychiatrist, a sociologist, an anthropologist (George), and various graduate students in education and the social sciences. George was assigned Roger Harker as a "case study," to be studied "anthropologically," whatever that was! Two afternoons and some mornings were devoted to a field study of nearly 5 months' duration.

At first, the field study was tedious, in fact, downright boring. George had just returned from another summer's fieldwork with the Menominee Indians of Northern Wisconsin. He had participated, in company with the most "traditional" Menominee, in the Medicine Lodge and Peyote Cult, attended funerals, gone to the "Chief's Dancing Ritual," attended feasts, and in general had lived their way of life. He and Louise had traveled, with Menominee companions, through the north-central states, interacting with Chippewa, Potowatomi, Winnebago, and Sauk and Fox on the "Indian Circuit."

To sit in a standard fifth-grade classroom very much like George's own fifth-grade classroom was a real comedown, as far as excitement was concerned. What to observe? What to do ethnography on? What to interview about? And who cares?

Then one afternoon, a pattern began to emerge and the classroom leapt to anthropological life. Roger, it appeared, was interacting differently with various students and these students represented different social statuses and various ethnic groups.

To make a long story short, and indeed it is a long story (see the references), Roger was—by his nods, smiles, winks, touches, postures, eye engagements, tone of voice, frequency of interaction, and voiced perceptions (to the ethnographer) of overall "adjustment," social position in the classroom, and peer liking—encouraging children who were his cultural counterparts (white, middle and upper middle class) and discouraging those who were different or, in subtle ways, oppositional to him and his culture.

He was quite unaware of what he was doing. In fact, he took special pride in being "fair to all my students," "open to their problems," in "not having favorites." Nor were his superiors at all aware of his selective behavior as a teacher, or, if they saw it, they thought it was all right. They ranked him high on all dimensions, as he ranked himself, and as he ranked how they would rank him. He was destined to move into administration soon, with enthusiastic approval.

It was George's responsibility as the team member doing the case study to give Roger the results of our work. He had volunteered himself and his classroom for study with the understanding that the experience would contribute to his professional growth. It did, indeed, but not exactly in the way he had expected.

George gave him the results of the study. It was clear, in the complex body of data collected, that Roger was acting out his own culturally phrased preconceptions and expectations, thus favoring some of the children and not others, as we have said. The first session of data feedback ended in his leaving in a huff. He didn't believe that he was denying his own idealistic, stated objectives by his behavior in the classroom and his declared perceptions of individual children. But he returned for the next session and the one after that, and yet more. He was determined to get what benefit he could from the experience, however distasteful and threatening it might be. He came to accept his unintentional biases, and to understand their source, and learned not to blame himself for them. *It became a professional matter.* We weren't dealing with his "personality" or his relationships with his mother; we were dealing with his culture and how it influenced his perceptions of and behavior toward the children in his classroom. He could improve his ability to relate to children who came from diverse backgrounds, some quite different than his own.

There is much more to be said about Roger Harker and it has been said in published form and for years in the lecture hall and classroom at Stanford and elsewhere. This case has become a metaphor for a range of phenomena centered on the unicultural teacher and the culturally diverse class. It is where *cultural therapy* was born, or at least our version of it.[1]

The first publication growing directly out of the experience with Roger, enhanced by studies of other teachers and schools, was *The Transmission of American Culture* (1959), a transcription of the Third Burton Lecture on elementary education at Harvard University in 1957. The title is an honest reflection of the importance George assigned to the observation and analysis of this teacher, who was effectively teaching only a minority of his students, and they weren't the minority students! If schooling was intended as a way of co-opting and cultivating the energies and intelligence of all the children, irrespective of race, creed, color, or social class, for the benefit of our whole society, it was not working, to the extent that the "Roger Harker syndrome" was widespread (and all of our experience indicated that indeed it was). The costs of failure have been enormous and we are today reaping a full harvest.

The model that emerged early in our careers as educational anthropologists has influenced much of what we have done in our studies of schooling at home and abroad. Our attention has been directed at teachers and teaching—their culture(s) and its selective projection in classroom behavior. Students were considered, and their perceptions of the teacher, each other, and themselves, elicited, but they were not the main focus. We therefore thought of cultural therapy, when we did think of it, as directed at teachers.

This book departs from that model and both enlarges it and confronts it. In the chapters that follow, the teacher is an actor on the stage, but not necessarily the lead in the play.

Phelan and Davidson describe and analyze group discussions by high school students reacting to "cases" of their peers negotiating discontinuities among their experienced cultural "worlds" as cultural therapy. Schram does an intensive study of a teacher with a Cuban refugee background who, unlike most of the faculty in a small New England town high school, identifies strongly with the Laotian refugee students. Her relations with the faculty, with the Laotian students, and with the schooling-resistant lower status American students are a complex whole that touches upon central questions of identity, motivation, and marginality in school life, for both students and teachers. Finnan, engaged in an accelerated schools project, finds that the school culture was an essential dimension that could block or promote change. How the actors in this scene found out about culture in their school, and how this culture could and did change, is described reflectively. Davidson provides extensive excerpts from in-depth interviews with an African American male who moved from St. Louis to California and reconstituted his situated self, and with a Latina who does well academically but feels at times quite misplaced and unrelated to non-Hispanics. The interviews are regarded as a form of cultural therapy for these two young people. Hauser describes her partial failure to engage the faculty of a small high school coping with an influx of refugees in a culturally "reflective" self-examination. She examines the reasons for her "failure." García-Castañón tells us how he used his own experience as a Chicano to help Hmong refugee-migrants to understand what was happening to them and their children, and why they felt about it as they did. Wilson builds bridges between counselors and students of culturally diverse backgrounds. Goldman, Chaiklin, and McDermott show how a form of cultural "therapy" without classroom, students, and teachers, or even a school, can be instigated through E-mail. Logan, in a fitting climax to the preceding chapters, reports on 10 strenuous days in a program where abused, troubled youths, both male and female, tell their stories to each other and strip away their street and gang identities—at least temporarily. He produces a telling critique of some of the model's propositions—the radical nature of these youths' experience goes beyond the capacity of the model to explain, at certain points, what happens.

The diversity of approaches to and interpretations of "cultural therapy" in these chapters is stimulating and challenging. The possibilities seem endless. And yet, at precisely this moment, it is time to remember that *therapy* won't cure deficits in funding, weak professionalization, or inadequate resources. It won't cure the disparate inequities in the distribution of American capital and opportunity or the miserable sinkholes of the inner city. Cultural therapy is something positive we can do more of to make things a little better—for some schools, some classrooms, some individuals, a lot better. But it is not a panacea.

Cultural therapy must be seen for what it is—a way of helping teachers and students to cope with cultural diversity and inequity in our society through the mediation of the school as a central institution for cultural transmission and maintenance. Surely no reader is unaware that most public schools in metropolitan centers are no longer dominantly European American, and that, by 2020 A.D. or sooner, the demographic profile will have shifted so that this ethnic group will no longer be the majority nationally. This development is unmatched by any contemporary European nation, though all are experiencing the impact of ethnic minorities in public institutions, especially the schools. We have analyzed the relationships in the United States in *The American Cultural Dialogue and Its Transmission* (Spindler, Spindler, Trueba, & Williams, 1990).

The shape of cultural therapy as we have conceived of it is presented in the next chapter. It is the product of our experience as field anthropologists over the years in five cultures and in their schools in the United States, Canada, and Germany. We take a strong cultural position in the presentation but include attention to the "self" and discuss the enduring self, the situated self, and self-efficacy as processes in adaptation that require attention in an effort to understand students and teachers as they interact with each other and among themselves in the context of the school.

Each author has read and discussed this framework, this model, with us, and has included attention to some part of it in his or her analysis. This gives this volume a degree of continuity and common purpose at the same time that it provides an opportunity for critical evaluation of the model.

We have requested that each author provide biographical information and a portrait—formal or informal to taste. It is important that identities be revealed in a volume dedicated to cultural therapy.

We hope that readers will share some of the enjoyment and inspiration we have experienced as they engage with the chapters of this book following our presentation of the framework. Each chapter presents a situation and processes in which the author has been intimately involved. Each is a pioneering, exploratory attempt to address the need for and utility of cultural therapy. Bon voyage!

Note

1. Henry Trueba has recently written at length on cultural therapy as one way to help "heal America" (Trueba, Rodriguez, Sou, & Cintron, 1993). He supplies in this reference relevant annotated references for background reading for anyone interested in cultural therapy.

References

Spindler, G. (1959). *The transmission of American culture* (Third Burton Lecture in Elementary Education). Cambridge, MA: Harvard University Press.

Spindler, G., & Spindler, L. (with Trueba, H., & Williams, M.). (1990). *The American cultural dialogue and its transmission.* London: Falmer.

Trueba, H., Rodriguez, C., Sou, Y., & Cintron, J. (1993). *Healing multicultural America: Mexican immigrants rise to power in rural California*. London: Falmer.

George and Louise Spindler

"What is Cultural Therapy" by George and Louise Spindler is reprinted
with minor changes by permission of the publisher from *Renegotiating
Cultural Diversity in American Schools*, edited by P. Phelan and A. L. Davidson, 1993, New York: Teacher's College Press. Copyright 1993 by Teacher's
College, Columbia University. All rights reserved.

1

What Is Cultural Therapy?

GEORGE AND LOUISE SPINDLER

George and **Louise Spindler,** both on the faculty of Stanford University and as visiting professors at the University of Wisconsin at Madison and the University of California at Santa Barbara, have collaborated since the beginning of their careers in research, publication, and teaching. Their interests include educational anthropology, psychological anthropology, and studies of culture change and modernization. Louise is a pioneer in the study of women's adaptations to culture change. They have lived and worked as anthropologists in three American Indian communities, the Rems Valley in Southern Germany and its schools, and communities and their schools in Wisconsin and California. They have edited more than 200 publications in cultural and educational anthropology, many of them in their series Case Studies in Cultural Anthropology. They have also edited and contributed to five major publications in educational anthropology used widely in this field as texts. In 1978 George received the Lloyd Dinkelspiel Award at Stanford University for outstanding contributions to undergraduate education and in 1984 was presented the annual award for outstanding leadership in publication, administration, and scholarship by the International Association for Diplomacy and Third World Anthropologists. In 1992 he received the Distinguished Career Contribution Award by the Committee on the Role and Status of Minorities in educational research of the American Education Research Association. In 1988 the George and Louise Spindler Award for Outstanding Contributions to the anthropology of education was established by the Council for Anthropology and Education of the American Anthropological Association. Between them, they have taught every grade, from kindergarten to the advanced graduate level. They enjoy teaching and are committed to its study and improvement.

Our basic premise is that culture is not simply "a factor," or "an influence," or a "a dimension" but that it is in process, in everything that we do, say, or think in or out of school. As a teacher, a gifted teacher, a mediocre teacher, a prejudiced teacher, a student, a delinquent, a superlatively good student, a miserably inept student, or an antagonistic, alienated, or resistive student, we are caught up in cultural processes. With this in mind, we designate the school a mandated cultural process and the teacher a cultural agent. Of course, the school is also a political or a social institution and a lot else.

We regard education as a calculated interference with learning. This applies to all education but particularly to that which is the most massive interference in learning in Western society, and excepting for total institutions in Erving Goffman's sense such as prisons and monasteries, the most massive interference cross-culturally—namely, the "school." What we intend to convey is that schools teach selected materials, skills, and ideas. They also carefully exclude a great deal of cultural content that is being or could be learned by the students. Schools define what is not to be taught and what is not to be learned as well as what is taught and learned. A great deal goes on in schools other than calculated *intervention* (which we will now use rather than *interference*) in learning. The calculated interventions themselves have unanticipated consequences. The students learn a great deal from each other that teachers don't control. Students also bring to school a great deal of learning that teachers would rather they hadn't acquired. A combination of what children bring to school and what they learn from each other causes teachers a great deal of trouble. It is "trouble" with which we are concerned in this chapter.

AUTHORS' NOTE: We wish to acknowledge the advice, reactions, and criticisms by colleagues and students at Stanford, the University of California at Davis, Sonoma State University, and the California State University at Sacramento on the occasion of various presentations and colloquia on cultural therapy and particularly Frank Logan, Patricia Phelan, Ann Locke Davidson, Henry Trueba, Luize Amodeo, Forrest Davis, and all of the participants in the workshops at the California State University at Sacramento.

Our strategy will be to describe and discuss certain models that we have generated in our research over the years in our attempts to understand how human beings adapt to changing circumstances in their lives. The chapter has a certain egocentric quality as we are not directly concerned with the models our colleagues have generated, though they have certainly been helpful.[1] We offer this chapter and the model of cultural therapy as *in process*, exploratory, in places tentative. We intend it as a way of getting into a dynamic and significant area of relationships and communication that is present in various forms in all schools, in schooling, and in the act of teaching. We will doubtless modify our thinking as we receive feedback and as we and our colleagues attempt further applications of the model in school situations.

Much of what we have done as anthropologists of education, as teachers of anthropology, as consultants in schools, and as authors of books and papers is intended to be "cultural therapy." We have, for example, long taught the introductory course in cultural anthropology to Stanford students as a form of cultural therapy—to widen their cultural horizons and their appreciation of diverse lifeways. We teach education graduate students ethnographic methods and self-examination as approaches to understanding cultural diversity. We work as consultants with individual teachers or with faculty groups through simulations of cultural experience and interpretation designed to increase understanding of cultural diversity. We have rarely labeled what we do as such. When we do label anything we have done "cultural therapy," people get quite excited and want to know very specifically what we mean by it. The answer that we just gave, that cultural therapy is virtually everything that we do as professional anthropologists, is usually not very satisfying. One of our purposes in this chapter will be to clarify what we do mean by this phrase.

As a preliminary orientation, we can state that cultural therapy is a process of bringing one's own culture, in its manifold forms—assumptions, goals, values, beliefs, and communicative modes—to a level of awareness that permits one to perceive it as a potential bias in social interaction and in the acquisition or transmission of skills and knowledge—what we later refer to as "instrumental competencies." At the same time, one's own culture, brought to this level of awareness, is perceived in relation to the "other" culture, so that potential conflicts, misunderstandings, and "blind spots" in the perception and interpretation of behavior may be anticipated. One's culture as well as the "other's" culture become a "third presence," removed somewhat from the person, so that one's actions can be taken as "caused" by one's culture and the interaction with the "other" and not by one's personality. A certain comforting distance and objectification becomes possible, and relationships, such as those between teachers and students, can be explored without getting personal (and upset) about it.

In our work with individual teachers, we have found, except in cases where psychopathology is indicated, that the sociocultural position and experience of the individual is a better predictor of classroom behavior, particularly in respect to selective bias (on the part of the teacher) in perception of and interaction with students, than psychological factors as such, as indicated by psychological tests or interviews. In the case of our "classic" fifth-grade teacher, Roger Harker, for example, his troubled relationships and identity problems with his father, and his overidentification with his mother and sister, did not have significant effects on his behavior as a teacher, but his narrow middle-upper-middle class, white, Protestant cultural background did (Spindler & Spindler, 1990).

Doing cultural therapy, as we do it, has psychological concomitants, but they are not the focus. The focus is the culture of the person and the way it biases relationships with children in classrooms. For teachers, cultural therapy can be used to increase awareness of the cultural assumptions that they bring to the classroom that affect their behavior and their interactions with students—particularly students of color. For teachers, cultural therapy is an intervention that can be used as a first step to affect and change behaviors, attitudes, and assumptions that are biased (and often discriminatory) and thus detrimental to students whose cultural backgrounds are different than the teachers' own. Our use of cultural therapy has been directed at helping teachers and other adults to understand their own cultural position and to reflect on and analyze the reasons they might find the behavior of a culturally different person objectionable, shocking, and/or irritating.

For students, cultural therapy is essentially a means of "consciousness-raising"—that is, to make explicit unequal power relationships in the classroom, the school, and the larger society. Further, cultural therapy can be used to help students clarify the steps necessary to obtain the instrumental competencies they need to gain access to opportunities within the school system (and, we hope, the larger society). For example, many students of color do not have access to the "cultural capital" necessary to compete for equal resources, knowledge, and experiences. The goal of "cultural therapy" for students (particularly minority students) is to empower rather than blame them.

The experiences of our colleagues working with minority youth suggest that many students fault themselves for their inability to navigate the educational system. Almost none are aware of the implications of tracking or are cognizant of the fact that they often receive inadequate help and assistance with respect to course work, college application procedures, and so forth, or that attitudes, values, and beliefs, as well as pedagogical methods and school policies, frequently mitigate their ability to succeed. Cultural therapy, as we conceptualize it, is intended as a method to increase students' understanding of the factors that work against them and to empower them to fight against the obstacles they encounter (rather than blaming themselves or engaging in behaviors that impede their access to the skills and competencies necessary to ensure their access to power and opportunity).

With this preliminary understanding in hand, we can turn to certain experiences and results from our field research as anthropologists in the manifold context of education.

Reflective Interviewing in Schoenhausen and Roseville

For some years, we have been researching in Schoenhausen, a village of about 2,000 in a semirural but urbanizing area in *Land* Baden Württemburg, Southern Germany. Schoenhausen was known, and still is to a considerable degree, as an *ausgesprochner Weinort* (emphatically a wine-making place). The native-born are Swaebish and Protestant. The *Grundschule* (elementary school) is charged with the responsibility of educating all of the children and preparing them for a changing Germany and world. Its 127 children are distributed in four grades staffed by six teachers and a *Rektor* (principal) and various other special services personnel.

The Roseville Elementary School, located in central Wisconsin, includes kindergarten through eighth grade and is somewhat larger than the Schoenhausen school but is comparable in every other respect. The school district is rural but has many commuters who work in nearby towns, some of them as many as 40 or 50 miles distant. The majority of the children attending the school come from small dairy farms. The predominant ethnicity of the Roseville School District is German.

Over the years, we have applied many different research techniques, some of which will appear in other parts of this chapter, but for our purpose at the moment we wish to emphasize some material that came out of an interview technique that we have most recently developed—the "cross-cultural comparative reflective interview" (CCCRI). It was applied in Schoenhausen for the first time in 1985 and had been applied in Roseville in 1983 and subsequently.[2] The CCCRI is designed to stimulate dialogue about pivotal concerns on the part of natives in comparable cultural systems. Some form of audiovisual material representing two cultures (conceivably more) is used to "bracket" the interview. That is, the interview is conducted as an inquiry into the perceptions, by the native, of his or her own situation and that of the "other," and the assumptions revealed in reflections about those perceptions. We regard both the perceptions and the assumptions as cultural phenomena.

We had taken films in both the Schoenhausen and the Roseville classrooms and our basic procedure was to show these films to our interviewees and thus elicit reflective discussion of their own and the other situations. We did this with teachers, administrators, and the children in both research sites. There is a very rich body of material that was generated by these interviews and we will select

only a few instances from interviews with two teachers, one in the
Schoenhausen school and one in Roseville.

The Roseville School (Mrs. Schiller)

GLS: Now with respect to your underlying objectives as a teacher, that
is, Linda Schiller as a teacher, not necessarily what you get in the
education courses, what would you say your basic purpose is?

Mrs. Schiller: To teach them to be an individual, to be all they can, to
their limits of their abilities and if I can get them to be a happy person
as well as get them to do their best, then I think I've done my job.
[Further discussion of the individual and of activity and of disruption in class.]

GLS: Here in Roseville wouldn't you be able to walk out of the classroom,
go down to the office, leave your class for 5 minutes or more?

Mrs. Schiller: Ah, yes. I left the first graders up in front without any
assignment just the other day and Jeremy grabbed the pointer and
started "A, B, C, D," etc. and the whole class repeated, and then went
on through the alphabet several times. I said, "That was so nice. You
didn't waste any time!"

Mrs. Schiller went on to discuss how children knew where the
materials were; they could get them whenever they wanted to or
if they had time after they had finished their assigned task and
that she expected them to work quietly and individually or with
others if they wished. The children used charts, tape recorders,
flash cards, and so on. She says, "They're all little teachers, it's just
built in." She claims that she doesn't really arrange the material
beforehand; they know where everything is and just go and get it.

Mrs. Schiller: I have a lot of faith in kids. I think kids are neat! If you have
high expectations, 98% of the time they will fulfill your expectations.

GLS: What would you feel like if you went out in the hall or someone
called you to the phone and you came back after 5 minutes and found
things in considerable disorder?

Mrs. Schiller: Well, I would tell them right off, "I am *very* disappointed!
I had this important phone call and you couldn't sit still for 5 minutes
while I answered it." I would let them know it hurt me personally.

It's kind of a personal thing. Oh yes! You start building that up the first day of school. Then they feel "we can't hurt our teacher."

Mrs. Schiller went on to describe an instance where a little girl had to go to the dentist and she had to take the girl out to the car where her mother was waiting and how she came back and found such a nice class and praised them for being so nice and quiet. "They just love praise!"

There was a great deal more in this interview about how she depended upon the personal trust between the children and herself and how she cultivated the feeling that they couldn't "hurt their teacher." She also discussed "curriculum." She pointed out that the teachers in the Roseville school had direct input into the curriculum themselves in contrast to the situation in Schoenhausen, where the curriculum plan (*Lehrplan*) comes down from the State (*Land*) Board of Education.

Schoenhausen Grundschule (Frau Wanzer)

For the first few minutes, we talked about what we wanted to do in her classroom and explained that we wanted her procedures and goals to be clear to the Roseville teachers when we showed the films taken of her (Frau Wanzer's) classroom. She had seen the Roseville films already.

Frau Wanzer: Ya, it was really difficult for me to see what was intended. Perhaps that was the ground for the feeling that many of us had, *"Was lernen sie eigentlich?"* [What are they learning really?]

GLS: The films shown were typical for this class and the *freiwillig* [freewill] character of the classroom activity was indeed characteristic.

Frau Wanzer: I can scarcely understand how the teacher working at the table with some of the children would work on without looking to see what the other children were doing in the rest of the room. How do the children working alone know what they are supposed to do? With us there are difficulties and fighting. This was apparently not the case in the Roseville school!

GLS: Naturally, the children have specific lessons, but then when they are finished—they can do what they want.

Frau Wanzer: *Sie können tun was sie wollen!* [They can do what they want!]

GLS: Well, they have various opportunities—such as tapes, computers, the library, flash cards, charts and posters, etc.

Frau Wanzer: There is naturally a great difference as compared to our school. In America they have so much more time and so when they are finished with their lessons they can do what they want, but with us there is no time.

GLS: To go back a little, so there is for every hour a specific goal you must reach?

Frau Wanzer: I have in my curriculum plan the goal that I must reach. Every hour has a part of the goal. I must find out as the hour progresses if I'm going to have enough time to reach that goal. It depends on whether the hour goes well or badly—how much time I will spend.

Here she is speaking of the *Lehrplan* (curriculum plan) from the Baden Württemburg (*Land*) office of education.

GLS: Well, if you did have free time, how would you arrange it?

Frau Wanzer: I would arrange materials beforehand that belonged to a specific theme. But in the framework of this theme, the children could do what they wanted. But I wouldn't just leave it up to them to choose from unorganized material. I would have the fear that they choose things that were just play.

She goes on at some length to describe just how she would work this out and what kind of product she would expect and ends with the comment: "This kind of procedure would work, but *völlig frie* [fully free]? *Dass macht nichts.* [That makes nothing—that's of no use!]"

We went on and discussed what would happen if she left the room and came back and found chaos.

GLS: What would you do if you heard a disturbance in the room when you returned?

Frau Wanzer: I would talk to the class. I would attempt to reach an understanding. Scolding does no good. Sometimes I have said that I am *traurig* [sad].

GLS: Would you say that you are *beleidigt* [hurt]?

Frau Wanzer: No, never *beleidigt, nur* [only] *traurig.*

GLS: Do you make the children feel guilty [*schuldig*]?

Frau Wanzer: I feel that guilt is not understandable for children of this age. How can they understand who is guilty, the one who started the trouble or the one who responded to the trouble and who carried it on further?

We carried on discussions of this kind with Frau Wanzer several times and her interpretation of her own behavior in the classroom and that of the Roseville teachers that she had seen on film was consistent. She saw the Roseville classrooms, as did the other teachers, as tending toward being directionless and without specific goals and not organized for the attainment of whatever goals existed. She did find the quiet orderliness of the Roseville school impressive and as exhibiting good "teamwork."

Interpretation

Frau Wanzer and Mrs. Schiller are two experienced teachers of about the same age, teaching the same grades, about many of the same things, in quite similar schools in parallel communities in Germany and in the United States. And yet their handling of their classrooms and the assumptions that guide their behavior are significantly different at some critical points. And their perceptions of each other's classroom reflect these differences. Mrs. Schiller's classroom is relaxed, quiet, low keyed, and diverse. Children carry out various activities on their own, in addition to those carried out by the teacher and the small group she is leading through a specific learning task. There is little or no disruptive behavior. These qualities were confirmed in many sessions of observation by us and are apparent in the films we showed to all the Schoenhausen teachers, the principal, and the *Schulamtdirektor* (superintendent of schools) and his assistants.

Frau Wanzer perceives Mrs. Schiller's classroom as undirected, as almost goal-less. At the same time, she acknowledges that there appears to be "teamwork," but this method would be unlikely, she says, to work well in the Schoenhausen Grundschule.

These perceptions are apparent in the interview. Frau Wanzer's assumptions are clear: that if children are undirected they, or at least a significant proportion of them, will do nothing at all, will become disruptive, or will choose to play rather than work. She also reports that when children have clear directions on an interesting topic they can become very enthusiastic about learning and will work hard at it. Frau Wanzer explains the differences observed in terms of time, which is short in Schoenhausen, and the fact that the curriculum plan there defines the goals to be reached quite precisely. She does not see these as *cultural* attributes but as given, practical preconditions to whatever she does, and the children do, in her classroom.

The differences run deep. Mrs. Schiller assumes that her goal is to help each individual develop to his or her fullest degree—to the limit of their individual capacities. Frau Wanzer assumes, as does the Schulamtdirektor, that her purpose is to help each child attain the standards set forth in the Lehrplan—that some will meet them fully and others only minimally. Frau Wanzer takes for granted the existence of a Lehrplan, that it is furnished to the school by the state education office, and that it will guide her management of her instruction directly. Mrs. Schiller takes for granted the fact that teachers in the school district develop their own curriculum and that it is only an approximate guide. Frau Wanzer assumes that the children eventually learn to continue working when she leaves the classroom, but that one can't expect too much of the younger first and second graders. Mrs. Schiller expects her first and second graders to be responsible for keeping a quiet, on-task classroom when she is gone for a few minutes. Frau Wanzer would "talk" to her class if there were a disruption, but she would not act "hurt," only "sad," and she would not try to make her children feel "guilty." Mrs. Schiller would develop personal liking and trust with her children, would be "hurt" if they misbehaved, and would leave them all feeling guilty if they did. And the two teachers have quite different conceptions of guilt.

For Frau Wanzer, guilt has to be established—there is a perpetrator, a reinforcer, and perhaps a victim. For Mrs. Schiller, there is a feeling state—guilt is internalized. The children feel guilty about their irresponsible behavior and about hurting their teacher.

These are the assumptions, as we see them, that lie behind both the behaviors of the two teachers in their classrooms and their perception of each other's behaviors in situ. These are cultural differences, we believe, that are expressed in and derived from the German and U.S. historical experiences, respectively. In our own terminology, they reflect the German and the American heritage cultures.[3]

The claim that we just made in the above paragraph always arouses criticism and rebuttal. We are properly abashed by the rashness of our interpretation. We do feel, however, that the elicited dialogue represents something that we can call "German" culture and "American" culture. We have recently represented the latter as a "cultural dialogue" (Spindler & Spindler, 1990) and we can understand certain of Mrs. Schiller's interpretations as expressions of (for instance) individualism, achievement, and internalization of authority and guilt as a part of this dialogue. We can understand some of Frau Wanzer's discourse, and that of the Schulamtdirektor (district director of education), as expressing certain aspects of a long-term German dialogue about authority, efficiency, collective effort, and the attainment of standards. To claim that the little elementary schools in Roseville and Schoenhausen somehow express their respective national *Zeitgeisten* goes further than most of us want to go, and yet the implications are tantalizing and, we think, important. The action in these classrooms and the interpretations by the "natives" seem to be the tip of a cultural "iceberg." The part of the iceberg that is under water is the enormous complexity of the national whole and its history. Just how to make the analytic connections remains obscure. Nevertheless, we feel that it is essential to take into consideration broad, pervasive aspects of cultural dialogue, such as those represented, when we talk about classrooms and confrontations in them. If the teacher goes into the classroom with undeclared, and possibly unverbalized (even to her) culturally patterned assumptions of this kind and the students come with other kinds of assumptions, also undeclared, there will be serious difficulties in communication. "Cultural therapy" in this instance would be to make it possible for both the teacher and the students to verbalize these basic assumptions. This is often actually done in "rap sessions" but the purpose of doing so is unclear and there is usually little reinforcement of the verbalization that does occur or a pursuit of the consequences and misunderstanding that may be ensuing.

The Enduring, Situated, and Endangered Self

In 1987 we were invited to participate in a panel for the American Anthropological Association meeting on the fieldwork experience in anthropology. Rather than simply talk about our experiences in what are now some 28 field trips in five different cultures, we decided to talk about the "self" and we treated this ambiguous concept in three dimensions: the enduring, the situated, and the endangered self in fieldwork.

The *enduring* self is that sense of continuity one has with one's own past—a personal continuity in experience, meaning, and social identity (Hallowell, 1955). It provides the ego—syntonic functions of the self—and functions as an integrating principle of the personality phenotype (LeVine, 1984). It seems to have, at least in our own experience, and that of some of our informants, a romantic-ideal quality that may be quite lacking in the more pragmatic *situated* self.[4]

The situated self may be thought of as encompassing those aspects of the person as he or she copes with the everyday exigencies of life. This self is situated and contextualized. It is instrumental in the sense that we use the concept (Spindler & Spindler, 1989a, 1989b). This self is linked to the attainment of ends defined within the framework of a lifeway or social context. One's sense of self-efficacy—a concept used by learning psychologists—is a product, as we see it, of instrumental success or failure. For further clarification of the "enduring" as against the "situated" self, important elements are that the enduring self provides a sense of personal continuity with the past while the situated self is oriented to the present and the contexts (situations) one finds oneself in. This may imply that the enduring self is entirely conscious, and indeed much of it is—particularly the idealized features of identity, obscured by time and selected out of memory. But there are events and situations that occurred in the past, that contribute to contemporary feelings and self-evaluation, that are not readily conscious.

For our purposes, this is not too important but in individual cases may be of great significance and would be brought to light with extended counseling or therapy. For us, what is important is that any given student or teacher will have a sense of self that is relatively independent of the situation he or she finds him- or herself in. If this sense of self (the enduring self) is violated too often and too strongly by the requirements of the situated self that is constructed as an adaptive response to situational contexts, the enduring self will be damaged or even endangered. This can occur in anthropological fieldwork and certainly occurs as children and youth of diverse cultural origins confront school cultures that are antagonistic to the premises and behavioral patterns of their own culture. This helps account, for instance, for the resistance of some minority youth to learning in school, where learning some aspects of what is being taught and accepting how it is taught may be regarded as a "sellout." We would regard this as evidence of a conflict between the enduring and the situated self (or selves). We will return to these considerations later.

In 1970, in *Being an Anthropologist*, we wrote that the ethnographer

if successful, is in truth friendly, in truth concerned with the welfare of his or her respondents, but in truth an observer. The job is to find out what the people think and feel as well as what they do. One must penetrate beyond the facade of rationalizations and diversions that all humans throw up around their activities and sentiments. But the ethnographer must not become one of the people being observed, though from the outside he or she may seem to become one. The ethnographer must keep his or her identity while he studies theirs. One may well observe oneself—this self-knowledge is necessary. But when the distance between oneself and one's respondents is lost and between oneself in the sense of personal identity and in the sense of the role as participant-observer, the ethnographer has lost his or her usefulness as a field anthropologist. (p. 298)

Another point of view was expressed by Michel Leiris in "Das Auge des Ethnographen" (Leiris, 1978, pp. 34 ff.) in anticipation of an expedition to Africa:

For me the trip has a prospect of fulfilling a certain child-hood dream—the possibility of fighting against age and death—to go against the river of time—to lose my time-bound person in contact with humans very different than myself. I also wish that my artistic and literary friends could travel with me, not as tourists but as ethnographers, and therefore come into contact [with the "natives"] in enough depth to forget their white, middle-class manners and to lose what they under their identity as intellectuals comprehend.

There are dimensions of the self embedded in these statements, and we will comment on them shortly in terms of our personal experience, but, for the moment, it is clear that the ethnographers, both ourselves and Michel Leiris, were doing what persons coming into a new cultural situation must do if they wish on one hand to "get along" and learn and at the same time to keep their identities. These are the problems, as we see it, of the ethnic minority student or the lower-class student in a middle-class school environment.

The problem, of course, is how to do this. The ethnographer has a role and in varying degrees is trained for it. The ethnographer is also highly motivated to perform adequately in the alien cultural setting. When we did our first in-depth fieldwork with the Menominee Indians of Wisconsin, we risked our health and at times even our lives to "get along" and obtain our "data."

We found the tradition-oriented group of Menominee most compatible. They were also culturally the most different (from us). They lived then (in the 1950s) in self-made shacks well back in the woods far away from the highway or amenities such as utilities, sewer systems, or electrification. These people carried on a way of life that was more than reminiscent of an aboriginal central woodlands culture. The ceremonial round, the subsistence activities, the language usage, the burial customs, sorcery, religious beliefs, all exhibited specific traditional cultural features (Spindler & Spindler, 1971/1984).

We were most interested in this group, spent the most time with them, wrote the most about them, and identified with them to a greater degree than with any of the four major groups of Menominee that we eventually described. We never thought we were Menominee Indians but we felt that we were members of that group and, indeed, were treated as such in many respects. None of this is too surprising. There was an obvious match between our romanticized, idealized, enduring selves and the place and the people we found interesting.

We both disliked urban life. We had experienced in depth the mountains of California (Louise) and the forests and lakes of northern Wisconsin (George) and had internalized the images and sensual appeal of nature. We chose to live in a tent on the boundary of the conservative Menominee community for seven seasons of fieldwork of about three months duration each. The nearby conservative Menominee often visited us there.

All of the people in this group under 50 had extensive experience with the outside world—in schools and in the workforce. Most had become disillusioned. They had come back to the "old people," as they put it, to learn and live their own lifeway again. All of them had traditional socialization experience, often with grandparents. All had experienced disruption and discontinuity. They came back, literally, to find themselves. The tradition-oriented group, we came to feel, was a kind of revitalization movement, guided by the surviving handful of knowledgeable elders.

It is an oversimplification, but it is not wrong to say that both the tradition-oriented Menominee and we, the anthropologists, were engaged in the same quest—rediscovering and reasserting our enduring, romanticized selves. But they were more clear about that than we were.

We were less objective than we thought. We managed our situated selves effectively and maintained a working balance between objectivity and involvement. We would not do it differently if we had to do it over again, but we understand better now our strong attraction toward this group. Other anthropologists who have worked with the Menominee were not similarly attracted. We think that such relationships are probably more common in fieldwork, and reflected more often in interpretation, than generally acknowledged.

We think that our experience, sketched above, suggests how complex self-other relationships may be. We were living and working in a social and cultural situation very different than the one to which we were accustomed. We were stimulated by this, as most anthropologists are in the field, and found it compelling in all sorts of ways. Our attraction was positive and we made a viable adjustment. But we did not fully understand what was happening—why we were so attracted to the "traditional" group of Menominee and why we were also quite unattracted by the acculturated portions of the Menominee population. To us, the latter seemed "stuffy"— too much like the people in small towns, or in big cities, for that matter, that we have tended to avoid in our personal lives. We might have seen the convergence in our romanticized-idealized-enduring selves if we had had those concepts worked out at the time but we might well not have seen the convergence between our selves and those of the traditional Menominee.

A matching of selves, whether enduring or situated, is not simple. The fact that a kind of convergence could occur in our case may suggest that there are all sorts of ways in which convergences may occur between students and teachers and between students and school situations that are not apparent on the surface. There are, quite apparently, divergences, as well. These kinds of relationships require a deeper penetration than we can provide at this time, but they are suggestive.

In this panel discussion at the AAA meeting, we also dealt with dangers to the self, both enduring and situated, that might be inherent in the fieldwork process. We felt that there were some dangers. For example, we feel permanently marginalized in our society. Many of our colleagues must feel this too. Knowing our enduring selves as we do and having found an alien identity with which to reinforce it, we feel we have left to us only our situated selves to be played out in our own society. Our relationships to all of our everyday affairs and aspirations seem at times shallow. But we cannot go back. Our friends and informants in the tradition-oriented Menominee group are either dead or themselves have left behind much of their revitalized native identity. Even their rituals, some of which they still carry out, seem removed from the traditional context that we first saw them in. The echoes of the past are faint and only the sociopolitical realities of the day seem alive. But is this feeling anything more than simple nostalgia for our own youth and the reinforcement of the enduring self that we found there among the Menominee?

This is a situation peculiar to the field ethnographer, perhaps, and yet the feeling dogs us that the children from a minority group in a mainstream-dominated school must have many of the same kinds of feelings. They *enter* marginalized and their marginalization is reinforced. This is exactly parallel to what happened to us. We entered the field situation with the Menominee already somewhat alienated and disenchanted with much of mainstream society as we knew it. We found reinforcement for this marginalization and emerged from the 7 years of intermittent field experience permanently marginalized. We do not claim that our experience and marginalization are directly comparable to that of a minority child or youth. We are empowered by our position, our status, and our ethnicity. They may not be. Nevertheless, our experience in the field where we made our adjustment to others' realities is suggestive and gives us, at least, some basis for empathy.

What may be most important here is that we learned how to make situational adaptations without destroying our enduring selves. Perhaps this is what many minority students with strong ethnic identities must do. They must keep their identity because this identity, in the sense of the enduring self, is essential to the maintenance of life itself. And yet they must get along in the world as it is. It is a world where instrumental competencies have to be acquired that are not required by the enduring self or one's ethnic identity; a sense of pervasive self-efficacy must be developed to cope with the exigencies of life as they happen in a complex technological society. Somehow minority youth as well as mainstream youth must be enabled to make this kind of adaptation and they will be helped in doing this if the necessary instrumental competencies can be deemotionalized—removed from the value matrix of mainstream culture. Perhaps if we have clear concepts of enduring self and identities, and situational adaptations, and can verbalize them, make them implicit and applicable to everyday lives, we can help ourselves (all of us) to make good working adjustments.

We end this section with another quote from our chapter in *Being an Anthropologist* (1970):

We have never had a truly bad time in the field, though we have not, to be sure, endured some of the extreme exigencies that some of our colleagues have. But we have fallen ill, been cold, wet, and insect bitten, suffered from having to struggle along in someone else's language, been rejected by the very people we wanted to know, harassed by children when we wanted to work with their elders, repulsed by offensive sights and odors (given our culturally conditioned sensibilities). Our lives have been threatened by people and by impersonal forces. But it was all the very essence of living. (p. 300)

If somehow the struggle of the minority student could be converted to a struggle with some glory in it as there was and still is for us, getting along in school would be perceived differently and reacted to with energy and determination rather than alienation. This may seem to be another kind of "blame the victim" concept but it need not be if counseling could somehow incorporate some elements from this kind of orientation—the orientation of the ethnographer. Perhaps both teachers and students have to become ethnographers, studying each other and themselves.

Getting Along in the Remstal

One of our major research efforts in Germany has been to study the ways in which people perceive and make instrumental adaptations to the changing environment in which they live. The Remstal in Germany is an area of some 21 communities, ranging from very small villages to midsize towns, but it is rapidly urbanizing and modernizing. One tool that we used, of our own invention and derived from field experience in Germany—but in all of the other places we worked as well—consists of some 30 line drawings of significant activities in which a person may engage or conceive of engaging in. These drawings are of occupations, houses, social situations, clothes, recreation, and places. They are clustered around two poles—the traditional way of life and a modern, increasingly urbanized way of life. The activities, the line drawings, and the conception of what is traditional and modern must be refit, of course, to each research site. The technique is *emic* in its evocative stimuli, but the underlying model or theory of relations (*etic*) remains constant. Respondents are asked to choose activities they would like to engage in, which means choosing certain line drawings, and to explain why they chose them. The drawings may be selected by the individual from the whole pile of drawings, as the Blood Indians (Kanai) insisted on doing, or presented one by one in any predetermined order. Alternately, the pictures may be presented in preselected pairs to groups of some size with two slide projectors, as we did in the Remstal with schoolchildren, their parents, and their teachers. The respondent makes choices, then defends the choices, either in writing for groups or orally under conditions of individual ministration.

Though not initially designed for that purpose, the Instrumental Activities Inventories (IAI) elicits data that seem relevant to concepts of self and personhood. We can say that we become what we choose as instrumentalities. The advertising profession recognized this long ago, and we are bombarded with invitations to identify with the sophisticated by drinking Perrier and to become a member of the "now generation" by drinking Diet Pepsi.

We cannot engage in a detailing of the results—which we found to be complex and revealing. What became abundantly clear was that there are indications of the enduring self and the situated self in the responses of the Remstäler. The enduring self is clearly ideal-romantic. It is represented in choices of the *Weingärtner* (vintner) profession, the *Selbständiger* (independent small shop owner), the *Kleinbauer* (small farmer), the *Grossbauer* (big farmer), the quiet evening at home, the traditional *Fachwerk* (open-beam structure) house, and the *Weinlese* (grape harvest). Images and values constituting an idealized lifestyle, now disappearing rapidly, were woven together in the "defenses" of these choices, the friendly village, kin, family, land and nature, fresh air and sunshine, history, beauty, independence, fresh natural food, freedom, and health. This cluster was represented in every IAI protocol, even when instrumental choices of a more pragmatic orientation were expressed. This cluster we regard as an expression of the romantic-idealized enduring self (Spindler & Spindler, 1989b).

The pragmatic lifestyle, represented in the choices expressing the situated self, centered on choices of the modern row house, white-collar work, factory jobs, the machinist and technical draftsman trades, the modern church, and the evening out in a festive pub. It is constructed of a cluster of quite different images and values: physical comfort, convenience, shopping, access to entertainment and medical care, regular income, paid vacations, less hardship, and clean work. This was the contemporary lifestyle actually available to most of the respondents. The ideal-romantic cluster represented in the enduring self was literally almost unavailable to the majority of the respondents.

We saw the cognitive management of these two opposing selves and supporting cultural clusters—the traditional versus the urban-modern ways of life—as the primary task the children learned in the school and that the teachers and parents taught. Every teacher knows that he or she lives and that the children he or she is teaching will live in the framework of the situated self (though teachers do not phrase it this way). And yet every teacher expressed the cluster of the ideal-romantic pole of the enduring self as desirable. Somehow the people of the Remstal seem to have been able to hold both the enduring-ideal-romanticized self and the pragmatic-situated self together without major breakdown. If they can do it, why do we have such difficulties with it in our schools?

We think the answer is that the enduring self is related to the traditional Swaebish culture, which is long standing in the Rems Valley. It is the traditional culture. There is a literature in Swaebish, the royal family of Baden Württemburg is Swaebish. The local Heimat-museums are about Swaebish home life, Swaebish artifacts, Swaebish quilts, and on and on. People speak Swaebish at home. The teachers, even though some of them are not from the Remstal area, speak Swaebish when they have to. The "newcomers," now third generation, from the outlying areas of Germany that had to be vacated after World War II, and from what was then the "East Zone," understand Swaebish. Although there are jokes about *die dummen Schwaben* (the dumb Swaebish) and their *unbeweglich* (unmoving) character, they do not really experience prejudice—being regarded as of lower quality, low status, or undesirable people. The fact that all children learn both Swaebish and *hoch Deutsch* is an indication of this. Speaking Swaebish is not discouraged in school but the teachers teach in hoch Deutsch excepting when sometimes they have to explain something to a very young child whose primary language is still Swaebish. In short, children are raised in and teachers work in an environment where cultural differences and distinctions are taken for granted and not considered invidiously.

The problem in America and in American schools seems to be that, to establish some kind of identity, mainstream American culture posed itself as dominant, supreme, moral, "right," to be observed, and to be taught at all costs to everyone. In the not-too-distant past, this involved punishing children for speaking their native language, shaving their heads, and "delousing" them (in residential Indian schools, for example) and in general letting them know that if they weren't pretty much Anglo-Saxon, weren't pretty much Protestant, or didn't at least act as if they were, they were inferior, on the back burner, and to be shaped up or shucked off. We are reaping the harvest of our history, and we are making efforts to change it but not fast enough, not thoroughly enough, not deep enough in our own psyches. There are very few consciously racist teachers but there are many teachers, perhaps even all teachers, who have very strong biases that are quite unmovable because they are integrated with their own sense of identity and self—in many cases, the enduring self. If we could just adopt a "Remstal" attitude about the whole business, it would help. Cultural therapy involves some self-examination along these lines on the part of both students and teachers. We do not mean that this should be a simple "confession of sins" by teachers and in effect a kind of apology to children (though sometimes this seems in order) but that there be an analysis of the cultural persuasions involved on all sides. We are currently doing this in an experimental course for people with bachelor of arts degrees returning to Sonoma State University to become teachers. We will have more to say about it at the end of the semester.

The Self and Instrumental Competence

It is not difficult to conceive of a global relationship of self, and particularly self-esteem, to instrumental performance, for which schooling, in modern complex societies, is a major arena. Children with various sociocultural backgrounds attend schools predicated on mainstream, largely middle-class, and largely white Anglo-Saxon North European Protestant cultural assumptions. Such children acquire deficits in self-esteem when they fail to master essential instrumentalities in this context. This self-esteem is damaged not only by actual failure but also by negative perceptions and low expectations of them by teachers and other students. The processing for failure begins when a child enters school.

The equation is direct: Instrumental competence acquired and displayed in school settings—positive self-esteem—and good self-concept equals competent school performance. Lack of instrumental competence in this setting—negative self-esteem and poor self-concept—equals incompetent school performance, alienation, and dropout. One condition feeds another that feeds back to the first.

The problem is more complex than that. The assumption that the whole self-concept is dependent upon school performance may be quite incorrect. The concept of *self-efficacy*, a subset of self-esteem, seems useful. We define self-efficacy as a prediction that one will be able to meet the demands of the situation effectively. A student with feelings of self-efficacy thinks that he or she can answer questions, pass exams, read adequately—get the work done as well as or better than most others.

Self-efficacy varies across different behaviors in different situations (Bandura, Adams, & Howells, 1980). This concept, like "instrumental competence," is not passive, as in Cooley's "looking glass self" (Gecas & Schwalbe, 1983). It is constructed of self-determined perceptions and predictions of behavior that interact with those of others in situations such as classrooms that are not simply a reflection of those "others." Instrumental competence and self-efficacy seem quite similar, though stemming from unrelated research projects and quite different disciplines. Instrumental competence requires that one understands what activities are linked to what goals and how to perform the activities. Self-efficacy in our terms is an expectation that one can exhibit instrumental competence in the appropriate context.

For example, minority children often fail to acquire instrumental competence in test taking. The importance of tests in Anglo-oriented schools is not appreciated. The skills and motivations necessary for getting one's control of the content to be tested up (and then letting it drop); the significance of time in testing; and the need for hurry and tensed, focused excitement (even anxiety)—the whole pervasive complex of configurations of test-taking in our schools—is not understood nor are the motivations for meritorious performance under the imposed and quite artificial conditions of test-taking present. The crucial linkage between goals, values, assignments and priority, and actual skills are not made. The child suffers failure, instrumental competence is not achieved, and self-efficacy is eroded.

Instrumental competence and self-efficacy are situational and may be considered to be expressions of the notion of situated self as employed in our interpretation of the Remstal case. We hypothesize that for minorities, as well as for Remstäler, there may be an enduring self that is sustained above and beyond the situated self, or estimates of self-efficacy, in school situations.

Children may fail in school because they do not perceive, understand, or master the instrumental relationships upon which schoolwork is predicated. They may develop low self-esteem and low estimates of self-efficacy in the school situation. But they may preserve an enduring self or identity that is comparatively intact and positive, formed and sustained in nonschool contexts.

Cultural therapy as relevant to these ideas would consist of trying to help children and teachers to acquire understanding of those instrumental competencies required in school. We are not thinking here of simply the competencies of test-taking, or writing well, or doing math, but the broader context into which specific competencies are embedded. The test-taking example is relevant. There's not only the content of the test, the rightness or wrongness of answers, but also the test-taking cultural complex. We see this every day in our teaching at Stanford. Stanford students have been selected out for test-taking instrumental competence in its most complex and subtle sense. They are not always necessarily the best students. Much of school is ritualized, complicated, made difficult for those who are not raised in its shadow in ways that are irrelevant to ultimate instrumental competence. Part of our effort within the framework of cultural therapy would be to try to come to an understanding of what essential competence is as against ritualized, culturalized competence—instrumental competence that has been embedded within the framework of the majority culture but is not necessarily a part of minority cultures. Teachers need to understand this and children need to understand it, though we are not sure that teachers would find it entirely comfortable to have students understand too much.

Adaptations

There is a further complication—if we read the possibilities correctly. Our researches have convinced us that under conditions of personally experienced culture conflict, especially where the conflict creates conditions for instrumental failure, people respond in certain predictable ways. These modes of response we can sum up as follows: *reaffirmation, withdrawal, constructive marginality, biculturalism,* and *assimilation* (Spindler & Spindler, 1971/1984, 1989a). There are various subsets to each of these modes; *withdrawal,* for example, can be vegetative or self-destructive. *Assimilation* can be adjusted or compensatory.

Among the Menominee, where our ideas about these modes of adaptation first emerged, the reaffirmative adaptation was represented by the "native-oriented" group. It was composed of a few older people who were essentially cultural "survivors" from the traditional past and a larger number of younger people who had met mainstream culture head-on in schools and in the work world and who were trying to re-create and sustain a recognizable Menominee way of life—and escape from the mainstream. They sought participation in the Dream Dance, Medicine Lodge, Chief's Dance, and Ghost Feast and tried to live "Indian style." They were fully aware of their choice. It could be called a "strategy" of adaptation (Spindler & Spindler, 1971/1984).

Various forms of withdrawal were represented by others who were so torn by conflict that they could not identify with either the traditional or the mainstream cultural symbols or groups. Many drank to oblivion and sometimes death. Others did nothing—they vegetated. "Constructive marginality" is represented by a number of Menominee who made a viable adaptation to culture conflict by avoiding strong identification with any group or any one set of symbols. They formed a personal culture that was instrumentally productive but was usually constituted of several different segments—some mainstream. They distanced themselves in greater and lesser degree from much of the conflict and maintained a wry view of it.

Among the "assimilated" Menominee, there were some "150 percenters"—people who were more respectable than most respectable mainstream whites and who wondered how we could live and work with those "dirty Indians." They were compensators. There were others who were undifferentiated culturally from mainstream whites in the surrounding areas and who did not denigrate others who were more "traditional." In fact, they were interested in Menominee traditions, as described by Walter Hoffman, Allinson Buck Skinner, and Felix Keesing—anthropologists who had worked with the Menominee decades before we did and who described the traditional culture in detail. There were also a few who appeared to be assimilated who had made a bicultural adaptation. They seemed equally at home in the traditional and mainstream context, though the latter was socially dominant. This adaptation is extremely difficult to make because the distance between the two cultures is very great—we think greater than that for most minorities.

There's one other adaptation represented by the Peyote Cult, or Native American Church. Menominee Peyotism synthesized Christian religious belief and traditional Menominee belief and symbolism. The Peyote tepee, for example, has 13 poles, 1 for Christ and 12 for the disciples. There does not seem to be anything exactly like Peyotism in the current adaptation of minorities, though one could probably make a case for it.

The underlying principle is that conflict resolution is likely to take defensive forms, particularly when self-esteem is threatened. For example, the reaffirmative mode is characterized not merely by a return to a traditional or neotraditional pattern of behavior but also by *exclusion* of perceived elements from the sociocultural context where one has suffered loss of self-esteem and has a low estimate of self-efficacy (contemporary "resistance" theory is an expression of this in a different theoretical framework). The assimilative mode may be characterized by a similar exclusion, but of perceived traditional cultural elements, if these elements are perceived as a handicap or cause for instrumental failure. We hypothesize that something similar happens to many minority students. When instrumental competence is not attained in school and situational self-efficacy is damaged, the individual response may be to reaffirm, withdraw, or compensate. There can be an active rejection of the whole schooling context—and a "reaffirmative" celebration of street life, or of home life, or diffuse ethnic images and symbols—or a withdrawal characterized less by compensatory reaffirmation and exclusion of threatening elements than by self-destruction. There may be important differences in the adaptations between males and females that, to our knowledge, have not been explored in the existing literature (Spindler & Spindler, 1990; L. Spindler, 1962, 1989). One could go on exploring these possibilities, but we hope our general intent is clear.

Cultural therapy with respect to this line of thought would consist of being able to bring out in free discussions the kinds of adaptations that students are making to the school, its culture, and its representatives. We are not inferring that the only adaptive strategies that are possible are included somewhere in the framework that we have delineated, but we do think that the framework orients us to some of the kinds of adaptation that are possible.

Knowing what one's adaptation is, one then can make a more cognitively based decision about whether or not this is the right strategy at the right time. It is very clear that some students are doing a kind of reaffirmative identification and in doing so withdraw from or become actively confrontive with school culture and purpose. Boundaries are created and in fact boundaries are necessary for this kind of identity work. These boundaries may seem quite irrational and destructive to outside observers who are not "in the skin" of the adapter. The ultimate driving force is to maintain self-esteem, at least not to damage seriously the enduring self, and to make the situated self, in relation to the enduring self, tolerable.

Summary

Cultural therapy is a complex and subtle process about which no one knows very much. Over the years, we have developed a model of interrelationships centering on certain dimensions of process, as follows.

Schooling is a *calculated intervention* in the lives and learning of the young that mandates that certain things be taught (whether they are learned or not) and certain things be excluded. This intervention is culturally constructed by the determinations of the mainstream, culturally speaking, of any society, however simple or complex. Much of the knowledge and some of the skills taught are extraneous and irrelevant to the situational realities of the lives of the young. This is true whether we are talking about Australian aborigines or twentieth-century Americans.

Instrumental competencies are the most important acquisitions of the school years. The three Rs are such competencies, but speaking correctly, having manners, learning how to present oneself, understanding something of the world beyond one's immediate environment are also instrumental to achieving position and material success. These competencies are embedded in a cultural matrix and may become emotionally burdened, so they cannot be taught or learned without emotional consequences. As gaining instrumental competencies increases and reinforces a sense of self-efficacy essential to confidence and productivity, it is a primary task of cultural therapy to make it possible to disengage instrumental competencies from their emotionally loaded cultural contexts.

Another important dimension of the model that we consider as standing behind any implementation of cultural therapy is the self. We have found it useful to separate the *enduring self* from the *situated self*. The enduring self transcends immediate reality, is developed early in life, is a central organizing process in the person, and is, for most healthy persons, romanticized and idealized at a conscious level—though there are unconscious dimensions of great influence. The situated self develops as a response to specific situations encountered repetitively by the person. There may be several situated selves, even within the school or classroom context. When the adaptation of the situated selves is incompatible with the enduring self, there is trouble—often in the form of resistance or opposition to demands placed upon the person, as in school. Where cultural diversity is the rule, as in contemporary American schools, this kind of trouble results in destructive relationships.

There are several kinds of adaptation that persons make to conflicts between the enduring self and situated selves that are internalized, such as reaffirmation of ethnic identity, compensatory adaptation, withdrawal, and oppositional behavior. These adaptations are influenced by the dynamics of relationships between the situational and enduring selves and may be regarded, at one level, as attempts to avoid self-destruction.

The underlying phenomena in all processes in person and culture relations is that basic cultural assumptions and perceptions held by persons of different cultures seriously influence behavior, perceptions of behavior, and communication. They are the starting point of differential rewards, punishments, oppositions, consequences, and the use of power to coerce, eliminate, damage, and promote.

Conclusion

Cultural therapy is an orientation for remedial efforts directed primarily (by us) at teachers or teacher trainers and by others at students—both mainstream and minority. The essential features of cultural therapy are making explicit the nature of conflict in cultural terms, the involvement of the enduring and situated self in this conflict, and the requirements for instrumental competence in the school situation. Cultural awareness, both of one's own culture (familial, ethnicity, class, gang, and so on) and of the "other" (usually mainstream or minority) culture is crucial for both students and teachers. When the nature of the problem is seen in this objectified manner, self-determined choices may be made on a realistic and less self-damaging basis.

Notes

1. We have drawn heavily in this chapter from our papers: "Instrumental Competence, Self-Efficacy, Linguistic Minorities and Cultural Therapy" (1989a), "Crosscultural, Comparative, Reflective Interviewing in Schoenhausen and Roseville" (1992a), and "The Enduring, Situated and Endangered Self in Fieldwork: A Personal Account" (1992b).

2. We presented the first paper on the CCCRI at the American Anthropological Association meetings in November 1986. The

first publication demonstrating it was not by us but by Mariko Fugita and Toshyuki Sano (1988), who had been instructed in it by us. The "reflective" interview technique was not inspired by recent work on reflective teaching or inquiry into teaching processes, though this work is not irrelevant to our purposes. It stems from anthropological concerns emerging particularly in the writings of postmodernists on reflective and reflexive ethnography and interpretation, anticipated by the work of people such as Mead and Collier. (The idea was generated in our minds by Margaret Mead's chapter on evocative stimuli in fieldwork in *The Making of Psychological Anthropology*, 1978, and by John Collier, Jr., and Malcolm Collier's, 1986, *Visual Anthropology.*) It has occurred to us that one way to encourage reflective, self-analytic, and self-aware teaching is to use culturally bracketed interview techniques such as the CCCRI. Our chapter "Crosscultural, Comparative, Reflective Interviewing in Schoenhausen and Roseville" (1992a) describes the technique, locates its origins, and demonstrates the results.

3. Our emphasis is on culture as a dynamic process (rather than a static historical experience) where the values and experiences of diverse groups of people play a significant role in an ongoing "American" cultural dialogue that is constantly being renegotiated. (We write about this topic extensively in *The American Cultural Dialogue and Its Transmission.*)

4. Our interest in the "self" is of long standing, as evidenced by Louise Spindler's memoir *Menomini Women and Culture Change* (1962). George Spindler used self-other concepts in this early research in California schools (see G. Spindler, 1959). The notion of a "situated" self was stimulated by a symposium paper presented at Stanford University by Dorinne Kondo (1987). There are other possibilities, such as the "constructed" self, made up from the interaction of the enduring and situated selves, or the "saturated" self, which is overwhelmed by input from frenetic, divisive, fragmented social communication, or "multiple" selves, more diverse than the enduring self but more cohesive as reactive systems than situated selves. We find that the "enduring" and "situated" selves represent the poles of cohesion and diversification possible

in the normal psychocultural constitution, and the "endangered"
self is a consequence of severe conflict between the two.

References

Bandura, A., Adams, N. E., & Howells, G. N. (1980). Tests of
    generality of self-efficacy theory. *Psychological Review, 84*, 191-
    215.
Collier, J., Jr., & Collier, M. (1986). *Visual anthropology*. Albuquer-
    que: University of New Mexico Press.
Fugita, M., & Sano, T. S. (1988). Children in American and Japan-
    ese day-care centers: Ethnography and cross-cultural inter-
    viewing. In H. Trueba & C. Delgado-Gaitan (Eds.), *School and
    society: Learning content through culture* (pp. 125-163). New York:
    Praeger.
Gecas, V., & Schwalbe, M. (1983). Beyond the looking glass self:
    Social structure and efficacy-based self esteem. *Social Anthro-
    pology Quarterly, 46*(2), 77-88.
Hallowell, A. I. (1955). *Culture and experience*. Philadelphia: Uni-
    versity of Pennsylvania Press.
Kondo, D. (1987, February). *Company as family? Ideologies of self-
    hood in a Japanese family enterprise*. Paper presented at the Stan-
    ford University Colloquium, Stanford, CA. See D. Kondo (1990),
    Crafting Selves, Chicago: University of Chicago Press.
Leiris, M. (1978). Das Auge des Ethnographen. *Ethnologische
    Schriften, 2*, 34-55 (Frankfurt/M: Syndikat).
LeVine, R. A. (1984). *Culture, behavior and personality*. New York:
    Aldine.
Mead, M. (1978). The evocation of psychologically relevant re-
    sponses in ethnological field work. In G. Spindler (Ed.), *The
    making of psychological anthropology* (pp. 87-139). Berkeley: Uni-
    versity of California Press.
Spindler, G. (1959). *The transmission of American culture* (Third
    Burton Lecture in Elementary Education). Cambridge, MA:
    Harvard University Press.

Spindler, G., & Spindler, L. (1970). Fieldwork among the Menomini. In G. Spindler (Ed.), *Being an anthropologist: Fieldwork in eleven cultures* (pp. 267-301). New York: Holt, Rinehart & Winston. (Reprinted 1984, Waveland)

Spindler, G., & Spindler, L. (1984). *Dreamers with power: The Menominee Indians.* Prospect Heights, IL: Waveland. (First published by Holt, Rinehart & Winston as *Dreamers without power: The Menomini Indians,* 1971)

Spindler, G., & Spindler, L. (1989a). Instrumental competence, self-efficacy, linguistic minorities, and cultural therapy: A preliminary attempt at integration. *Anthropology and Education Quarterly, 10*(1), 36-50.

Spindler, G., & Spindler, L. (1989b). The self and the instrumental model in the study of culture change. *Proceedings of the Kroeber Anthropological Society* (pp. 109-117). Berkeley: University of California Press.

Spindler, G., & Spindler, L. (1990). Male and female in four changing cultures. In D. Jordan & M. Swartz (Eds.), *Personality and the cultural construction of society* (pp. 182-200). Georgia: University of Alabama Press.

Spindler, G., & Spindler, L. (1992a). Crosscultural, comparative, reflective interviewing in Schoenhausen and Roseville. In M. Schrätz (Ed.), *Qualitative voices in education research* (pp. 106-125). London: Falmer.

Spindler, G., & Spindler, L. (1992b). The enduring, situated, and endangered self in fieldwork: A personal account. In L. B. Boyer & R. Boyer (Eds.), *The psychoanalytic study of society: Vol. 17. Essays in honor of George and Louise Spindler* (pp. 23-28). Hillsdale, NJ: Analytic Press.

Spindler, G., & Spindler, L. (with Trueba, H., & Williams, M.). (1990). *The American cultural dialogue and its transmission.* London: Falmer.

Spindler, L. (1962). *Menomini women and culture change* (Memoir No. 91). Menasha, WI: American Anthropological Association.

Spindler, L. (1989). A comment: Gender differences neglected. In H. Trueba, G. Spindler, & L. Spindler (Eds.), *What do anthropologists have to say about dropouts?* (pp. 135-136). London: Falmer.

Patricia Phelan

Ann Locke Davidson

2

Looking Across Borders

Students' Investigations of Family, Peer, and School Worlds as Cultural Therapy

PATRICIA PHELAN
ANN LOCKE DAVIDSON

Patricia Phelan graduated from Oregon State University with a B.S. in elementary education in 1967. Motivated to expand her horizons, she moved to Washington, D.C., where she obtained an interesting and challenging position with the National Trust for Historic Preservation. Her experiences during the discourse and activity of the 1960s, combined with her continuing interest in the lives of children and youth, led her to return to the West Coast in 1973 to a position with the Urban/Rural School Development Program at Stanford University. Pursuing her master's degree in anthropology and her Ph.D. in anthropology of education at Stanford, her first graduate course, "Cultural Transmission," taught by George Spindler, who was later to become her doctoral adviser and esteemed mentor, provided the catalyst and the base upon which she has now built a 12-year career. Her work has been dominated by three themes thus far: first, a persistent interest in the context of social life and the ways in which people find meaning and operate within the general and immediate social situations in which they find themselves; second, a concern with the lives of children and adolescents, particularly those of varying cultural backgrounds and those who experience difficult life circumstances; and, finally, the relationship between students' contexts and experiences and their engagement in educational settings. Her current position is Associate Professor of Education at the University of Washington, Bothell.

Ann Locke Davidson began her career in education in the People's Republic of China, teaching Western literature, composition, and conversation to university students. These and other experiences teaching in diverse U.S. classroom settings made her well aware that social differences can play a major role in classroom interactions. An interest in better understanding these issues led her to graduate work in education at Stanford University, where she received her Ph.D. in curriculum and teacher education and M.A. in anthropology in 1992. Her research focused on the social construction of ethnicity across two northern California high school settings. She was particularly interested in the role that school and classroom practices play in shaping students' sense of their ethnicity in relation to schooling. Today, she is working as a postdoctoral fellow at the Learning Research and Development Center at the University of Pittsburgh, and as an ethnographer for a portfolio-based assessment research effort associated with Harvard's School of Education. Her major research interests center on the relationship between school and classroom practices, school culture, and youths' construction of school self. She recently completed coediting (with Patricia Phelan) *Renegotiating Cultural Diversity in American Schools* and is coauthoring (with Patricia Phelan and Hanh Cao Yu) a second volume describing the ways in which cultural aspects of students' family, peer, and school worlds combine to affect youths' involvement in schooling.

In this chapter, we relate the results of a group investigation[1] involving 12 culturally diverse youths, with respect to the tenets of cultural therapy as described by George and Louise Spindler (this volume). While cultural therapy was not our original purpose, it turned out to be one result of seven 1-hour sessions that involved high school students in an examination of data and a critique of the Students' Multiple Worlds Model and Typology, which we had generated during the course of a previous 2-year investigation (Phelan, Davidson, & Yu, 1993).

AUTHORS' NOTE: The group investigation project reported here was conducted in collaboration with Don Hill, Director of the Professional Development Center, Stanford, Schools Collaborative; Brooke Knight, a high school counselor; and Hanh Cao Yu, doctoral candidate, School of Education, Stanford University. Without the vision, inspiration, and collaborative efforts of these colleagues, this project would not have been possible. The work reported here is part of a larger study conducted under the auspices of the Center for Research on the Context of Secondary Teaching with funding from the Office of Education Research and Improvement, U.S. Department of Education (Cooperative Agreement No. OERI-G0087C235).

findings from their perspective. In essence, the students served as apprentice researchers as they examined data, generated hypotheses, and assessed the applicability and relevance of the model and typology to their own lives.

We proceeded inductively by asking students to read and discuss case studies of adolescents we had compiled from our research data—rather than presenting the model and typology at the outset. Our intent was to elicit their understanding of the circumstances portrayed, their thoughts about the accuracy and fit of the cases to the typology we had developed, and their view of the overall significance of the findings.

While our purposes as researchers were explicit, the group sessions resulted in a number of other outcomes that have particular relevance to cultural therapy. For example, as the students read and discussed the cases (which included descriptions of cultural factors affecting adolescents' relationships with peers and school), they began to relate the ideas and themes embedded within to their own lives, reflecting on the ways in which they personally respond to pressures emanating from their own cultural backgrounds. Further, they began to articulate and examine their own presuppositions about other social and cultural groups. Finally, they began to notice and talk about social stratification within their school setting. Their reflections relate directly to two of the desired outcomes of cultural therapy as described by the Spindlers: (a) to bring one's own assumptions, goals, values, and beliefs to a level of awareness that permits one to perceive these as potential biases in social interactions and in the acquisition or transmission of skills or knowledge and (b) to make unequal power relationships in the classroom, school, and larger society more explicit.

Overall, the group investigation project resulted in lively discussions, thoughtful comments, and ultimately an elaborated typology of students' various adaptation patterns. Equally as important, the processes that occurred during the sessions enabled the participants to broaden their views and develop a richer and more complex understanding of themselves in relationship to the culturally diverse peers in their school environment.

Background

The content of the group investigation sessions was derived from a 2-year study concerned with identifying factors that affect students' engagement with schools and learning. From data collected during interviews and observations with 54 ethnically and academically diverse youths, we generated a model to describe the ways in which sociocultural aspects of students' family, peer, and school worlds combine to affect students' thoughts and actions with respect to school and learning. Particularly important is our focus on the nature of borders and processes of movement between worlds. Figure 2.1 visually represents these relationships.

The emergence of the Multiple Worlds model was an important development of the first year of this investigation. Unlike most other approaches that focus attention on stable characteristics of individuals (e.g., gender and ethnicity) or concentrate on language acquisition or achievement level alone, the Multiple Worlds model is generic. It is not ethnic, achievement, or gender specific but transcends these categories to consider multiple worlds, boundary crossing, and adaptation for all students.

As our study proceeded, we found a good deal of variety in students' descriptions of their worlds and in their perceptions of boundaries. At the same time, we also uncovered distinctive patterns and strategies that students employ as they make the transition between and adapt to different contexts and settings. These patterns are summarized in the following typology.

Students' Multiple Worlds Typology

I. Congruent worlds/smooth transitions: These students describe values, beliefs, expectations, and normative ways of behaving as similar across their worlds. Moving from one setting to another is harmonious and uncomplicated. *Many* of these youths are white, upper middle class, and high achieving, but not always. Some minority students describe little difference across their worlds and experience transitions as

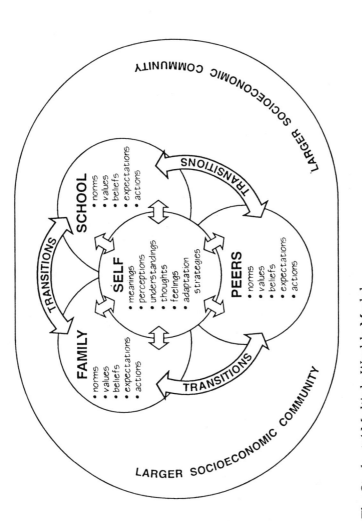

Figure 2.1. The Students' Multiple Worlds Model

smooth. Likewise, academically average students can also exhibit patterns that fit this type.

II. *Different worlds/border crossings managed:* For some adolescents, differences in family, peer, and/or school worlds (with respect to culture, ethnicity, socioeconomic status, and/or religion) require students to adjust and reorient as movement among contexts occurs. Students in this category perceive differences in their worlds but use strategies that enable them to manage crossings successfully (in terms of what is valued in each setting). High-achieving minority youth frequently exhibit patterns common to this type.

III. *Different worlds/border crossings difficult:* In this category, like the former, students define their family, peer, and/or school worlds as distinct. These students, however, have not learned, have not mastered, or are not willing to adapt all of the strategies necessary for successful transitions—thus they often experience difficulty adjusting and reorienting as they move across borders and among settings. Common to this type are students who adapt in some circumstances but not in others; that is, they may do well in one or two classes and poorly in the rest.

IV. *Different worlds/border crossings resisted:* In this type, the values, beliefs, and expectations across worlds are so discordant that students perceive borders as insurmountable and actively or passively resist transitions. Low-achieving students (seemingly unable to profit from school and classroom settings) are typical of this type, although high-achieving students who do not connect with peers or family also exhibit Type IV patterns.

While these categories matched the descriptions of the circumstances and experience of the high school students in our original study, we were interested in exploring whether the patterns we described had relevance to other adolescents as well. Therefore, in collaboration with a high school counselor and teacher, we generated the group investigation sessions referred to previously.

The 12 high school juniors who participated in this project were diverse with respect to cultural background, gender, ethnicity, social class, and academic achievement. The six males included three European Americans, one Chinese immigrant, one Central American immigrant, and one East Indian American.[2] The six females included one Tongan American, one East Indian American, one European American, one Chinese American, one African American, and one Central American immigrant. While these students varied with respect to academic achievement, with some participating in advanced classes and some in regular (general track) classes, none was failing or appeared to be at imminent risk of dropping out of high school.

The sessions were conducted over a period of 7 weeks. During the first five meetings, students read and discussed eight case vignettes that described youths in our original study. The cases were selected to illustrate the four types described in the Students' Multiple Worlds Typology and were written to portray the experiences, perspectives, and views of one adolescent. These 2- to 3-page cases, condensed from much longer in-depth case studies, were compiled from background data, interview excerpts, and observation notes. The themes in each reflected our focus on the interrelationships between students' family, peer, and school worlds as well as the importance of transition and adaptation patterns.

During the final two sessions, we presented the Students' Multiple Worlds Typology and asked the students to consider the cases they had read and discussed in light of the framework. Further, students were encouraged to reflect on the relevance and accuracy of the framework in terms of their own experiences. In the following section, we describe in detail the processes that occurred during this group investigation project.

Phases of Group Inquiry

In describing cultural therapy, George and Louise Spindler (this volume) point out that what cultural therapy is may vary depending on the orientation and starting point of the individuals involved. We found the experience of working in a group particularly conducive to capitalizing on where students were (e.g., with respect to their experiences and starting points). Because these cases contained a great deal of variety, students found themselves sometimes quite familiar with the circumstances in one case and quite unfamiliar with those in another. In other words, students were more or less competent with regard to analyzing the thoughts and actions of a particular student depending on the congruence of the case with their own life experiences. When youths were more competent, they frequently assisted other participants by communicating their understanding of the situation. This led to chains of collaborative reasoning about a variety of socially relevant topics, for example, the source and meaning of ethnic divisions, whether or not teachers can be prejudiced, and what it means to be an American. This assistance grew naturally out of the group process. In other words, students were not told to help one another and they were probably not conscious of the fact that they were doing so. As such, much of the cultural therapy that occurred during the sessions was student directed, with group members assisting one another in the interpretation of a given situation.[3] Exposure to same-aged peers' explanations and points of view enabled students to begin to understand and empathize with the feelings and perspectives of others in a way that probably would not have occurred in a one-on-one setting.

Overall, the group process was characterized by seven distinct phases: (a) confrontation with the cases, (b) personal recognition, (c) communication to others, (d) recognition of others, (e) consciousness of tacit social assumptions, (f) analysis of social stratification, and (g) theory generation and critique. The group phases are described in detail below.

Phase 1: Confrontation With the Cases

The first phase of the group process was characterized by students' responding directly to the content of a given case. Facilitators' questions (for example, "What do you think about Trinh?" or "What stands out to you about this case?") prompted students to reiterate their understanding of a particular student's life and comment on difficulties they saw the student facing. They also made suggestions, often evaluative, about how things could be different. In essence, the cases provided a thematic perception stimulus to which the students responded. In other words, all contained the themes of the importance of interrelationships between students' multiple worlds and the significance of transition and adaptation patterns. While the cases provided the content, the students were not told how to deal with what they read. In short, their initial responses were analogous to how they might respond to a short story or piece of literature in one of their high school classrooms. For example:

Black American female: I think she is trying to fit in but at the same time she doesn't feel it right to be a part of both cultures and she wants to shed one and just be part of one. Which I don't think is right. . . . You shouldn't have to necessarily shed all of one culture to be a part of the other. I mean, that is what America is about, right?

European American male: At the beginning, this guy sounded a lot like myself. Where he lost me was when he started to say he doesn't want to mingle. When he says he wants to stay with his own kind and not mingle I think that's where he goes wrong. I think that's stupid.

By initially focusing on the content that was introduced, students were able to maintain a certain comfortable distance from one another—in other words, they did not have to talk about their own lives but could focus on the substance of the material provided. The first phase of the group process gave them a chance to test their own responses against the reaction of other group members, assess the situation in which they found themselves, and gauge the extent to which it might be safe to reveal more personal information.

Phase 2: Personal Recognition

Central American female: I think reading all the different cases about the different kinds of teenagers gave me an opportunity to think about people's situations in the same way I live them. I was able to relate to many of them or some of them and was able to express my feelings about problems. . . . I hadn't really found a place where I felt comfortable enough to say my problems out loud until now.

European American male: While I was sitting in the conference room for the first time I was thinking, "Oh boy! We have to do this *six* times!" Then we did a case study. I was so intrigued by reading about a person and then finding a way to relate them to my life. It helped me to realize who I am as a person. Talking about the pros and cons of each study, relating them to me, and then using that to change the way I act in a positive manner.

While students' initial responses were almost always concerned with the content of a specific case, they quickly began to relate the cases to their own experiences. Not surprising, students could identify more closely with some cases than others. The circumstances of the students portrayed, however, provided enough variety so that all of the participants could find parallels in their own lives. For example:

Central American female: That's me. It's very much like me. I came to the U.S. when I was 7 years old. By third I could speak fluently. My family couldn't believe it, I got it so quickly. But I remember the first day of school. I came home crying and I said, "I never want to go back." 'Cause everybody looked at me and they are like, "Oh, she can't speak English, leave her alone." And I was like all to myself in a corner at school.

European American male: The guy [referring to the case study of a high-achieving European American male] has gotten turned the wrong way—like David Duke . . . but sometimes I feel that way when someone walks along in the hall and is acting like they own the place and knocks my girlfriend down. And either I do nothing or I find myself targeted, I find myself being jumped, and that upsets me sometimes and that's the only time I feel myself feeling that way . . . but like I don't think he's seeing the rest of the population. He's just like looking at one little piece of the population and saying, "That's the way they are."

While each case triggered different issues and concerns for individual students, common themes arose in group discussions as well. For example, the case study of Carla, a high-achieving Latina student who adopts one set of behaviors with her primarily European American peers in high-track classes and other behaviors with her Latina friends and family (see Chapter 5, this volume), triggered students' immediate recognition of the various selves they themselves reveal as they move across settings. Their comments bear remarkable similarity to the Spindlers' descriptions of enduring and situated selves:

Central American female: I know how she feels. For example, here [at school] I hang about with my Spanish friends and when I get home, I mostly hang out with Black and White people.

East Indian male: I feel that way [like Carla] because when I'm with my friends outside of school—they mostly speak Indian, and I feel strange because sometimes I slip up by speaking Indian with English combined and they think that I'm strange or something. . . . It's a shame to have to change. I wish that I could just be myself.

European American male: Because I'm in CP [an academic track] I'm like this. And when I go out, I join my honors friends and I have to change to fit with those friends.

East Indian female: I go to Indian wedding festivals and I feel strange, like I go with the flow and don't express myself much. I don't know, it's like I don't think much about readjusting. I just don't want to think about it.

African American female: I think that with friends, I can be myself the most. In class I feel that I have to act all proper and not use street talk.

Attention to the details of students' family, peer, and school worlds and the explication of patterns used to navigate settings in the case studies were themes with which the group participants resonated. The interactive group process provided a catalyst for all students to explore the relevance of these themes to their own lives.

Phase 3: Communication to Others

While students readily moved to considering similarities between their lives and those of the case study youths, communicating their understanding to others was a process that evolved more gradually. As mentioned previously, evaluative comments about the case vignettes were frequent and made by almost all of the participants. This was particularly true as students considered case study youths who voiced negative attitudes toward peers or teachers. For the most part, students did not question or respond to their classmates' evaluative interpretations in initial sessions. As time went on, however, students began to respond to others who voiced critical comments—particularly when they saw comparisons between their lives and that of the case study student being criticized. For example, after reading about Sonia, a Latina student who responded negatively to a teacher for making comments she perceived as prejudiced, the following conversation ensued:

European American male: First of all, I think it's sad that she says that her teachers don't care. That's, that's . . . they care. It's just her perception of them not caring. And she is probably negative towards them so she doesn't see them as being positive back. And I think the saddest part is that her parents can't help her. Like she said, they don't know the educational system so she can't expect help from them. And if you can't expect help from your family, you are in trouble if you start hanging out with the wrong people. You've got nobody to tell you to do any better. I feel bad for her because I'm sure we'd all like to think everything ends up all cheery. But there are some people it doesn't turn around for.

Central American male: I pretty much know how she feels about the teachers. I mean kinda. I came here in '86 when I was in the sixth grade. I felt like the teachers really encouraged me to learn English. But then when I got to middle school I started getting in the wrong group and the principal really got me on the wrong side 'cause he told me like I was going to end up bad. I was going to end up a bum and he even bet me $20 I wouldn't graduate from high school. I gotta go find him. (laughter) And when I came here [middle school] I pretty much got a bad impression of the teachers. Thought they were prejudiced and stuff like that.

Counselor: What did they do?

Central American male: Like if you got sent to the central office they'd say, "Oh, you again," like you Mexican guys are all alike. He was very prejudiced about Hispanic people.

European American male: Do you think he was really prejudiced or do you think that was your perception?

Central American male: I think he was pretty prejudiced, that, "I'm going to get that kind of people [Mexicans] here in the office." And when I first came here [to this high school] it was different.

African American female: I agree that he says teachers here are understanding and want you to do better, but I had an experience my sophomore year—I worked my butt off in his class and he wouldn't give me the grade. He would like make comments. . . . It was like the way he looked at me, the way he talked to me. And I can understand where she was coming from when she said the teachers are prejudiced.

The two youths speaking above are communicating an important message to their European American classmate who cannot conceive of prejudice from teachers. They are in essence telling him not to discount the possibility of racism in school environments. From their perspective, Sonia's description rings true, for they also have had similar experiences.

A similar incident occurred during a later session, after students completed reading a case study describing a Vietnamese female who made negative comments about several student groups at her high school. The particular case study sought to illustrate that the remarks were made in response to harassment from peers about her Vietnamese heritage. Nevertheless, some of the group participants voiced strong negative reactions toward the case study student.

European American male: It's like she is racist. She started off with Black people and then she started hitting on the Mexicans. She doesn't want to be here [in the United States]. And I don't know why anybody would force her to be.

Teacher: Why do you suppose she feels that way?

European American male: Because they probably did it to her first. My guess. Or she never wanted to move in the first place, and it was a forced move. They stay around in their own little groups. But Ryan [referring back to another case study in which a European American male says several negative things about other groups] never, he never got into fights or anything. He didn't do it as badly as she did.

Researcher: What are some of the reasons behind people having a lot of fear of others?

Tongan female: Not comfortable in their surroundings.

European American male: She hasn't really given them a chance.

Chinese American female: Some of the Asians who don't speak English—who just moved from Hong Kong—they get a lot of flack from the Blacks and the Mexicans and they will say mean things and these Asians don't even understand what is being said to them. [But] they get the feeling, the tone. They are, we are very passive people. We don't like to antagonize others, so they won't say anything back.

The Chinese American student speaks to her classmate, trying to help him understand that this experience is not unique. By suggesting that the Vietnamese student may well have experienced negative comments from youths in other groups, she tries to encourage a more complex and empathic understanding of the behavior described.

In seeking to communicate, students were forced to search for a way to voice their implicit understanding of the behaviors, values, and assumptions that underlay a given case study student's behavior. In so doing, students took a first step toward bringing their culture, in relation to the "other's" culture, to a level of conscious awareness.

Phase 4: Recognition of Others

> [European American male:] I found the experience very enlightening. It was a good way for me to "break out" of my usual group of friends and talk openly about issues that are important to me. The cases were a good spark for discussion of ourselves. Each of us had a first impression, which then changed as the discussion went on. It was a good experience for me to keep on shattering my preconceptions about people. (Written response)

While students sought (albeit unconsciously) to change each other's first impression of a case, we were not certain whether the discussion that occurred had actually affected students' perceptions of other group members. It was not until the sixth session, when students were asked to provide a written response to the probe, "Write about what comes to mind about this experience and what you think about this experience," that we became aware of the extent to which the group interaction served to heighten students' awareness of not only their own but others' social and personal contexts. It was surprising that, although many of the students knew each other, their written responses indicate that, prior to participating in this project, they had little knowledge of one another's experiences, feelings, or circumstances. For example:

> Perhaps my most interesting discovery through these meetings is that of the many different types of people who attend this high school. Strange. I knew it in the back of my mind that they were there. I just never truly acknowledged them as "people." A fault of society? Tracking in schools? (Written response)

> I found the experience very enlightening. It was a good way for me to "break out" of my usual group of friends and talk openly about issues that are important to me.

While we do not know if, in fact, the processes that occurred in this group will actually help to promote intergroup communication or prevent future misunderstandings, we do know that group participants did become more aware of themselves in relation to others. In this sense, we view it as a positive beginning.

Phase 5: Heightened Consciousness of Tacit Social Assumptions

> As a preliminary orientation, we can state that cultural therapy is a process of bringing one's culture, in its manifold forms—assumptions, goals, values, beliefs, and communicative modes—to a level of awareness that permits one to perceive it as a potential bias in social interaction. (Spindler & Spindler, this volume)

As group members listened to each other and responded to one another's remarks, it appeared that they began to hear themselves in a new way as well. For example, over time, group members became more conscious of the evaluative statements they made and of the assumptions their statements contained. The following examples, in particular, illustrate the group's increased sensitivity to issues of status. These statements were made over time in reference to the case of Carla Chaváz, who, as we mentioned earlier, moves between high-track classes dominated by European and Asian American peers and a group of Latina friends in regular and lower-track classrooms.

Session 1:

European American male 1: She's learned to cope with different pressures and has the desire to succeed. She also leads two lives where she had to get out or drop down to a different level with her Hispanic friends.

European American male 2: When I go from my honors classes to basketball, I step down like Carla—well, not exactly step down, but I certainly get more vulgar with my basketball friends.

Session 2

European American male 1: School was hard. She really concentrated on getting good grades. It was stressful for her. She had to appeal to her upper friends and then wanted to maker her lower, her lower-class friends proud—[to be] kinda a role model type thing.

Counselor: Was it tough for her?

Hispanic male: Yes. Adjusting from group to group. Like hanging around her so-called upper-class friends and then going [with her Hispanic friends] when lunch comes around. Having to do a 360 degree turn.

European American male 2: Maybe she'll find the self-confidence [to know] that it is not a matter of going to her upper or lower-class friends, but that they are both good.

Session 4

Counselor: Thinking about the four cases [that we've read so far], how do they experience transitions?

European American male 2: I think Carla transitions very well. She can be with her superior friends and not superior friends. I don't know what to call them.

Chinese American female: Don't call them "superior."

Students' readiness to equate academic achievement with being "high class," "superior," or a "step up" is a vivid illustration of the extent to which these youth have internalized the cultural messages embedded in their school environments. But over time, as students heard themselves speak and began to challenge one another's assumptions by persuading others to look with more complexity at youths who are different than themselves, group members appeared to become more aware of the tacit assumptions they hold.

Students' written comments about the value of this process also appear to support this premise. For example, one European American male wrote:

> I think that talking about these situations would be ex-
> tremely helpful to someone like Ryan (or myself!) because
> it brings out the realities behind behaviors of people from
> different worlds. I think Ryan's fear of Vietnamese people
> (or whomever) would be abated by knowing the pressures
> put on someone like Trinh, and the conflicting forces of her
> culture and American culture. I certainly found that I had a
> much better understanding of the people in our group, and
> it became very important to me at a time in my life where I
> was locked into all white and Asian classes, white and
> Asian sports, etc.

In a sense, the group process enabled students to obtain a symbolic handle on the underlying beliefs and assumptions guiding their thoughts and actions—not unlike the process that occurs in psychotherapeutic settings. Unlike therapy aimed at bringing underlying psychological dynamics into consciousness, however, what occurred here had very much to do with making explicit the tacit messages embedded in the school and broader social environment.

Phase 6: Analysis and Critique of Social Stratification

> For students, cultural therapy is essentially a means of consciousness-raising—that is, to make explicit unequal power relationships in the classroom, the school, and the larger society. (Spindler & Spindler, this volume)

As mentioned initially in this chapter, cultural therapy was not our purpose when we began to work with this group of students. Moreover, our emphasis on determining the validity of our research focused our efforts on promoting students' self-examination and recognition of others rather than social analysis. Nevertheless, issues relevant to social stratification were embedded in many of the case vignettes. Over time, group members began to notice and discuss these points. For example, in early sessions, students identified some of the personal consequences of social categorization. In particular, they analyzed the ways in which groups work to mitigate individuals' developing bicultural or constructive marginal personalities (Spindler & Spindler, this volume) and began to analyze group politics that give rise to such pressures.

African American female: I grew up in a White neighborhood, went to a White middle school and people feel I should join the Black Student Union. And I don't think I have to join a group to understand my culture.

Central American female: It's not only Blacks. I see it happening to my Latino friends. It's like a line divides certain things. They put themselves on one side of the line (*boundary?*) yes, boundary, and you can't pass that certain boundary, otherwise you are going to be like someone else. You have to try and stay the way you are. So it's like you don't want to admit a change for the good 'cause you don't want anybody talking about how you prefer to change than stay yourself. So more or less it's like people care more about what others think if they do good than what they think if they're not.

[Continuing, this Central American female describes an instance when a group of Tongans asked her and her friends, "What are you guys doing over here? You're supposed to be over there."]

European American male: I think their [Tongan's] culture is really important to them. 'Cause I go to a church which is 90% Tongan. I think culture is just really important. Each group has their culture and it's important to them. And any other culture is not as good.

European American male 2: That's how it can be in our culture too. When we see some kind of danger trying to overthrow our culture or trying to change it of course we're going to put up a barrier to try to protect it. I assume it's like that with every culture. That people are very strong about keeping it and that they will do whatever is in their power to keep it. . . . [This male goes on to explain that his friends are thinking of starting a European Club in response to the other ethnic clubs at the school.]

African American female: I don't know why, 'cause Black culture is certainly not mentioned in the textbooks.

European American male 2: I think they are feeling really threatened by all of these people that they are not used to being around.

In a manner reminiscent of Foucault (1983) and other scholarly writers (see Anzaldua, 1987; Kondo, 1990), these youths identify the ways in which power, embodied in personal relationships, affects and constrains their lives. In seeking to locate the source of this power, students do not usually go beyond psychological explanations (e.g., "wanting to keep one's culture," "feeling threatened") to consider the economic, historical, and political sources of group alliance and conflict. Yet, with the aid of a few well-placed questions (e.g., Are there other things, in addition to culture, that ethnic groups are seeking to protect? When is it that one group begins to perceive another as a threat?), a conversation such as the one above could lead to a detailed discussion of social stratification and group alliance.

Students did examine an aspect of social stratification when discussing differential student achievement in terms of parental involvement in schooling. For example, during the fourth group session, students compared Sonia, coming from a Mexican immigrant family in which no one attended college, to Ryan, coming from a European American family in which both parents attended college. During this discussion, the group began to locate and analyze the type of knowledge that enables some students and not others to attain or maintain status and privilege. In essence, they were exploring Bourdieu's (1977) concept of "cultural capital."

European American male: I'm like Ryan but not socially. My family and school match. Parents look out for you. If your family believes in what the school is doing then everything will be all right but if not, then they'll express what is wrong.

[Seeming to recall that Sonia's parents *did* believe in what the school was doing, this group member then modified his comment as follows.]

> Sonia's parents didn't go to college. 'Cause they didn't have the experience of Ryan's parents and didn't know. And I think they might want to help and they do want to help. But how to help, they don't know. Even if someone told them to go to the school and talk about it, I don't know if they would have the guts or self-will to talk to the school about it.

European American male 2:   I don't know about anybody else, but we have the PTA parents. Our families, like you can't do anything wrong [at school] 'cause everybody knows. My dad used to teach here and my mom was PTA president so people don't mind calling my folks. It's an advantage in a way 'cause if we need someone, I know they are willing to help me out because they are my parents and stuff.

East Indian female: My parents look out for me. They're not PTA parents, but my mom's here to defend my case. My mom has been up here so many times. It's very hard for a person to come in who doesn't know the system.

East Indian male: Basically, my parents expect . . . actually, listening to [name] talk, I wouldn't mind having someone watch me a bit more.

Central American female: My parents, especially my mom, doesn't feel comfortable speaking English.

In a later session, when considering the case of a Latina female who earned primarily Cs and was working to be the first in her economically poor family to graduate, students referred more explicitly to the power differences between families vis-à-vis the school system:

European American male: She's just a normal student. . . . She has to go along with a school system that does nothing for her. But if she wanted the school system to change—like Ryan and his parents would go down and have the school changed, but her parents can't.

In seeing the power differences between case study students' families, the group participants also appeared to become more aware of the power differences between themselves. Such is a first step toward encouraging students to critically examine the extent to which equal opportunity exists in their high school and, by extension, in American society.

Phase 7: Theory Generation and Critique

> [Chinese female:] Originally when I first saw the model [the one with four types] I knew that there had to be other types. I treated the model like scientists treat the five criteria necessary for the Hardy-Weinberg [theorem] to work—in other words, the exceptions prove the rule or, in the case of the two new types that have been developed, the exceptions make the rule. (Written response)

In the last two sessions, we presented the Students' Multiple Worlds Typology. The students then discussed the cases they had read and attempted to classify them according to the typology. In so doing, they also began to think about their own family, peer, and school worlds and transition patterns generally. "But what about students whose worlds are different and have smooth transitions?" remarked the Chinese American female. "That sounds like the way it is for you," replied the counselor. "Yes, I think it is," she responded.

"I don't think Robert [a case study student] really fits one of the types," said a student. "How would you describe him?" asked another. "Well, I think his worlds are really pretty much the same but even so he can't transition." And so the discussion continued.

With this group analysis, it became clear that our typology could be expanded to include two additional types: (a) students whose worlds are different but transition smoothly and (b) students whose worlds are similar but find transitions impossible. Further, we realized that, while the types represented fairly distinct patterns, they might better be illustrated along a continuum. Thus the group investigation process led us to revise and expand our original typology (see Figure 2.2).

Discussion

[Chinese American female:] I do think reading and talking about this model will be beneficial to other students (and even adults!). An analogy for this model might be (before learning about it) trying to read a map with the paper stuck right on your forehead and covering your eyes. After learning about the model it is like reading a map with the map with the paper at a comfortable and readable distance away. (Written response)

Students' written comments following the sessions confirmed our perception that the participants very much liked reading and talking about youth their own age. The content had indeed engaged their interest and stimulated thoughtful and prolonged discussions. Further, the experiences of these youth confirmed the relevance and validity of our research—they too felt that the interplay of meanings from family, peer, and school worlds was critical to their experiences in school. Finally, with respect to our original objectives, we found that involving students as partners in the research process is not only feasible but also profitable.

Students' participation and analyses led us to further develop our original framework by expanding our descriptions of the range of transition and adaptation patterns. By reflecting on the model in terms of their own lives, students were able to help us see ways in which the typology could be expanded. At the same time, they articulated some cautions. For example, one student wrote:

[East Indian male:] In this world also there is much more tolerance of other people now than there was 20 years ago. I believe the best advantage to "our" model is that it helps

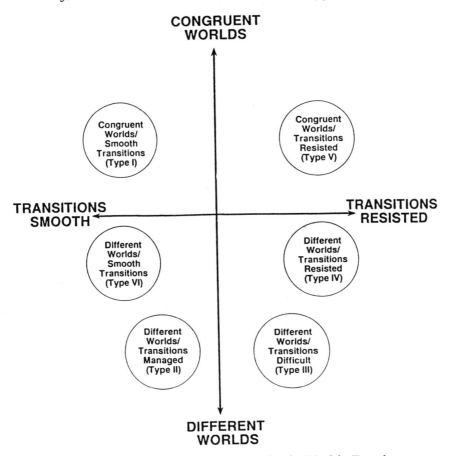

Figure 2.2. The (revised) Students' Multiple Worlds Typology

us understand where people do come from and what problems are associated with their personal lives. If this model will enable us to be more tolerant and understanding of people then more power to it. But, if this model leads to the grouping of individuals and separation of people then there must be a better way to study the problems and personalities of people. I think the best thing about this model is that it creates a space for everyone, but everyone should *not* be confined to their space. I think it is safe to say that people can and will change. (Written response)

Beyond these results, we observed that the group process in many ways bears remarkable similarity to the Spindlers' articulation of cultural therapy. In this group investigation, first, students became more aware of their own assumptions, goals, values, and beliefs, and, second, they began to perceive these as potential biases in their social interactions with others. Further, students began to examine unequal power relationships in their classrooms, school, and the larger society. Thus what began as an informal exploration—trying to learn how adolescents would perceive and respond to a model and typology—turned out to clearly resemble cultural therapy or at least approximate the core of the Spindlers' purpose.

We do believe, however, that had cultural therapy been an explicit focus at the outset, the potential for "consciousness-raising" during these sessions would have been even greater. While students were certainly capable of identifying and discussing themes and relating them to their lives and those of others, they lacked the background necessary to formulate, without assistance, questions about social and structural factors that limit access and perpetuate inequalities in their school and in the broader society. A more in-depth and complex consideration of such issues and problems by students might well have been possible had the tenets of cultural therapy guided us as we began.

Notes

1. The group investigation we describe is similar to the group investigation model described by Joyce, Weil, and Showers (1992) and Sharan and Shachar (1988).

2. We use the suffixes *American* or *immigrant* to indicate place of birth.

3. In this sense, much of the learning that took place during these six sessions can be analyzed in terms of a Vygotskian framework. Vygotsky (1978) refers to a zone of proximal development, which is "the distance between the actual developmental level as determined by individual problem solving and the level of poten-

tial development through problem solving under adult guidance or in collaboration with more capable peers" (p. 86). With such assistance, "learning awakens a variety of internal developmental processes that are able to operate only when the child is interacting with people in his environment and in cooperation with his peers. Once these processes are internalized, they become part of the child's independent developmental achievement" (p. 90).

References

Anzaldua, G. (1987). *Borderlands/la frontera: The new mestiza.* San Francisco: Spinsters/Aunt Lute Book Company.

Bourdieu, P. (1977). *Outline of a theory of practice.* Cambridge: Cambridge University Press.

Foucault, M. (1983). The subject and power. In H. L. Dreyfus & P. Rabinow (Eds.), *Michael Foucault: Beyond structuralism and hermeneutics* (pp. 208-226). Chicago: University of Chicago Press.

Joyce, B., Weil, M., & Showers, B. (1992). *Models of teaching* (4th ed.). Boston: Allyn & Bacon.

Kondo, D. K. (1990). *Crafting selves: Gender, discourse and identity in a Japanese workplace.* Chicago: University of Chicago Press.

Phelan, P., Davidson, A. L., & Yu, H. C. (1993). Students' multiple worlds: Navigating the borders of family, peer, and school cultures. In P. Phelan & A. L. Davidson (Eds.), *Renegotiating cultural diversity in American schools* (pp. 52-88). New York: Teachers College Press.

Sharan, S., & Shachar, H. (1988). *Language and learning in the cooperative classroom.* New York: Springer-Verlag.

Vygotsky, L. (1978). *Mind in society: The development of higher psychological processes* (M. Cole, V. John-Steiner, S. Scribner, & E. Souberman, Eds. and Trans.). Cambridge, MA: Harvard University Press.

Tom Schram

3

Players Along the Margin

Diversity and Adaptation in a Lower Track Classroom

TOM SCHRAM

Tom Schram is Assistant Professor of Education at the University of New Hampshire. He completed his Ph.D. at the University of Oregon in 1990, with a major in education and minor in cultural anthropology. His dissertation research, under the guidance of Harry Wolcott, focused on the life history of a veteran teacher and her transition to a new work setting. For his study, Schram received the outstanding dissertation award in teaching and teacher education at the annual meeting of the American Educational Research Association in 1991. Prior to his graduate work, he was an elementary school teacher in rural Wyoming, where he also had worked as a cowboy, ambulance attendant, and wilderness guide. He first became interested in educational anthropology through his undergraduate program in Native American studies and education at Dartmouth College and subsequent work on the Flathead Reservation in western Montana. In this chapter, he draws upon his most recent 2 years of work with an ethnic Lao community in northern New England.

"Hello. My name is Ms. Navarro and I'm going to be your English teacher for the rest of the year." It was the fifth week of the fall semester. Mary Navarro's hands shook noticeably as she reviewed the circumstances that led to the previous teacher's

AUTHOR'S NOTE: The research reported in this chapter was supported by grants from the Central University Research Fund and the Graduate School Faculty Fellowship program at the University of New Hampshire. Special thanks to George and Louise Spindler, Cyrene Wells, and Harry Wolcott for their editorial assistance and helpful comments on earlier drafts.

departure and her own sudden arrival at Millshore High School. The economy was in recession and she was grateful to be in a classroom. Replacing a teacher who had been deemed incompetent, however, was hardly the auspicious start to a teaching career that Mary, a second-career beginning teacher, had envisioned. Nor had she expected to face such culturally diverse students in a rural New England community.

In this class, one of six separate courses she prepared for daily, Mary taught American Literature to 11 "lower track" juniors. Three of these students were Laotian refugees with limited understanding of the English language and limited experience with American culture. Each received one or two periods of supplemental English-as-a-second-language (ESL) instruction daily in a self-contained resource room. The other eight students shared an American working-class background and a fundamental ambivalence toward schooling. Five students from this latter group attended an afternoon vocational training program in another community. All eight were designated as "problem" or "low-ability" students. Individuals from both groups, Laotian and American,[1] bore the burden of social and cultural marginality and academic stigmatization.

For the 10 months prior to Mary's arrival, I had been collecting data on the social and cultural adjustment of Laotian refugee adolescents within this small and, until recent years, ethnically homogeneous high school. The focus of my inquiry was the role of teachers and peers as mediators among students, lesson content, and the structural arrangements that made it easy or difficult for language-minority students to participate meaningfully in classroom interactions (reported in Schram, 1992b).

Mary's arrival proved serendipitous. Her own perspective as a Cuban refugee and as a newcomer both to Millshore and to the teaching profession, I felt, could highlight taken-for-granted aspects of the local school experience. These tacit understandings might prove to be most significant in understanding cultural conflict and adaptation within the classroom. Mary had foreseen early on that she would receive little support or guidance from her Millshore colleagues. She viewed my proposed collaborative study of her class "as a positive way to improve my technique and my understanding of the students."

This chapter is devoted to a discussion of cultural therapy as manifested in the study of Mary's classroom over a period of 8 months. As a deliberate remedial effort, this study drew the two of us into a joint exploration of the role of culture and social background in shaping opportunities for success in the classroom. Our exploration took the form of a reflective and culturally bracketed dialogue focused upon Mary's perceptions of herself and her students. Drawing in part upon the Spindlers' framework of an "own" and "other" reflective analysis of similar or shared situations (Spindler & Spindler, 1992), we attempted to clarify cultural assumptions revealed in Mary's behavior and in the behaviors of her students. Application of concepts of self and culture, and the relationship of cultural self-awareness to acquisition of competence, suggested several orienting questions:

1. In what ways do the behaviors and coping strategies of individuals within the classroom reflect and enhance their respective cultural perspectives?
2. To what extent, and to what effect, are the teacher's cultural assumptions and values projected into her interactions with her students?
3. How does the teacher's awareness of cultural assumptions informing individual behavior in the classroom translate into responsive educational practice?

The interpretation of cultural therapy as advanced in this chapter presupposes that the key to effectively managing personally experienced cultural conflict is to become functionally aware of the degree to which behavior is culturally informed and influenced. By functionally aware, I refer to an awareness that translates into an ability to manage or adapt one's behavior in response to situational demands. The underlying assumption is that, consciously or unconsciously, individuals exhibit behaviors that fit their cultural assumptions and enhance their cultural perspective

(Trueba, Jacobs, & Kirton, 1990, pp. 133-137). As presented in this case, cultural therapy provides a means to explore an individual's perceptions of her interactions with others and, through focused reflection upon those perceptions, to come to terms with the cultural embeddedness of her behavior.

A fundamental issue was how Mary and her students dealt with the marginal status attributed to them by others in the school and community. I direct particular attention toward the manner in which Mary's intermittent obscurity and exposure along the margin sharpened the focus of our cultural interpretations and facilitated her ability to "step back" from the school setting and reflect critically upon actions, events, and behaviors.

In the following section, I describe the school and community context in which classroom events and teacher-student interactions occurred. The next section provides a focused description of Mary and her lower track English class, with particular attention directed toward issues of marginality and group identification, patterns of interaction mediated by the teacher, and conflicting perceptions of classroom life.

In the final section, I apply concepts of self and culture to an understanding of Mary's present situation. Here the attempt is to operationalize cultural therapy, with an emphasis upon clarifying the relationship between cultural self-awareness and the mediation of social interaction and cultural conflict in the classroom.

The School and Community Setting

A former mill town of 7,000, Millshore represents one of a growing number of small, rural communities affected by the secondary migration of Southeast Asian refugees within this country. Its location within northern New England, identified in the 1990 census as the most ethnically homogeneous region in the United States, accentuates the challenges faced by culturally distinct "outsiders" who enter the local scene. To the surprise of many local observers, these factors have not deterred the emergence of a sizable ethnic Lao community within Millshore, a town that affords ample rental housing and easy access to nearby factories, where many refugees find work.[2] The community's response to such change, while not antagonistic, has been less than receptive. As one longtime resident noted,

> I guess we're somewhere between a holding tank and a melting pot. But for all the good feeling you get from this town, there's still some sense of underlying tension. It's just not like the days when you could walk from home to the mill every morning and recognize everybody on the street.

At the heart of the "traditional" Millshore community, and lending its influence to both the school board and the town government, was an extended core of families that proudly traced their descent through generations of Millshore residents, some as far back as the town's founding in the late seventeenth century. Local residents confirmed the community's strong sense of tradition, noting that construction of low-income rental housing in recent years had contributed to increased transiency and a "breakdown of the local socioeconomic and family structure." Others described a weakening of the town's historical rootedness while at the same time noting the persistence, in one form or another, of an "us versus them" mentality: "You're never really considered a true member of Millshore unless you're born here. My husband and I have lived here 13 years and we're still considered among 'the new people.' It's a funny community that way." The proud but beleaguered faculty I encountered at Millshore High School traced the general lack of appreciation for their teaching efforts to townspeople frustrated with the costs of supporting the school for an increasingly "new" and "needy" local population.

At the time of my fieldwork, Millshore High served approximately 220 students, 9% of whom were Laotian. With the exception of one African American, the remaining 91% were white students of predominantly northern European ancestry, though most identified themselves as "typical, small-town New Englanders." Class sizes averaged 10 to 15 students, with some lower and upper level courses numbering as few as 4 or 5 students.

Students were placed for their regular academic classes into one of three tracks: college preparatory (C Level), "average to above-average" (A Level), or remedial (Basic or B Level). Laotian students receiving ESL services and generally deemed unable to keep up with the demands of either A- or C-level classes were placed in the B-level track. Systematic observations of student and teacher behavior at Millshore highlighted a number of concerns commonly associated with lower track classrooms (for detailed examination of tracking-related issues, see Page, 1987, 1991; Schwartz, 1981):

1. Millshore teachers generally had lower expectations for B-level students. Comments and actions by teachers and other school personnel regarding the Laotian B-level students, in particular, pointed at the presumed disability or lower mental ability of these students.

2. American students in the B-level classes were felt to be less tolerant of the Laotian students than were American students in the faster track classes.

3. The Laotian students tended to view their American B-level classmates as social outcasts whose friendship offered limited social or academic advantages. Several Laotians expressed confusion and resentment due to their seemingly automatic placement with students whose behavior they found disrespectful and who, according to general student and faculty perceptions, were regarded as "slow" or "dumb."

4. The American B-level students' social differentiation from the top tracks tended to be expressed academically in an unwillingness to participate or perform voluntarily in the classroom. In contrast, the Laotian students in B-level classes did not tend to lower their expectations and succumb to peer pressure to "take it easy" in school.

The Millshore faculty's definition of Laotian student success hinged on cultural assimilation, with an implicit bias toward facilitating the students' social adjustment and "getting them through" high school. For all lower track students, comparatively little emphasis was placed upon enhancing academic performance. One teacher offered this blunt assessment:

> The feeling I get is that the school administration is contemptuous of these lower track kids, including the Laotians. I know in part that's a function of the way the community looks at them. The guidance department just pays lip service to these students and shoves them through—no guidance, just a small Band-Aid on an open chest wound. What's most important is making sure the students are under control.

The Laotian students, in turn, seemed intent upon minimizing the more conspicuous aspects of their ethnicity yet did not necessarily seek primary integration into the social sphere of the high school. Reflecting the wishes of their parents, most Laotian adolescents assumed an instrumental perspective toward formal education. Courses were deemed valuable only insofar as they could be tied to future employment aspirations. Participation in informal social activities was viewed as drawing unwanted attention to cultural and linguistic differences.

As noted by Gibson (1988), immigrants and refugees, on the whole, are more determined than nonimmigrants of comparable class background to use education as a strategy for upward social mobility. Fueled by high expectations and assumptions about the value of schooling, this strategy assumed particular significance in Millshore, where a number of Laotian parents had experienced the demoralizing shift from high-status occupations in Laos (e.g., pilot, government official) to less highly regarded factory work in the United States. The Laotian students' attitudes toward school and employment, especially those of the boys, were shaped by a determination to be more successful than their parents. (For

discussion of changing family dynamics during the refugee resettlement experience, see Wiseman, 1985.)

In this regard, the Laotian students were like their lower track
American classmates, who, by individual choice or institutional
steerage, tended to place greater emphasis upon vocational than
upon academic training. In contrast to the Laotian adolescents, the
American students typically indicated that they would be satisfied to achieve the same occupational level and status as their
parents. Others felt they were never offered any alternatives: "I
was born to be a Vo-Pro [vocational professional], and I'll be one
'til I die," remarked one disaffected student. One veteran teacher
responded:

> So many of these voc-ed kids aren't really part of the school.
> Much of that comes from the larger community. There's a
> definite division between the kids who have and the kids
> who don't. By "have" I don't mean money, I mean they have
> parents who care and communicate with teachers—they
> have a better life.

In sum, Millshore's lower track and language minority students
found themselves in conflict-ridden roles that virtually guaranteed
they would be at odds with some relationship. With few excep-
tions, their classroom experiences were framed by a deficit view
of their abilities and experiences, an administrative perspective
that stressed social fit above enhancement of academic performance, and differing expectations from school and community.
The "working-class identity" (Moll, 1992, p. 20) of the education
received by these students shaped their academic stigmatization
and reinforced their status as social and cultural marginals.

Mary Navarro and Her Classroom

Although my stated intention was to engage in a process of
"cultural therapy" with Mary, much of what I did under that label

resembled nothing more and nothing less than what I had done in previous anthropologically oriented fieldwork. Hindsight reveals the primary difference to be one of emphasis and timing rather than approach: I had never before been so explicit about, or dependent upon, my role as cultural translator. Nor had I so deliberately "laid my cards on the table" as I did in this case by inviting Mary to share my developing interpretations from the start. Our cycle of feedback and analysis signaled a shift in my role from unobtrusive recorder of change to interactive facilitator of change.

I had devoted the latter half of the previous year to intensive observation of student-student and student-teacher interactions throughout the school. For at least 2 days each week, I immersed myself in Millshore High, using the scope of activities and contacts of the Laotian students and their teachers to determine the study's boundaries. The school's ESL resource room provided regular opportunities for intensive contact with the Laotian students and also served as a base from which I made observations throughout the school. The ESL instructor became my "anchor" and confidant. (For a description of the role played by this earlier informant, see Schram, 1992a.)

As I shifted into a collaborative phase with Mary, the following data collection procedures supplemented my regular classroom observations and proved especially valuable and appropriate to the cultural translation process: (a) the regular exchange of a "dialogue journal" in which I fed back to Mary selected observations and my developing interpretations of classroom life, to which she responded in writing; (b) the construction of Mary's life history through taped interviews, supplemented by interviews with her parents and colleagues; (c) interviews with students in Mary's class and the elicitation of informal ratings of themselves and of Mary; (d) Mary's formal and informal assessment of each student, including estimates of academic performance and potential, peer interactions, home background, and personal feelings toward members of the class; and (e) my continuing observations of faculty and school board meetings, community events, and other activities that helped define the broader context of Mary's classroom experiences.

Marginality and Identification

My observations of Mary confirmed the idea suggested by
Finley (1984), Metz (1987), and Goldstein (1988) that teachers'
status within a faculty culture is in large part derived from the
status of their students. Colleagues' perceptions of Mary's teaching
or interpersonal skills were tempered not only by her status as
newcomer and novice but also by the fact that she taught students
who were marginal to the faculty's desired image of the school.

The Laotian students' experience revealed basic contradictions
in the manner teachers perceived them. On the one hand, they
displayed the quiet, cooperative, and studious behaviors valued
by Millshore's faculty. On the other, their status as good behavioral and motivational models was framed by low expectations for
their academic achievement and persistent frustration with cultural
and communicative difficulties. These latter concerns, set within a
dominant school culture that tended to categorize refugee and lower
track students together regardless of actual placement, sustained
the Lao students' position as both social and academic marginals.

Mary's feelings of identification with the Lao students and her
overall confidence in the abilities of her lower track students put
her both on the margin of the dominant faculty group and in the
central position of defending her students as competent, under-
rated individuals. Her status was further framed by an institutional context in which teachers generally felt undervalued and
unempowered and that ascribed limited influence and support to
her as a beginning teacher.

Uncertain of how she was perceived by her colleagues yet
convinced that the academic potential and self-esteem of her
lower track students were being undermined in other classrooms,
Mary chose to avoid identifying too closely with the high school's
dominant faculty group. Frustrated as well by the disconnected-
ness and self-defensive posture she perceived among many of the
secondary teachers, especially those within her department, she
frequently sought support and advice within the junior high
school wing of the building.[3] In her words:

I am much more like the junior high teachers than the high school teachers. The junior high teachers are activists in many ways—they're vocal, they're not complacent, and they care very much about the kids. . . . You have to be fearless to do this job, but we have quite a few high school teachers who are afraid of the kids. So, to get through the day, they don't make the kids do anything. They don't want to deal with the flak. I know, because I get that feeling sometimes.

Soon after Mary's arrival, one of the junior high teachers described the "unspoken contract" that existed between a number of the high school teachers and their students: "I won't make you work too hard, you don't give me a hard time." When asked to elaborate, this teacher explained that the lower track students' behavior and achievement did not reflect what some teachers believed was necessary to portray teaching success and effectiveness to a demanding Millshore community. To compensate for this, teachers distanced themselves from these students and, in some measure, categorized them as unteachable. In a few isolated cases, teachers invested effort in students who demonstrated promise and a willingness to work. But this investment in individual students coexisted with a dismissive attitude toward the lower track students as a whole. As one faculty member stated it: "I think some of these kids threaten the teachers' ability to demonstrate whatever victories they attain in the school."[4]

In contrast to teachers who rely upon a faculty culture to free them from total dependence on student feedback as a source of rewards (Lieberman & Miller, 1984, pp. 48-49), Mary's actions suggested a deliberate rejection of the dominant peer group and a primary identification with her students and with her role as teacher. Ultimately, she negotiated her own unaffiliated course between and around groups in the school, informed and inspired by her students' advocacy needs and by her own uncertainties and enthusiasms as a beginning teacher.

Patterns of Interaction

The learning environment jointly constructed by Mary and her students was marked by contrasts and complex interdependencies. In previous work, I described how participation patterns of the Laotian students in both formal and informal classroom activities were characterized by extraordinary efforts to remain inconspicuous, though not necessarily uninvolved in the task at hand (Schram, 1992b). American student participation, on the other hand, was generally characterized by selective, often resistant engagement in activities, with occasional bursts of focused involvement by one or two individuals.

Through teacher-mediated pairings and small group work, the Laotian students learned that their academic and social worth in teachers' eyes rested not on solidarity with but on differentiation from their lower track American classmates. They found it demoralizing to be in the position of constantly requiring assistance, especially from individuals regarded as social outcasts in the school and whose behavior and foul language they found disrespectful. At the same time, they acknowledged that the type of help provided by the American students (e.g., providing contextual clues in vocabulary exercises) could not be obtained from their limited-English-proficient Laotian peers.

The American students, in turn, viewed cooperation or friendship with the Laotian students as offering no social or academic advantages. Their openly expressed indignation at the reinforcement and higher expectations they felt Mary granted their Laotian classmates—an accurate assumption, as detailed in later sections—translated more broadly into a resentment toward any reminder of their own status as academic inferiors within the school. The intensity of this resentment was revealed in the response of one American girl who had been shifted into Mary's class from a higher track. Her sense of worth apparently rested upon distancing herself from all lower track students, Laotian and American alike. Mary described this student's behavior:

Libby tries to make herself out to be better than all the rest of the people in the class. It's important that she separate herself image-wise . . . by the way she dresses . . . by asking questions the others don't ask. On the outside, she likes to appear as someone who's on top of her work. On the inside, in private, I get nothing from her.

Despite such feelings, the American students frequently assumed the role of "more competent other" in their classroom encounters with the Laotian students—whether directly, through paired interactions mediated by the teacher, or indirectly and unpredictably, through the questions and answers they provided in class discussions (Schram, 1992b). Interview data suggest that the Laotians viewed such "indirect instruction" as helpful but frustrating. Constantly having to rely upon others' dialogue exacerbated the magnitude of their perceived incompetence and highlighted desired knowledge as something located beyond their immediate grasp.

In sum, Mary's attempted mediation of student interaction was compromised by students' negative perceptions about the worth and attractiveness of their peers as well as by students' negative feelings about their own academic situations. Reinforcement bestowed upon one group of students typically fostered resentment in another group. Those most highly motivated to meet Mary's expectations, the Laotian students, occasionally and paradoxically found themselves dependent for their learning upon those most resistant, the American students. In turn, Mary occasionally and reluctantly compromised the long-term aim of developing the Laotian students' communicative competence in the classroom (e.g., knowing how and when to participate in group discussions) for the sake of their immediate acquisition of knowledge.

Perceptions of Classroom Life

Four culturally informed perspectives were especially significant in the daily functioning of Mary's classroom. Shaping the context for classroom activities was a school culture in which tracking had become the organizational and expectational framework defining the options of students and teachers. Prevalent among the faculty, this perspective reflected a deficit view of the abilities and experiences of Millshore's lower track and language minority students.

The lower track American students upheld a version of classroom life framed by the "unspoken contract" between teachers and students described earlier. Mary's own characterization of this perspective suggests how it reflected and reinforced the "getting-them-through" philosophy that prevailed among Millshore's faculty:

In this low-level situation, I think their [the American students'] minds are made up. They just look at a teacher as someone else who is telling them what to do and what not to do. Some of them are 18 and 19 years old. What's their motivation to do well in school? They just want a grade so they can get out of here.

The Laotian students in Mary's class were not party to this unspoken contract and demonstrated little awareness of it. They proceeded according to Lao community-sanctioned assumptions regarding the instrumental value of formal education. School was a place where they could learn English, learn to cope with the new American environment, and, most important, prepare for entry into the labor market. This perspective was manifested in a positive attitude toward learning. In Mary's words, "They're all hope and dreams and high expectations."

Finally, there was Mary's version of classroom life—a unique blend of assumptions and values derived from her family's Cuban refugee experience and her middle-class, achievement-oriented American upbringing. This lived experience with oppression and opportunity, to be explored in the following section, significantly influenced her beliefs and behavior as a teacher. Much of what she did in the classroom was aimed, directly or indirectly, at offsetting the costs of her students' stigmatized ethnic or social class identity. Although her primary frustration remained "how to find connections between the social and academic needs of the Laotian and American students in the class," her stated goal for each individual remained consistent across whatever boundaries separated the disparate subgroups: "I want each student to *reach* in this class, not just get by."

Mary's statement of frustration suggested that a key instructional challenge for her lay in the different expectations brought to the classroom by the Laotian and American students. Mary admitted to identifying more closely with the Laotians and punctuated her descriptions of them with exclamations of respect and amazement. But she also empathized with the American students' resistance to reminders of their already low status. In one of our early conversations, she acknowledged her selective perceptions and the complex interplay of student attitudes:

> I feel so bad for the Lao kids because intellectually, they don't belong in this class. I admit I feel differently towards them than I do towards many of the American kids. My expectations are higher. But it seems that any positive reinforcement I give them for their studious behavior only puts more distance between them and the American kids [and] they become targets of resentment.

Less obvious to Mary were two other dimensions of the American students' tacit culture—their perception of the high costs of accepting Mary and her instructional program and their response to her attitude toward the Laotian students. Part of our effort within the framework of cultural therapy was to clarify how Mary's own cultural perspective played out against these other dimensions shaping classroom life. I turn now to an examination of this process.

Application of Concepts of Self

A Culturally Based Process of Self-Appraisal

My approach to cultural therapy developed along two comple-
mentary paths. The first dealt with the Spindlers' important distinction between the *enduring self* and the *situated self* (Spindler &
Spindler, 1989, this volume). I was drawn to their suggestion of an
interplay between the deep-seated sense of continuity one has
with one's own past (the enduring self) and the adaptive capabilities manifested in the goal-oriented, context-specific aspects of
the person (the situated self). The former provides, without constraint, a "psychological cohesiveness" to individuals (Trueba et
al., 1990, p. 134). The latter, as an adaptation to immediate demands,
is revealed more explicitly in the attainment of specific ends. One
value of this framework lies in the integrative quality of these concepts. Adaptation does not mean that individuals have to deny or
disregard their deep-seated values, but it does mean that they
must draw upon them in the light of new options and constraints.

My second line of inquiry was more conjectural. I remained
focused on the nexus between the enduring and situated selves
but sought additional explanation of the basis upon which shifts
toward or away from the enduring self took place. On the one
hand, I was attentive to the immediate, practical constraints of
social interaction as catalysts of self-appraisal. On the other, my
work with Mary convinced me that the "romantic-ideal" quality
of the enduring self as identified by the Spindlers pointed to a
culturally embedded "measuring up" process that shapes one's
adjustment to immediate situational demands.

My initial strategy was to posit the interplay of a third construct of self. In previous life history research (Schram, 1990), I had
drawn upon selected elements of Watson and Watson-Franke's
(1985, pp. 187-203) notion of the *ideal self* to direct attention to one
teacher's efforts to cope with the exigencies of a new position
while also measuring up to her image of the "good" teacher. The

basic assumption underlying the ideal self is that, in any society, there exists a set of implicit standards about ideal or proper behavior pertaining to specific roles and revealed in normative statements. How individuals "measure up" to these standards has direct bearing upon the manner in which they approach and meet the demands of interpersonal situations.

Frustration with efforts to establish the enduring and ideal selves as distinct constructs prompted me to reconsider my formulation. Mary's dealings with the ideal appeared clearly embedded in her own historical and cultural experience. In this light, they made sense as a distinct and functional component of her enduring self. References to the ideal proved useful insofar as they highlighted bases of self-appraisal and affirmed the lasting influence of values acquired in early socialization.

Watson and Watson-Franke (1985) provided some organizational guidance by suggesting orders of analysis I might use in applying concepts of self to an interpretation of individual experience. I draw upon general aspects of their model here. My analysis begins with normative statements from informal conversations and from Mary's life narrative that help define qualities of her enduring self, including implicit standards against which behavior across contexts seemed to be measured. I then consider the cognitive dimension in which Mary used standards embedded in her deep-seated cultural values to appraise and adjust her responses to immediate situational demands, including experiences of success or failure. Within this framework, the modes of adaptation demonstrated by Mary are viewed as expressions of the situated self.

Qualities of the Enduring Self

In implementing cultural therapy, I stress the need to maintain a distinction between the personal or idiosyncratic dimensions of an individual's experience (personal or psychological traits) and the qualities embodied and revealed in normative statements about what is expected or ideal or proper with respect to one's role and dealings with others (culturally significant behavior). My focus is on the latter, and my concern in this case is to describe a set of meanings or values appropriate to the cultural contexts that frame Mary's enduring self.

My interviews and field notes are interspersed with normative statements that express the kinds of behavior Mary deemed necessary and proper for social performance and presentation of self. From an analysis of these statements, I identified certain values that constitute something of an ideal configuration against which her behavior across contexts could be measured. With notable consistency, this set of attributes included a strong sense of justice, respect for family and for authority, and belief in the importance both of individualism and of "a sense of belonging."

In expressing notions of justice, Mary evoked the influence of her Cuban heritage and her family's refugee experience. Both her father and her grandfather—the latter of whom served as a representative to Cuba's first constitutional assembly—were briefly imprisoned by Castro in the late 1950s for their political views. The Navarro family's subsequent flight from Cuba to the United States was prompted not by desire for "the good life"—politics aside, they enjoyed a comfortable, middle-class, and professionally oriented existence—but because they were persecuted and they feared for their well-being. They arrived in the United States with little in their pockets and no immediate prospects for support. A lawyer by training, Mary's father worked as a janitor, shoe salesman, teacher, and, after years of struggle and relocation, obtained a position as professor of history at a small state college in northern New England. "We experienced the American Dream," proclaimed Mary's father.

As the eldest daughter and the only child in her family born in Cuba, Mary learned from an early age to appreciate "the old country and customs." Her parents and grandparents fostered in her a steadfast respect for their Cuban heritage and an equally unbending resentment toward injustice and oppression. Mary's mother shared this insight:

There has always been the persistent longing to right something that was wrong. Mary came to see the injustices not only to her family but to a whole nation—the constant lies, the misinformation. For 33 years, she has seen that we and other Cubans still say, "Don't give up until that injustice is addressed!" So, too, will you see that justice is always woven into whatever Mary does.

The persistence of a sense of justice was revealed in many contexts. It appeared explicitly in the form of Mary's analysis of herself and her background:

> The Cuban part of me has always affected the way I look at things. I've always been a very righteous person, always looking out for the underdog. You know those save-the-orphaned-baby-seal television specials—I used to write letters and try to fix things. I used to get into arguments all the time about Castro, but I always behaved as any proud American would.

In the classroom, Mary gave expression to her justice-seeking ideals when describing her perspective on the school's mission and on her role as a teacher:

> I've come to accept that life isn't fair and you need all the help you can get. I really feel that school should be the Great Equalizer . . . the one place where kids don't have to fend off labels and don't have to compete for what they need . . . the oasis in what's become a hard life for them. . . . I'm the type of person who likes to clue people into better ways of "making it" through life. I know my effect on students is—and should be—emotional as well as academic.

Mary's righteous side was evoked most commonly in response to students' refusal to acknowledge and act upon the opportunities afforded by school. She resented the students' easy acceptance of

their negative labels and exhorted them to assume greater responsibility for their futures. Exasperated on one occasion with the
off-task behavior of several American students, she interrupted
the lesson to address the class:

> You guys come in here with your little tags and refuse to
> take them off. You want me to accept you that way, and I
> won't! I accept you for the people you are in my classroom.
> If you want to continue being the goof-offs, I'll eventually
> have to accept that, because I can't seem to get you to accept
> the fact that I see you differently. Maybe I can see something
> in you that other people don't want to see—you don't let
> them see it—but that's not being fair to me.

Reflecting upon this incident later, Mary clarified some of the
difficulty she had identifying with her American students:

> It makes me so angry that the [American] kids in class don't
> realize how wonderful it is that we live here and not in a
> place like Cuba or Laos. They just don't see it. And here are
> these three Laotian kids who have surmounted incredible
> odds just to be able to sit in this classroom and read in peace.
> I just want to kick all [the American kids] and tell them how
> spoiled they are: "Life is hard, yeah, but you have opportu-
> nities that are staring you in the face every day and you
> *waste* them!"

Mary's statements also suggest the extent to which she had
acquired from her family a sense of middle-class morality and an
ethos of working hard to achieve success. By all accounts, these
values affected her family life in Cuba as well, but they assumed
even greater significance through their struggles and achieve-
ments as refugees in the United States.

Given the feelings of loss and uprootedness generated by the
refugee experience, family ties were understandably prominent in
Mary's life narrative. Respect for family, and for authority gener-

ally, emerged as a key attribute of appropriate social performance. "In the old country," explained Mary's mother, "you gain self-respect by cherishing your elders." In Mary's case, a youth spent largely within small-town New England had the effect both of challenging and of reinforcing these cultural values. After my visit with her parents in her New England hometown, Mary offered this explanation:

> We were nobodies because we had no roots in the town. Your family has to be there at least 300 years to be considered true New Englanders. Growing up with friends who had that rootedness, I saw in the example set by my parents and grandparents a different kind of pride and connectedness. I saw what my family represented, how they overcame hardships to attain positions in this country. I was always proud to say I was from Cuba.

Mary's relationship to authority entailed a strong commitment to individual expression as well as a healthy concern for the established way of doing things. "She respects authority," noted her father, "but then she does what she wants, working in and around things in her own quiet, tenacious way to change what she feels is not right." She affirmed in her statements the importance of a sense of belonging—to family, society, a profession—and saw in teaching the opportunity to work within a field that held meaning for her and that sustained her justice-seeking ideal.

> As a teacher I can express myself as an individual within a system I respect. When I was younger, especially during the 1960s, I used to think changing the system from within was "wimpy" or hypocritical. If I wasn't bulldozing through things, then I really wasn't a true mover and shaker. I never backed down from a fight. Now I see that changes one can make within the system's rules might take longer, but they also last longer. I take great pleasure in the power of that kind of "subversive" activity!

Expressions of the Situated Self

To the extent that she viewed herself as an equal participant in the social and cultural conflict within the classroom, Mary was an exception to the norm among Millshore's faculty. She was sensitive to the marginalization and academic stigmatization of all her lower track students—a sensitivity sustained in part by her own experience as a refugee and as a player along the margin of Millshore's mainstream. By itself, this sensitivity could provide shape but only partial substance to the constructive teacher-student and student-student relationships she envisioned for her class.

Mary's largely independent stance on the margin of Millshore's faculty culture prompted me to consider how she might use the status attributed to her to benefit her students and herself. Mary acknowledged both the boundedness and the boundary-spanning quality of her marginal position. She chose to accept the former but emphasize the latter. It became apparent to both of us that the marginal role defined for Mary offered the opportunity to shape an instrumentally productive perspective informed by selective identification with different groups and selective avoidance of conditions that might set her up for failure or feelings of inadequacy. We also realized that a positive orientation toward her marginal status contributed significantly to her effectiveness in objectifying relationships and events in the Millshore setting.

The deliberate, defensive, and, in some measure, productive nature of this strategy reflects the Spindlers' notion of "constructive marginality" as an adaptive and sometimes predictable response to personally experienced cultural conflict (Spindler & Spindler, 1984, 1989, this volume). As a means to maintain or enhance self-esteem, this strategy made sense for Mary. At the same time, she could not totally escape the boundedness of her situation. By choice and circumstance, she was denied some of the social "free play" and access to local knowledge made possible by a more extensive sharing of assumptions with others in the school. This resulted in an internally positive but isolated learning environment for her students and herself. Reconceptualized as a form of insulation (see Flinders, 1989, p. 76), this largely self-imposed isolation enabled Mary to maintain a sense of self that was relatively independent of the constraining influences she felt characterized the school as a whole.

In contrast, the behavior of Mary's American students reflected both a deliberate rejection of the classroom context and what the Spindlers term a "reaffirmative celebration" of their world beyond the classroom. Mary's early efforts to structure paired activities with Americans and Laotians, for example, typically resulted in the American student "deschooling" the instructional context by drawing the Laotian student into accounts of events far removed from the classroom (e.g., partying, "getting busted"). On other occasions, these same students skillfully encouraged teacher digressions as a means to shift the focus of discussion more substantially to their real and imagined lives outside of school. From the American students' perspective, such activity proved an effective strategy to enhance self-esteem—replace attention to academics with conversations about a world where they knew more and, in a sense, could assume the expert role.

To some degree, Mary always had seen in the American students' actions a desperate, daily struggle to survive and to maintain their own identity in the face of difficult odds. As the year progressed, our more explicit translation of the students' behavior into something compensatory rather than deliberately antagonistic enabled her to make realistic, thoughtful decisions regarding her instructional approach. Open acceptance of her and of her teaching, Mary realized, was threatening to a number of these students. She responded by creating discreet channels of assistance that freed them from worrying about conspicuous displays of need or commitment. Simultaneously, she tried to project herself as someone who also was fighting off a label and who, in her words, "could see something in these kids that other people have chosen not to see."

They find it very difficult to come across to someone who is taking them at face value. They don't trust it. The key, I think, was creating ways to have private conversations with

each of them—response journals, for example. I'm not trying to tear down their walls—they presently rely on those
barriers—but I am reaching over, around, or through those
walls to encourage them in areas where they need encouragement. I think it's a trickle-down effect: "Yeah, Ms. Navarro's
really serious about this stuff, and she'll help you if you ask
her."

Less obvious to Mary in her efforts to make the classroom
experience more supportive and student centered was the influence
of the American students' own narrow expectations for proper instructional activities. Their rejection of so many aspects of classroom
life was offset by rigid, almost inviolable assumptions regarding
activities they considered appropriate for school work. Student
interviews revealed consistent notions of the ideal classroom—a
structured and straightforward curriculum transmitted by an efficient but indifferent teacher with minimal expectations. Resistance and confusion awaited the teacher bent on undoing established
habits and initiating change. Mary learned this when she instituted
a "reading workshop" format characterized by less teacher-cen-
tered instruction and more individualized and small group work.
What she perceived as granting more control to the students was
viewed by some students as "slacking off" and "teaching less."
Mary expressed her frustration:

Unless you really know what you're doing and what your
objectives are, the students won't like it if you jump in and
try to follow *their* lead. They're used to having the teacher
say, "This is the story, these are the questions, this is the
quiz." It's hard to improvise when the audience is expecting
one show and you say to them, "It's your show, you tell me
how you want this to be done." It's like they've been conditioned not to think!

Differences in the perceived locus of responsibility for student
learning contributed to conflicts in communication and behavior.

Mary embodied the norm among American teachers in that she felt students bore the primary responsibility for their successes and failures in the classroom. The lower track American students, socialized into the passive learning role and conditioned over the years to believe that they were academically deficient, viewed teachers as responsible for student learning. Teachers who did not communicate this style and sense of responsibility were perceived by the students as neglecting their primary educational role. As one American student remarked, "Ms. Navarro's not so much teaching us now; she's just giving us work and expecting us to do it."[5]

The American students' indifferent response to her instructional strategies had a dual effect. On the one hand, Mary began to lose confidence in herself and in some of her students. In this case, *too much* awareness of her students' situations softened her ambition to change them:

> I think back to the things I tried to do with them and realize it was better to be naive than to know what I have come to know about these kids. I've definitely become more hesitant about trying new things because I know how they will react. Whereas before I had pretty high expectations about my ability to motivate students, knowing what I know now has brought me crashing down to reality.

On the other hand, the general resistance she encountered from the American students reinforced her already significant feelings of identification with the Laotian students. She recognized the importance of the Laotians' embrace of normative expectations for learning responsibility. Their strong commitment to the aims of schooling and to their responsibilities as students affirmed the middle-class, achievement-oriented perspective that had informed her own family experience with the American Dream—and that she now projected into her interactions with all her students. The aspirations the Laotian students expressed to Mary appeared to her a fair expression of her belief in school as the Great Equalizer and in her own role as one who could help others "make it" through life. She responded positively to their respect and receptivity: "It's easy for me to help them," she noted, "because they want it. I feel that what I'm giving them is being accepted." This acceptance translated into a selective dedication to their success and a comfort with being more academically demanding of them.

Mary was less accommodating to the Laotian students' deliberate exclusion of traditional cultural elements perceived as compromising their chances for success in the mainstream environment. In marked contrast to the American students, the Laotians were hesitant to share the realities of their lives outside of school. To openly reaffirm a family and community life in which little English was spoken and that otherwise accentuated differences between themselves and their American classmates contributed little to their images of social fit and success in the mainstream. Theirs was an assimilative mode of adaptation.

Mary expressed to me and to the Laotian students her resentment at the circumstances that prompted them to deny their cultural heritage. Given her persistent and positive identification with her own cultural background, it was hard to accept such denial in her students.

> It's difficult to resist making speeches every day. I've toned that down quite a bit. Now there's just a little pain in my heart because they [the American students] don't get it, they won't get it. They'll never go through anything like a refugee experience—leave their country, leave everything behind, have their family scattered, have to be in a country where no one speaks their language, and have no idea how anything runs.

Mary's attempts to reconcile the disparate needs of her American and Laotian students highlighted aspects of her struggle to maintain a sense of continuity with her own deep-seated values. Her measured effectiveness on both fronts reflects the degree to which she had become consciously aware of the cultural identities and differences of her students and herself. This awareness, in one instance, facilitated her understanding of the American students' behavior as compensatory rather than deliberately antagonistic. In other cases, it led to a thoughtful assessment of her selective identification with students whose experiences and educational aims more closely mirrored her own.

Ultimately, her awareness of the manifold forms of culture operative in her classroom enabled her to see that she was a coproducer with her students of the behaviors and conditions that lead to academic success or failure. She realized that "catching students up" made little sense without first developing some awareness of where they already had been and what they already understood that enabled them to cope in the classroom on a daily basis. She developed avenues of expression and assistance that capitalized on the students' knowledge and capabilities, for example, encouraging them to generate text materials based on their own experiences (a strategy reinforced in Trueba, 1989). In broad terms, she created opportunities for herself and her students to verbalize the basic culturally patterned assumptions that each carried into the classroom. Insights thus gained helped her to identify the learning contexts in which students would most likely experience academic success and develop a sense of competence.

Summary

Mary expressed in her teaching both an ideological and an idealistic vision of the world and a personal need to identify with her own roots and culture. She envisioned her classroom as an arena in which social and emotional needs would be addressed on an equal basis with academic demands. But the embodiment in her teaching of a deep-seated sense of justice was offset by an institutional and cultural context that prompted colleagues and students to misread or resist her intentions in the classroom. Mary sought accommodation and compromise without having to deny her basic values.

Within this framework, cultural therapy was not simply a means to understand the idiosyncrasices of personal experience. It was a collaborative process in which Mary and I explored the cultural embeddedness of her enduring values and adaptive capabilities and then highlighted the linkage between these attributes and other dimensions of classroom life. Similar efforts in other classrooms may help teachers to clarify their roles in the cultural conflict that affects the learning process and empower them and their students to act with competence.

Notes

1. These admittedly general designations reflect the labels popularly used in Millshore. The Laotians who resided in Millshore were predominantly representative of the *Lao Lum* (lowland or ethnic Lao), a group that includes rural villagers from the lowlands, former government bureaucrats, and soldiers of the Lao faction that supported the United States in Southeast Asia from 1954 to 1975. Following local usage, I employ the term *Laotian* when referring to members of the ethnic Lao community in Millshore, and *American* for Millshore's white majority population.

2. I have drawn heavily in this section upon earlier descriptions of the Millshore setting (Schram, 1992a, 1992b).

3. This connection with the junior high faculty mirrored the behavior of the ESL teacher with whom I worked at Millshore, as documented in Schram (1992a). She, like Mary, was ascribed limited influence by the dominant high school faculty group, due in part to her position as a part-time instructor and in part to her exclusive identification with the Laotian students. Not surprising, she emerged as Mary's only confidant among the high school staff.

4. Such "distancing" is a well-documented phenomenon. For example, Mary Metz (1987) found that teachers who worked within an institutional context that undervalued them as teachers put their energies into self-defense and constructed "a culture which

frees them from responsibility to develop effective teaching and constructive social relationships with students" (p. 130).

5. Diane Hoffman (1988) describes a similar phenomenon in her insightful discussion of communication and cultural adaptation among Iranian students in American secondary classrooms. One contrast lies in my documentation of this behavior among lower track American students, an observation that appears to support my characterization of them as involuntary players along the margin of the mainstream. Hoffman's overall critique of the cultural conflict model of intercultural relations is significant for its alternative emphasis upon learning rather than conflict in the examination of cross-cultural interaction.

References

Finley, M. K. (1984). Teachers and tracking in a comprehensive high school. *Sociology of Education, 54*, 233-243.

Flinders, D. J. (1989). *Voices from the classroom.* Eugene, OR: ERIC Clearinghouse on Educational Management.

Gibson, M. A. (1988). *Accommodation without assimilation: Sikh immigrants in an American high school.* Ithaca, NY: Cornell University Press.

Goldstein, B. L. (1988). The interplay between school culture and status for teachers of immigrant students. *Educational Foundations, 2*(1), 52-76.

Hoffman, D. M. (1988). Cross-cultural adaptation and learning: Iranians and Americans at school. In H. T. Trueba & C. Delgado-Gaitan (Eds.), *School and society: Learning content through culture* (pp. 163-180). New York: Praeger.

Lieberman, A., & Miller, L. (1984). *Teachers, their world, and their work.* Alexandria, VA: Association for Supervision and Curriculum Development.

Metz, M. H. (1987). Teachers' pride in craft, school subcultures, and societal pressures. *Educational Policy, 1*(1), 115-134.

Moll, L. C. (1992). Bilingual classroom studies and community analysis: Some recent trends. *Educational Researcher, 21*(2), 20-24.

Page, R. (1987). Lower-track classes at a college-preparatory high school: A caricature of educational encounters. In G. Spindler & L. Spindler (Eds.), *Interpretive ethnography of education: At home and abroad* (pp. 447-472). Hillsdale, NJ: Lawrence Erlbaum.

Page, R. (1991). *Lower-track classrooms.* New York: Teachers College Press.

Schram, T. (1990). *Coming to terms with becoming a teacher: An anthropological perspective on the veteran as newcomer.* Unpublished doctoral dissertation, University of Oregon.

Schram, T. (1992a, January). *Negotiating a positive marginality for researcher and informant.* Paper presented at the Qualitative Research in Education Conference, University of Georgia, Athens.

Schram, T. (1992b, April). *Teacher and peer mediation in the schooling of language minority students: Contexts and encounters.* Paper presented at the annual meeting of the American Educational Research Association, San Francisco.

Schwartz, F. (1981). Supporting or subverting learning: Peer group patterns in four tracked schools. *Anthropology and Education Quarterly, 12*(2), 99-121.

Spindler, G., & Spindler, L. (1984). *Dreamers with power: The Menominee Indians.* Prospect Heights, IL: Waveland.

Spindler, G., & Spindler, L. (1989). Instrumental competence, self-efficacy, linguistic minorities, and cultural therapy: A preliminary attempt at integration. *Anthropology and Education Quarterly, 20*(1), 36-50.

Spindler, G., & Spindler, L. (1992). Crosscultural, comparative, reflective interviewing in Schoenhausen and Roseville. In M. Schratz (Ed.), *Qualitative voices in education research* (pp. 150-175). Bristol, PA: Falmer.

Trueba, H. T. (1989). *Raising silent voices: Educating the linguistic minorities for the 21st century.* New York: Harper & Row.

Trueba, H. T., Jacobs, L., & Kirton, E. (1990). *Cultural conflict and adaptation: The case of Hmong children in American society.* Bristol, PA: Falmer.

Watson, L. C., & Watson-Franke, M. (1985). *Interpreting life histories: An anthropological inquiry.* New Brunswick, NJ: Rutgers University Press.

Wiseman, J. P. (1985). Individual adjustments and kin relationships in the "new" immigration: An approach to research. *International Migration, 23*(3), 349-367.

Christine Robinson Finnan

4

Studying an Accelerated School

Schoolwide Cultural Therapy

CHRISTINE ROBINSON FINNAN

Christine Robinson Finnan is currently serving as director of the South Carolina Accelerated Schools Project at College of Charleston (South Carolina). She studied folklore and anthropology at both the University of California, Berkeley (B.A.), and the University of Texas (M.A.). She received her Ph.D. in education and anthropology at Stanford University and has since worked in a number of research and teaching positions, including SRI International, a nonprofit research organization. While at SRI, she was engaged primarily with multiple case examinations of educational and refugee resettlement policies in her research. She also taught at Stanford University, College of Charleston, and Chabot College (Pleasanton, California). Her involvement in the Accelerated Schools Project began in 1990, when Henry Levin, director, asked her to conduct a study of the implementation of the project at a local middle school. As this study progressed, she realized that significant changes will not last in schools if the members of the school community do not make the changes their own—in effect, make the changes a part of their school culture. During the 1991-1992 school year, she had the opportunity to move from a research to a program development role within the Accelerated Schools Project. She was responsible for starting the Accelerated Schools Center at the College of Charleston and has been working with several schools in the Charleston area as they progress through the Accelerated Schools process. The experience of trying to implement the project gave her insights into the dynamics of project implementation that are difficult to attain, even in the most participatory of participant observations. She has published articles on children's play, Southeast Asian refugee resettlement, ethnography, and the Accelerated Schools Project.

Is school culture necessarily a barrier to school reform? According to many accounts (Sarason, 1990; Schlechty, 1991; Wehlage, Smith, & Lipman, 1992), school culture, that web of understanding that is agreed upon by members of a school community, protects the status quo by blocking or watering down change efforts. This has been true especially when interventions have been designed to create specific changes in schools but have not been designed to work with the existing school culture. Few educators intent on reforming schools realize that any intervention, except the most superficial, is actually an intentional attempt to create school culture change and that the success of an intervention rests on its ability to work with, not against, a school community interested in changing its own culture. Reformers become frustrated when they find that their good ideas are taken in by the agents of the existing culture and are reshaped to the point that they are hardly recognizable as new ideas (Wehlage et al., 1992).

The idea of working with, rather than against, the existing culture shared by members of a school community is consistent with the Spindlers' concept of cultural therapy as presented in this volume and previous publications (1989, 1991). I will assert that it is also the primary reason that one recent educational reform effort, the Accelerated Schools Project, has been experiencing success. This chapter is based on an examination of the first year of implementation of the Accelerated Schools Project in a California middle school.[1] As this chapter describes, the middle school studied was quite successful in implementing the Accelerated Schools Project, and changes were already evident after 1 year. This was contrary to what I expected to find, because most studies of implementation point to failure or only limited success of interventions (Bardach, 1980; Berman & McLaughlin, 1977; Sarason, 1990; Wehlage et al., 1992). I assumed that the Accelerated Schools Project would be like most other reforms—an intervention filled with good ideas created by well-meaning intelligent people from the

AUTHOR'S NOTE: I extend my thanks to George Spindler and Henry Levin for their comments on an earlier version of this chapter.

university. It would be politely received by a group of dedicated teachers who would ignore most of what the reformers said and continue to do what they knew worked for them. This did not prove to be the case at the school studied; significant changes did occur.

Looking for an explanation, I realized that two features of the design of the Accelerated Schools Project contributed to its success. The first feature involves the commonsense philosophy of the project with its focus on the strengths of all members of the school community, especially those of the children. The second feature lies in the Accelerated Schools process, which allows members of a school community (teachers, administrators, support staff, parents, children, community members) to first understand their own school culture and then make the changes they want to make in the school.

Both of these features of the Accelerated Schools Project relate to the philosophy and process underlying cultural therapy. The Accelerated Schools Project does not explicitly address school culture and does not claim to do cultural therapy, but when the project is viewed through the eyes of an anthropologist, it is clear that there are direct parallels with theories of culture change and with the Spindlers' design for cultural therapy. A key element of cultural therapy is to make people aware of their own culture. People participating in cultural therapy engage in exercises to better understand their culture and to understand the influence of culture on their attitudes, values, and behavior. The Accelerated Schools Project provides the members of the school community an opportunity to understand their existing school culture before they initiate changes.

Another key element of cultural therapy is its goal of changing behaviors and attitudes of members of the school community toward each other. The Spindlers assert that this is best done by sensitizing people to their own culture. Once aware of one's own culture, a person is better able to adjust to the demands of cross-cultural interaction. Cultural therapy facilitates dialogue between cultures. The Accelerated Schools Project encourages school culture change, but toward mutually agreed upon goals and through a process that involves all members of the school community.

Cultural therapy's primary goal is to improve relations within a school culture and a by-product of this will be change. The Accelerated Schools Project's primary goal is to create school culture change with a by-product of improving relations within the school culture. The relationship between the Accelerated Schools Project and cultural therapy will be discussed further following a description of the school culture at Calhoun Middle School[2] and the changes observed during the first year of Accelerated Schools implementation.

School Culture and Calhoun Middle School

The concept of school culture is not new in educational literature. Most examinations of the daily life in schools explicitly or implicitly describe school culture (for example, Fine, 1991; Goodlad, 1984; Page, 1987; Peshkin, 1978, 1986; Sizer, 1992). The school culture provides a web of meaning to all members of the school community (Geertz, 1973). It shapes how members of a school community use resources, structure experiences, and relate to the wider world. School culture includes the values, traditions, attitudes, and interpretations that are understood by members of the school community. As Sarason (1990) writes, it is the "interlocking ideas, practices, values, and expectations that are 'givens' not requiring thought or deliberation" (p. 228).

The existence of a school culture does not necessarily indicate harmony and shared goals. Each person brings to the school culture a perspective that is shaped by his or her race, ethnicity, class, family structure, and social, occupational, and spiritual experiences and interests. The school culture serves as a veil of cultural interpretation that binds members of any organization together; it allows subcultures that appear to have divergent goals and attitudes to coexist. Through a school culture, people with strong commitments to certain ideals can work side by side with others who have no interest in such ideals. No two people share the same interpretation of the school culture, but their interpretations are within an accepted framework that helps all members of the culture make sense of the school together. George and Louise

Spindler (1987, 1990) describe this process of creating meaning as a "cultural dialogue." Any person's description of the school culture will be his or her own, but the person should also be able to describe (in varying degrees of accuracy) the cultural interpretation held by others. His or her ability to describe the cultural interpretations of others depends on the nature and amount of cultural dialogue the two parties share. For example, a teacher will describe his school according to his cultural interpretation. His ability to include in this description the interpretations of students, other teachers, or members of the support staff depends on whether he engages in cultural dialogue with others and on the nature of the dialogues.

The description of the school culture at Calhoun derives largely from discussions with teachers, support staff, and administrators. A complete description of school culture would be based on a comprehensive examination of the culture from all perspectives (teachers, support staff, students, administrators, parents, and community members). All of these school community members were included, to some degree, but my initial study design led me to pay more attention to staff members. I set out initially to examine the influences on the implementation process from the perspective of those engaged in the process. The focus on school culture grew out of my fieldwork, and as the concept of school culture change became more compelling, I sought voices of other members of the school community.

This chapter focuses on the influence of an intervention— Accelerated Schools—on changing a school culture. There are other influences that also shape a school's culture. I have divided these influences into historical and environmental influences. Historical influences are events, actions, and decisions that occurred in the past and have shaped the existing school culture. These include prior reform efforts, prior district policies toward curriculum and instruction, influential former staff members, prior staff relations, and changes in student population. Environmental influences include the demographic makeup of the student body, community, and staff; resources, policies, and federal, state, and district mandates; resources available in the community; occupational and educational possibilities; and deviant alternatives to schooling (crime, gangs, and drugs). The following is a description of the key historical and environmental influences that have played a role in shaping the school culture that existed at Calhoun Middle School prior to the implementation of Accelerated Schools.

Calhoun Middle School is a downtown school in a large school district serving over 30,000 students. The district is both geographically and demographically diverse. The immediate surroundings of the school are dominated by the city and county government buildings, including the courthouse, jail, and police station. The homes are largely older bungalows, and although many are well kept, drug activity does occur in some of the vacant homes. Most of the residents of the neighboring bungalows and apartment buildings are low income and Hispanic. The larger community served by the school district is one of the most affluent in the country. Until recently, jobs have been plentiful, but most of the jobs require specialized training and higher education. Unskilled and semiskilled manufacturing jobs have become increasingly scarce because the high cost of living in the area drives manufacturing operations to other communities. Although the school district serves a racially diverse population, many schools were segregated until the school district agreed to comply with a 1985 federal court order to desegregate. Until 1986, prior to the desegregation order, Calhoun's student population was almost completely Hispanic.

When the Accelerated Schools Project began in September 1990, the school resembled a traditional junior high school, despite its label of "middle school."[3] The curriculum, instruction, and organization were like those found in many junior high schools. The school day was divided into six periods, 50 minutes long. Students changed classrooms at the sound of a bell.[4] Students were grouped in classes according to their ability. Language arts and social studies were labeled "accelerated," "regular," or "sheltered."[5] Math classes were tracked according to students' readiness to take algebra. Many students were also served in special classes, such as a Chapter 1 compensatory class, special education classes (self-contained and pull out), and an "opportunity class" for children who appeared destined to drop out because of behavior problems.

The governance of the school was primarily from the top down. The principal and vice principal for curriculum made most of the decisions.[6] Teacher input into decisions was primarily through their department heads. The 42 teachers were represented by seven department heads who met monthly to discuss school issues.[7] The classified staff (teacher's aides; campus supervisors; secretarial, janitorial, and cafeteria staff; bus drivers) had little or no input into schoolwide decisions; they did not attend either faculty meetings or steering committee meetings. Parent involvement was limited. A Home School Club existed, but only a few parents were active, and few of the active parents were members of minority groups.

The student body represented an ethnic mix, achieved largely by the desegregation order. In fall 1990, Calhoun served 617 students of whom 55% were Hispanic; 39% were white, of which 64% were of Portuguese descent;[8] 5% were Asian/Filipino/Pacific Islanders; and 2% were African Americans. Calhoun was under-enrolled because it could not admit Hispanic students, even though there were many on a waiting list, unless it could attract more white students.

The ethnic mix at Calhoun was a result of the 1986 plan to desegregate the district. At that time, Calhoun was closed, and it reopened as a learning/technology magnet school. The school had a new principal who was able to hire her own staff; the school staff had considerable money to spend on equipment and curriculum. White students were recruited from across the district and were promised an exciting, innovative curriculum focusing on mastery of technology. Many teachers remember this time as a golden age for the school. The school culture at Calhoun allowed veteran teachers to glorify this era as a time of great change, even though evidence to the contrary existed. One teacher reported:

> One of the things that [the new principal] was able to do because they closed it down and returned it to a magnet, she was able to hire a whole new staff. . . . She picked people who

wanted to make a difference, people that wanted to make a change and to build a program. So she got a really high caliber group. . . . We put together a fabulous program. I was so excited about our magnet program, and the three years that we had it, it was wonderful. The level of academics here—the whole atmosphere of the place changed. It really was positive. We had parents who were excited about sending their kids here, and it was really successful.

These beliefs were held firmly by many members of the staff and describe a key phase in the history of the school. Teachers did work hard, and no doubt did develop some exciting curriculum. Their reports, however, mask some very serious problems. The rosy glow of memory seems to have blocked the fact that student achievement at the time was poor, and internal segregation was the norm. The student body was polarized both ethnically and academically. Of all students, 20% were in gifted or accelerated classes and 60%-70% were eligible for compensatory programs. Very few students were in the middle. Internal segregation was quite visible. The top 20% of the school was composed primarily of white and Asian students, while Hispanics were disproportionately in the compensatory programs. Not only did large numbers of students test poorly on standardized tests, the curriculum did not really incorporate the technology theme, and rapport with many parents, especially Hispanic parents, was low. Calhoun was chronically underenrolled because it could not meet the desegregation formula.

In June 1989, the staff was informed that the principal was being transferred to a different school. The transfer was not clearly due to problems at Calhoun, as the principal was still very popular with the staff and some of the parents. The superintendent of schools conducted a major reshuffling of administrators throughout the district 2 years in a row, and Calhoun was part of that activity. In September 1989, the staff met the new principal for the first time, and they found that he was very different than their former leader. Many of the teachers were very upset, and morale plummeted. The new principal was placed in a difficult position.

He was replacing a very popular principal, and the reports he received from the central office did not confirm the glowing accounts of positive change that the teachers relayed. A central office administrator said:

> The district had not given [the principal] all the cards when they interviewed him, and didn't tell him that this was a school that was in—had a red alert with the state because their test scores were so rotten. And their students were failing, and they weren't attracting students . . . they didn't tell him half this stuff.

The principal did not seem to realize the extent to which the school culture of the teachers differed from the district office accounts. His actions, directed at changing what he saw as a bad situation, were misinterpreted by many of the teachers. He felt that he needed to make changes to improve a bad situation, but many of the teachers felt that he was intentionally trying to undermine their hard work. One teacher relayed her frustration:

> It was horrible. For those of us that had worked so hard, it was like getting slapped in the face because our new administrator came in and, I guess maybe he heard too much about, well this is the way we do things. We didn't want to see our program destroyed, and he got very defensive, and it was like we learned right away we couldn't talk about that.

By the end of the first year, the members of the administration knew that they needed to make some significant changes in their relationship to the staff as well as to the school to overcome the negativity that characterized most interactions at the school. The principal sought outside help to bring in new ideas and additional funds to Calhoun. One of the most promising opportunities was the Accelerated Schools Project.[9]

The preceding provides the historical and environmental context for the school culture that existed at Calhoun when the school community became a part of the Accelerated Schools Project. The

school culture at Calhoun is much more complex than described
below but, for the purpose of this chapter, I will limit my description to the four features of the school culture that influenced the
Accelerated Schools implementation process and that changed
most significantly during the first year.

The first feature of the school culture involves expectations.
This includes expectations staff members hold for the children and
for themselves, and the expectations the children hold for themselves. Although there was a general perception that Calhoun had a
strong staff composed largely of good, hardworking teachers, there
was also a realization that the staff did not hold uniformly high
expectations for all students. The expectations for the GATE[10] students were very high, and these students received a stimulating,
demanding curriculum. Most teachers' expectations for the average or low-achieving students, however, were low. This was especially evident to teachers who had transferred to Calhoun from
other schools. For example, one special education teacher said:

> When I compare this to other schools I've taught in, there
> is almost a uniform low population. Teachers who have
> stayed here a long time—it's just like what happens to you
> in special ed. If you stay and you never go out of it, you lose
> touch with what reality is. You know that the regular classes
> are higher, but you kind of forget how much higher
> . . . . Why are so many of our kids [special education stu-
> dents] able to make it in classes—I mean, even be main-
> tained? Why the teachers aren't screaming? This blows my
> mind that they can maintain in, and even get a C or a D and
> sometimes a B with their level of functioning. So gradually,
> I have gotten the picture that we are talking about an
> academically very low functioning school. The special ed
> kids don't stand out much. What stands out are behavior
> problems.

According to some members of the staff, students do not push
themselves because they have learned how to progress through
school with little effort. For example, many of the students have

been labeled "special" (e.g., limited English proficient, Chapter 1, or special education) since they entered elementary school, and they know the easy way to slide through. An instructional aide described how she feels many language minority students pass through elementary school and then Calhoun without having to work:

These kids can read and write English. They can speak English too. The thing about it is that they have been labeled since they were in kindergarten, and they just don't want to try. They think they're going to pass anyway. It's easy for them. They can come to that other class and just do whatever they want to, and they have to pass them anyway.

Staff members reported that many students have low expectations for themselves and express disdain for education. By the middle of sixth grade, many students had learned from their peers that it was not "cool" to care about school and that to be accused of being a "school boy" or a "school girl" was grounds for a fight. A teacher explained:

We see the incoming sixth graders come in ready, ready to be in middle school with their little binders and their papers. And, by this time—midyear—the little sixth graders are now like seventh graders. They don't have their pencils. They don't have their binders. They are no longer prepared; they no longer care about homework because that's the attitude.

The school culture at Calhoun allowed for a great deal of variation in the expectations teachers had for themselves. Although there was considerable grumbling, hardworking dedicated teachers worked side by side with teachers who clearly put in minimal effort. Many of the teachers worked hard to keep their classes alive and challenging, but others were content to fall back on tried-and-true methods. One teacher described a veteran teacher's attitude toward training. The teacher interviewed was upset that her colleague felt in-service training was only for young teachers:

I think that teachers can't get complacent. . . . One teacher
at one of the meetings said, "Well, I think that would be
great for the younger teachers to observe," and I looked at
[my friend] and said, "Gee, I mean, that's where I get my
inspiration and a lot of my ideas, is by going to workshops
and watching the people and talking." . . . Why go into
teaching if you think you know everything?

The fact that the entire faculty voted to become involved in the
Accelerated Schools Project indicates that most of them were
willing to work hard for the students, and they wanted an opportunity to incorporate into their school culture higher expectations
for the students.

The second feature of the school culture at Calhoun involves
trust, communication, and shared goals. As described above, the
school culture in most public schools provides a web of meaning
for the many divergent attitudes, values, and behaviors existing
at the school. Schools rarely have shared goals that all members
of the school community work toward. Calhoun was no different.
The school community members did not have a set of common
goals, a vision, or a mission for Calhoun when they began the
Accelerated Schools process. Levels of trust and avenues for communication were not adequate for creating a shared vision. Because of the administrative shuffling and miscues the previous
year, the level of trust and communication was very low, especially between the teaching staff and the administration. Many of
the teachers resented the fact that a beloved principal was replaced, especially by one with a completely different style and
focus. Where the former principal was very accessible to teachers
and ever present in the classroom, the new principal spent most
of his time in his office or away from the school at meetings. The
new administration did not encourage the teachers to talk about
their recent past, which made it something private rather than
public, legend rather than merely the past. This may account for
why some teachers venerated the former principal. Teachers felt
that the principal and vice principal did not care about them

because they rarely visited their classes, and the teachers felt the administrators were often defensive when approached with questions or problems.

Communication channels between teachers were limited primarily to department meetings and to occasional grade-level meetings. Teachers had few opportunities to interact with each other outside of department meetings. The support staff was completely cut out of schoolwide communication. They did not attend faculty meetings or department meetings. Instructional aides had close working relations with one or two teachers but barely knew most of the others, and other support staff had only passing relations with most of the teaching staff. Support staff had no input into schoolwide decision making.

Students were represented through a student council that focused primarily on school spirit. The council did not seem to have any role in schoolwide decision making, and it did not provide true representation of the student body. A disproportionate number of representatives came from the white, high-achieving population. Discipline was a serious problem at the school. Teachers were frustrated, and students did not feel they had anywhere to turn with their problems unless they developed a special relationship with a teacher or support staff member.

A third feature of the school culture involves personal and group efficacy. As the preceding describes, communication and trust were low at Calhoun, which contributed to a sense of powerlessness. Teachers and support staff felt powerless in relation to the school-level decision making and district decision making. They also felt the impending gloom of state budget problems that were sure to affect them. The district actions led many teachers to consider transferring to other schools. When they found that they would not be allowed to transfer within the district, some said that they just withdrew into their classrooms:

When people are coming and going constantly, and you never know if this person is going to be here next year or if you're going to have a new principal to get used to—I think

> what it does to me is it has a tendency to make me want to withdraw into my room and not get involved with anybody else.

The administration alienated many of the teachers by appearing inaccessible and autocratic. Many decisions were made by the principal and vice principal for curriculum without any teacher input. Rapport between the administration and teachers hit a new low when the principal asked the staff to vote on a scheduling system, and he subsequently ignored their vote. The staff felt that even their vote was meaningless.

The fourth critical feature of the school culture at Calhoun involves the educational practices considered acceptable. No common agreement existed at Calhoun on how best to teach the students. As described above, students were grouped by ability, and, generally, the more interactive, creative teaching was reserved for the more advanced students. Teachers who did not teach the "accelerated" classes disagreed on the most appropriate teaching methods for their students, although they found during the initial phase of Accelerated Schools—taking stock—that many teachers relied heavily on lectures and work sheets. Some of the teachers believed strongly that the students needed a great deal of structure:

> I've been teaching downtown for 19 years, so I've worked with kids that have been low achieving. They come to school, and usually their only stability in their life is the teacher. So when you're a structured person, and they come in they know exactly what you expect of them. They know that you're going to be the same way, that you are not going to tell them one thing one day and then do something else the next day. I get comments like "She's a strict teacher, but you learn a lot in her class." . . . I work hard to be mean. I said, "I want you to learn." But they want that.

Other teachers put more stress on holding high expectations:

It's how you manage it and how you approach it—the expectations that you have. If they are high, then magic happens. If you believe that it can't be done, then it isn't done, and somehow the kids know the difference. They know when they are doing something just to—remediation kinds of things—and they know when they are doing something that everybody is doing, and is worthwhile.

Other teachers were more lax, both with themselves and with their students. They said that they needed to keep "realistic" expectations for the students and, in some cases, they spent more time cultivating the friendship of students than teaching them. Some teachers never assigned homework, claiming that the students never did it anyway. Where most classes were quiet and orderly, others were chaotic with little learning occurring. Based on essays written by all eighth-grade students, students preferred order over chaos.

On first glance, it seems like the situation described above would stifle any efforts at positive change. The negativity and antagonism that existed when the Accelerated Schools Project was introduced could have easily overwhelmed the project. The veteran teachers at the school, however, had already demonstrated an interest in change and a willingness to work hard to achieve it. Many of the newer teachers were also committed to change. The administration and central office saw the wisdom in the Accelerated Schools model and were committed to making it work. In one sense, given the negativity of the preceding year, they had nothing to lose.

Changing the School Culture
Through the Accelerated Schools Project

The Accelerated Schools Project was designed to bring at-risk students into the educational mainstream so that they would be academically able and capable of benefiting from a high-quality and high-content school experience (Hopfenberg, Levin, Meister, & Rogers, 1990). The Accelerated Schools Project launched pilot elementary schools in 1987. This chapter describes the launch of a middle school in 1990. By fall 1992, 300 elementary and middle schools in 25 states had begun the process of transformation to accelerated schools (Levin, 1993).

The Accelerated Schools Project provides both a philosophy and a process to schools interested in making radical change. The philosophy is built on three principles. The first principle is *unity of purpose,* which ensures that all members of the school community—teachers, administrators, support staff, parents, students, and the community—agree on a vision for the school and agree to work together to achieve this vision. The project holds that, if everyone in the school community is committed to shared goals, the fragmentation that characterizes most schools will disappear, and the energy of all members of the community will be channeled toward the shared goals.

The second principle is *empowerment coupled with responsibility,* which is based on the belief that the people who are in the position to make the best decisions for children are those who work with them daily—parents, teachers, support staff, building administrators, community members. Although well meaning, many of the decisions made at the federal, state, and district levels do not meet the specific needs of a particular school. Teachers feel powerless and either follow mandates that do not always make sense or close their doors and do what they want to do despite the mandates. Principals become compliance monitors, and parents are typically out of the decision-making loop altogether.

The third principle, *building on strengths,* is crucial to acceleration. Accelerated schools build on the strengths of all members of the school community. The project holds that schools seriously undervalue and underuse the strengths that exist in their school communities and need to change their focus from looking for weaknesses in children and each other to building programs based on strengths.

The Accelerated Schools Project guides participating schools in pursuit of what is referred to as *powerful learning.* The Accelerated Schools Project does not provide a kit with manuals for how to "do powerful learning"; it provides a process that helps a school community determine for themselves what is best for their children. The project encourages schools to think carefully about how they teach, what they teach, and the context in which learning occurs. Rather than focus all energy on changing one aspect of learning—say, the curriculum—schools examine how changes in curriculum will require changes in instruction and the organization of the school or the classroom. The Accelerated Schools Project works with schools to make systemic, not superficial, change.

Accelerated Schools provides schools with a systematic decision-making process. The process is a slow one, designed to avoid the tendency many schools have to jump at any interesting idea. It emphasizes the importance of creating a thorough baseline understanding of the school as it embarks on change and a shared vision of what the school should be like in the future. These two goals are accomplished in the first phase of the project through the taking stock activities and the vision creation. It is through the taking stock process that school communities begin to make their school culture more explicit, and it is through the vision creation process that the school community articulates the dreams that are also a part of the school culture. This phase of the project is usually accomplished in several months.

The second phase of the project, the inquiry phase, is a time for ongoing problem definition, hypothesis development and testing, solution seeking, and assessment. The inquiry process allows small cadres (composed of teachers, support staff, parents, students, administrators, community members) to thoroughly examine issues and design solutions that are appropriate to the school. The governance structure that is initiated as a part of inquiry encourages democratic decision making because many of the decisions related to curriculum, instruction, and organization of the school, student activities, and parental outreach are made by the inquiry cadres, refined and approved by the steering committee (composed of representatives of all cadres and others as determined by the school), and agreed upon by the school as a whole. The inquiry phase of the project becomes a permanent feature of an accelerated school. The school community will always use the inquiry process to identify, understand, and solve problems.

Calhoun school community members began the first phase of the Accelerated Schools process in September 1990. During the next 4 months, they participated in training and engaged in the taking stock and vision development processes. The Accelerated Schools Project designates these activities as the first steps in capacity building, but they can also be seen as a part of the cultural transformation of the school. The training was conducted over 2 days prior to the start of school. The training focused heavily on the Accelerated Schools philosophy and was designed to help participants integrate the three principles into their own concept of appropriate education. The training provided an opportunity for participants to examine their own beliefs, values, and behaviors. This was a welcome process for some of the staff because the philosophy of Accelerated Schools fit their own closely. For example, several teachers explained why they became involved in Accelerated Schools:

> Nothing in my philosophy has changed—not one thing. This is the thing that attracted me to the program, was that it was so consistent with my philosophy. My own personal philosophy of the way things should be done. And I said, "Hear! hear! Finally I have somebody [the Stanford project director] who knows what's supposed to happen."

> I'm not the kind of guy that says, "Hey, this looks good! I'll jump on the bandwagon." I think the concept of the project is a valid one. It is grounded in a lot of common sense. I regard myself as a commonsense, practical kind of guy. When I read the original proposal, it just made a lot of sense to me. The approach was right.

As a part of the training, the school community began both the taking stock and the vision development processes. Seven taking stock groups were formed to examine current practices, student outcomes, and student, staff, and parent attitudes. The groups collected data primarily through surveys sent to staff, students, and parents, although they also reviewed documents, conducted interviews, and collected data from central office records. These data were analyzed and presented to the entire staff in mid-December 1990. The tendency of many of the groups was to look for the positive in the data. This is not surprising given that there was a pervasive sense in the school culture that the staff at Calhoun was composed of strong, caring teachers who were striving to create a positive environment for the students. Data that pointed to possible shortcomings in their teaching or in students' attitudes toward Calhoun were often downplayed in the reports. For example, the staff members were asked on their survey if they would send their own children to Calhoun: 50% of the staff said that they would, while 50% said they would not. The committee saw this as a positive finding, even though half of the staff did not feel the school was challenging or comfortable enough for their own children.

When the data were reported to the entire staff, a number of groups presented data that challenged the accepted image of the school. For example, the achievement committee revealed that 57% to 70% of the students were below grade level at every grade. The staff was previously unaware of how high this percentage was. Many of the teachers were initially defensive about these data, explaining that the students come to them well below grade level. The discussion continued when the committee leader pointed out that students' expectations of attending high school and college exceeded the staff's expectations and that the staff's low expectations might be creating self-fulfilling behavior on the part of the students. A heated discussion broke out, as many teachers felt their teaching and their attitudes were being challenged. The discussion ended when an influential teacher spoke up and said, "Look, this is our present reality. We're going to create a new reality together—our Vision." This comment helped calm fears of criticism.

While the taking stock process serves as a fact-finding reality check on the perceptions that make up the school culture, the vision development process serves to bring to light the ideals held by individual members of the school community. The ideals are as much a part of the school culture as the more factual data collected during taking stock, even if they are at odds with current practices and expectations. The vision development process at Calhoun offered all members of the community a chance to express their dreams for the school, the children, and themselves. These dreams were very much a part of the school culture, but they were not articulated. Vision development was a powerful process at Calhoun because all members of the school community were given an opportunity to contribute to the vision and because, once it was created, it was publicly celebrated. The vision celebration—a whole-school assembly followed by a parade from the school to the government center several blocks away to present the vision to the mayor and a county supervisor and ask their support—made the vision, and the entire Accelerated Schools philosophy, meaningful to everyone in the school, even to some of the more skeptical staff members. One teacher described her reaction:

> I would suspect that a lot of people thought like I did, before. Why are we doing this? This is really stupid. A waste of time. A lot of people dragged their feet. A lot of good teachers said, "Oh well, I'm not going to go on that walk." "Well, I don't have a class that period so I won't have to do that." It turned out everybody in the school did it. I mean everybody. . . . Everybody, and I think that we had one person left at the school to answer phones. It was requested that everybody join us on the walk. It turned out to be pretty amazing. I mean, I wish you could have seen 700 people walking. It could have been a total disaster—on public streets! Kids were absolutely amazing. It was really neat.

The second phase of the Accelerated Schools process, inquiry, began in January. The taking stock data were compared with the vision, and five areas where the current situation did not meet the vision were identified. Five cadres (curriculum, instruction, student interaction, family and community involvement, and culture) were formed and each began the inquiry process. Each cadre had a mix of administrators, teachers, and support staff. They all attempted, with varying degrees of success, to include parents and students in the cadres. The cadres met at least twice a month through the school year.

The inquiry process, as described by the official Accelerated Schools documents (Hopfenberg et al., 1990; Hopfenberg & Levin, 1993), is very clear, logical, and linear (although the project staff members are fully aware that actual implementation cannot be "textbook clean"). Cadres define their problem, develop and test hypotheses about why the problem area exists, develop solutions, pilot test the solutions, and evaluate the effort. Each of the cadres at Calhoun tried to work systematically through the stages of inquiry, but they found that actual implementation is not clear, logical, and linear. This does not mean that they failed to implement the process. They actually made good progress, but they did so in their own way within the context of their existing school culture.

Several factors influenced the cadre members' movement through the stages of inquiry. People were often impatient to "see results" and they did not want to spend the time to move carefully through the stages of inquiry. Some had pet explanations for why the problems existed and found hypothesis development and testing unnecessary. The following discussion occurred in one cadre meeting as they were moving from hypothesis development to testing.

The facilitator asked the group for suggestions on how to test the hypotheses. There was quick agreement that they did not want to conduct another survey:

Cadre member 1: We've done some by observation, and we're tired of surveys.

Facilitator (a teacher): Can we go out to other students and see whether these really are issues?

Cadre member 2: Let's look at test scores and referrals and observations.

Stanford staff member: But, we have to be sure that these are the problems.

Cadre member 1: *We can just use our eyes.*

Cadre member 2: Didn't we do that when we came up with these?

Cadre member 1: *We tested them before we came up with them.*

Cadre member 2: That's not very good social science.

Cadre member 3: Some are just generalizations.

Cadre member 4: You know, the culture cadre is frustrated because they have sort of junked their activities. They aren't doing anything.

Stanford staff member: Look, we've done most of this [hypothesis generation] now. Let's see which ones we can do something about.

Opportunities or issues also arose that had to be dealt with even though the cadre was not at that stage of inquiry yet. For example, the instruction cadre was asked to determine if the school wanted to become a pilot middle school for the Complex Instruction Program.[11] This program might be a solution to problems in instruction, but the cadre had not developed and tested hypotheses yet, and it was being asked to evaluate a possible solution. After careful consideration of the program, they determined that they needed to complete the earlier stages of inquiry before making a decision about Complex Instruction. The curriculum cadre had a crisis disrupt its progress through inquiry. The cadre members were using the inquiry process to set a different class schedule for the coming year. They assumed they would have until the end of the year to accomplish this task. In mid-March, however, they were asked to help the principal and vice principal develop a new schedule in one week in response to district pressure for schedules that would accommodate budgetary reductions demanded by anticipated state funding cuts. The inquiry process had to wait until their involvement in the crisis was over.

The movement through the stages of inquiry was also affected by the ability of cadre members to work in small groups. At Calhoun, each cadre was composed of teachers representing different departments, support staff members who had never been involved in school decision making before, a member of the administrative team, parents, students, and community members. All of the cadres had three challenges: to develop a unity of purpose, to accommodate members with whom they had rarely worked before, and to develop a system for distributing the work and developing ownership in the project among all of the members. Cadres met these challenges differently and with varied success.

Although differences existed in how the cadres implemented the inquiry process, some patterns emerged. A rhythm developed in cadres (and in individuals) as they internalized the principles and process of the Accelerated Schools Project. The following are stages through which most of the members of cadres passed. They were not always in this order, but the stages illustrate the ebbs and flows of excitement and exhaustion that characterize this kind of school-level change. One stage was characterized by concern over the amount of work involved in the process. At this point, the tasks looked insurmountable and the resources (time, money, personnel) insufficient to address them.[12] Another stage was excitement over the possibilities for change. The world of new ideas was open, and creative energy was flowing. There was an awareness that long-held ideals and dreams might be realized. This stage can be overwhelming because an unlimited array of possibilities opens up. In another stage, there was eagerness to *do* something. Cadre members felt frustrated over the tedious nature of group work and the unwillingness of others to jump quickly to solutions. For some, this was a time for them to initiate their own "little wheels," or smaller projects that tapped their latent creativity and initiative. For others, it was a stage of disappointment and frustration. A final stage was the realization of accomplishment. A few tangible changes occurred during the first year (e.g., they eliminated ability grouping and created a new schedule with a humanities core to facilitate interdisciplinary study and to offer electives), but most of the cadres could not point to such tangible results. It was not until people reflected on their activities that they realized that they had made major structural and attitudinal changes.

Changes Observed in the School Culture

As described above, the Calhoun school community was ready for change. Serious shortcomings in relation to expectations, trust and communication, group and personal efficacy, and acceptable educational practices had been excused or tolerated within the web of meaning provided by Calhoun's school culture. Once these shortcomings were made explicit through the taking stock process, and ambitious goals to eliminate them were laid out in the vision, the Calhoun school community turned to the inquiry process to make the changes. After only 1 year, most of the changes were attitudinal, but these attitudinal changes served as the foundation for systemic changes.

The most critical change in the school culture was to expect that everyone hold high expectations for all students, in terms of both academic performance and behavior. Most of the teachers felt that they had always been fair to all of their students, but through their introduction to the Accelerated Schools philosophy, and through their taking stock and cadre work, they realized that some students at Calhoun were not receiving as high a level of instruction as others and that some teachers did not hold high expectations for the students. One teacher vividly described how the Accelerated Schools Project transformed his attitude toward teaching. He had been experiencing problems with his sixth period class and was frustrated by their behavior. As he listened to the principal explain the Accelerated Schools philosophy to a group of parents, he realized that he was remediating this entire class; he was watering down the instruction he gave them. He explained:

> The philosophy that *all* kids will succeed and achieve and stuff—I started thinking—I looked at myself, and I was putting these kids in the second track instead of the same track. For that reason, I think it was a pearl of wisdom in there that made me survive and actually we did a much better job in the last five weeks than the five weeks before it. . . . The testimony—just that all kids can succeed. You kind of assume that, but when you find yourself giving them easier stuff because it's such a hassle to try to keep them going with kids that you think are going faster and cooperating. . . . Actually, the kids in that sixth period, in the four weeks we spent [after he realized he was remediat-

ing them], did almost as much as the other kids did in the seven or eight weeks that they were spending with it.

Even some of the most staunch critics of the project began to change their attitudes as the school culture began to change. Compare the attitudes expressed by one teacher.

> February 1991—I deal with a specific skill area, and that's math. It's easy to accelerate with an accelerated group, OK? But I have one Math 8 class. . . . Well, what I've seen is it's kind of a dumping ground, and the kids that we have in here are—I've got this one class that has been very difficult . . . four kids out of a small class who were fresh out of Mexico and had very limited English. . . . Up until this quarter, I had four special ed kids who were real discipline problems, all in one class. And they talk about accelerating them? Well, it bothers me.
>
> May 1991—Definitely, there have been changes. No one can deny the fact that the time has been well spent to get to a sense of common purpose. The project has pulled the school together. It has helped the attitude of students. It is a self-esteem builder for students.

The staff began to have more trust for students as reflected in the frequency of whole-school assemblies. The vision celebration was the first time that all of the students had attended an assembly together. Prior to the celebration, separate assemblies for sixth, seventh, and eighth grades were held because of fear of bad behavior. After the success of the celebration, all-school assemblies became the norm, and student behavior was never a problem.

The decision to eliminate ability grouping was a clear sign to the entire community that Calhoun was going to hold high expectations for all students. With almost no debate, the school community decided that, as an accelerated school, they could not divide students between classes based on their academic ability. They felt that it was antithetical to continue to track students if the school embraced the philosophy of holding high expectations for all students. They also saw that this practice can lead to internal segregation, which they also wanted to eliminate.

There was also some evidence that students were beginning to change their expectations for themselves. Teachers noted that the children were better behaved and more responsible than they had been in the past. One teacher commented:

> The kids have changed a lot in attitude. They're more responsible this year. I think it's part of the Calhoun Accelerated Program. Because we try to tell the kids, you know, "We are an accelerated program. We're doing special things, and you have to show to this community that you're special, that we're special, and strive very hard for that."

Change in students was most evident in the students who became actively involved in the project. One boy who was actively involved in one cadre changed from being a poor student and a discipline problem to a conscientious student, concerned about the future of the school. He became more involved in his classes, no longer created problems, and even publicly spoke about the Accelerated Schools Project. He spoke at a school board meeting to try to persuade the school board to spare Calhoun from budget cuts that might slow the progress made by the Accelerated Schools Project and at the graduation ceremony about how involvement in Accelerated Schools changed him and Calhoun. On both occasions, he credited participation in the Accelerated Schools process with reengaging him in school.

Changes related to the expectations the staff members held for themselves and each other were evident in the behavior of individual staff members and in some of the decisions they made by the end of the school year. Social studies and language arts teachers did not complain that a shift to a humanities core might mean more work for them, and none of the teachers voiced concern that they would have to change their teaching styles to accommodate heterogeneously grouped classes. Some teachers who previously felt that they were doing an adequate job if they did no more than teach their classes became more interested in issues affecting the entire school. Teachers were also changing their expectations of what they could do in the classroom. These changes are related to changes in communication patterns, personal and group efficacy, and acceptable educational practices. These changes will be discussed further below.

The Accelerated Schools Project had a profound impact on the level of trust and the nature and level of communication among members of the Calhoun school community. Teachers found that they were working with colleagues they previously would not have known. One teacher commented:

> This is how I view Accelerated Schools. Well, first of all, the Accelerated Schools Project has done more to get all the teachers working together than anything else in the school—anything. So if it's going to happen, something like this is going to do it.

Many teachers credited the Accelerated Schools Project meetings with opening communication between departments. One teacher said:

> The departments now talk to each other. The departments stayed to themselves, but now there is better interdepartmental communication. There is a higher degree of unity for common goals. Before, they just worked to keep the status quo.

By the end of the year, there was considerable talk of interdisciplinary work. Teachers were actually talking to colleagues in other departments about joint work rather than sitting in department meetings bemoaning the obstacles to interdisciplinary work. The curriculum cadre's creation of a humanities core was visible evidence that interdisciplinary work is possible.

The Accelerated Schools Project became a vehicle through which classified staff and teachers could interact. Prior to the project, most of the classified staff had little interaction with teachers.

Instructional aides worked closely with one teacher, but campus supervisors (people who patrol the school grounds) and office staff had only passing involvement with the teachers. Through the Accelerated Schools process, they became active participants in cadre work and were encouraged to attend all school-as-a-whole meetings. One campus supervisor described the changes she has experienced:

> It gives us closeness, togetherness—before it was like the teachers were on one side and the other staff was on the other side, but I don't know, with these meetings, it's like—I can't say it's like they're equal to us, but we feel just the same as they do.

Communication with the administration also improved greatly during the year, and the level of trust began to rise. Because members of the administrative team served on inquiry cadres as members, not leaders, other staff members had a chance to talk to them as colleagues, not superiors. Teachers began to seek out the principal for informal chats, which had been rare the year before. The principal noticed a definite change in the attitude of teachers:

> Many of those who are committed to the school in a leadership way now were the constant gripers. [They] used to come in braced for a fight. It was a real "us and them" feeling before. That is gone.

The teaching staff also demonstrated increased trust in the administration. Given that trust was at a low point before the project started, many members of the faculty responded to overtures by the administration with caution. With increased communication with the administration, a unity of purpose, and growing evidence that the administration was willing to share power and responsibility, teachers began letting down their guard.

Avenues for increased family involvement were opened through the Accelerated Schools process. Although few family members were actively involved in the Accelerated Schools process, efforts were made to involve them and their input was sought during the taking stock and vision development phases. One parent who was actively involved found it to be a profound experience. He described the changes he saw at Calhoun since the Accelerated Schools Project began:

> It is like night and day. Teachers talk to parents. They talk to children. There is excitement. Excitement in the kids. They are part of meetings; they make speeches; they want to be visible. If parents know what's going on at school— even if it is just one teacher, they will try to have the same relation with all teachers. We must expect teachers to care about kids.

The sense of powerlessness that pervaded Calhoun was being replaced by a growing sense of personal and group efficacy. Staff members were realizing that they could make a difference at the school. As one teacher said:

> We are starting to feel that what we decide will be put to use and practice. Before the cadres, there was a sense that input would be put to us—that decisions were made without us. We are seeing our work put in place for the next year.

The staff was both excited and frightened by the thought of having influence and responsibility. One teacher said:

> I think the faculty is really happy about having the empowerment, the right to make decisions and be in on the process. They don't realize as many other people don't—fail to realize—that rights also carry their burden of responsibility.

The principal commented that he likes the idea of empowering teachers because it gives them more freedom to do what they want:

The best curriculum is what the teacher is excited about. It doesn't matter what it is. Accelerated Schools has done that. It's hard to convince teachers that they have the freedom to do it—to get over doing what the principal wants.

The increase in group efficacy resulted largely from the Accelerated Schools decision-making process and structure. In one year, Calhoun moved from centralized authority to democratic decision making through cadres and the steering committee. The process was not always smooth or perfect, but it created a very different governance structure than the one that existed before. As the vice principal explained, the level of democratic decision making achieved by the Calhoun staff was unusual:

The structure received from Accelerated Schools was important. I've been in education for so many years, and I've never seen a structure for team building. Usually we make some decisions and others complain.

Related to an increase in group efficacy was increased personal efficacy, most obvious in a blossoming of creativity and initiative. As one teacher commented at the end of the year, "Accelerated Schools rejuvenated us. It made lots of us more creative." There were many examples of teachers taking chances within their classes that they might not have taken before. Several teachers seemed to rediscover creativity that had lain dormant, or they felt more freedom to try the things that previously they may have been afraid to try (see Brunner & Hopfenberg, 1992, for examples).

The most dramatic example of blossoming creativity involved a teacher who decided to hold an egg drop contest. In egg drop contests, students (and interested staff and parents) build containers capable of protecting a fresh egg as it is dropped from a great height. The teacher did not initially intend for the contest to be a major event, but the event grew as the enthusiasm of the teacher, his colleagues, and the students grew. By the time of the contest, most of the students and staff had created entries, parents had become involved, and the teacher had obtained sponsorship from local businesses. At each step, the teacher was surprised at the support he received and he repeatedly encouraged his colleagues to "think globally rather than locally" when they decide to try something new.

The increase in personal efficacy relates to the changes in acceptable educational practices. As the staff began to realize that they could make changes in their teaching, some of them became increasingly creative. By the end of the year, there was considerable talk of interdisciplinary courses. The development of a humanities core was a concrete beginning. Changes in instruction were also evident, although less visible than the curricular changes. The process of examining the Complex Instruction Program made them realize that they have untapped resources within the school that might be more efficiently and effectively used. Through discussion of alternative instructional practices, individual teachers began experimenting in their classes. Teachers began thinking of ways to move from work sheets and textbooks to more interactive teaching techniques.

Accelerated Schools and Cultural Therapy

This chapter illustrates that schools can change, but not necessarily in the ways prescribed by outsiders. Schools change when the members of the school community are ready for change and are ready to take a close look at themselves. This process is not easy; it is occasionally painful. Members of the school community have to examine long-held beliefs and confront inconsistencies between their ideals and their current behavior, interactions, and expectations. Once an entire school community has done this, lasting change should occur. Some critics (e.g., Cuban, 1984) might say that the changes observed in this study were due only to the excitement of engagement in something new and that evidence of the changes will disappear after a few years. This does not appear to be the case in other accelerated schools (McCarthy & Still, 1992), and it seems unlikely given the changes in the school culture that were taking root at Calhoun during the first year.

Although this chapter has focused primarily on the Accelerated Schools Project, this book examines another school intervention—cultural therapy. Some of the parallels between cultural
therapy and Accelerated Schools have already been discussed. I
will end this chapter with a discussion of the implications of some
design features of Accelerated Schools for those practicing cultural therapy.

The initial success of the Accelerated Schools Project is due
largely to its ability to work with members of a school community
as they change their own school culture. The project provides a
philosophical base and a process for achieving change. Often
when school communities first hear about the Accelerated Schools
Project, their school has already been identified as a problem
school. Once they learn about the process, a significant portion of
the school community recognizes that the project will allow them
to make the changes they want to make in their school. Experience
has shown that, if a school community is not committed to making
attitudinal and behavioral changes, the project will not succeed.
A school community would also need to be committed to engaging in cultural therapy. Cultural therapy requires that participants
carefully examine their values, attitudes, and beliefs. This is not
an easy process, and it might alienate some people who really only
want to be taught how to tolerate culturally different people.

The Accelerated Schools process is critical to its success for two
reasons. First, without a process, members of a school community
would not have examined their existing school culture, developed
a shared vision, and engaged in systematic problem solving and
implementation of solutions. Second, the process is ongoing; an
accelerated school never stops doing the inquiry process, and the
governance structure remains in place. School reforms usually fail
because there is nothing there to ensure that the changes are
perpetuated. This could happen to cultural therapy without a
meaningful mechanism for keeping the kind of introspection,
reflection, and action that characterize cultural therapy an ongoing process at the school. No matter how meaningful the experience might be to participants, they are likely to fall back on
comfortable habits unless an extension of cultural therapy is inte-

grated into the accepted practices at the school and into the school culture. Cultural therapy is not unlike clinical or medical therapies; without regular interaction with the therapist, or a clear process for dealing with the problem alone, the "patient" often backslides into the undesirable behaviors or patterns.

The Accelerated School Project's three principles clearly facilitate school culture change. The principle of unity of purpose leads to the development of shared goals and makes the dreams of all members of the school community explicit. Too often, school communities embark on reform efforts without any unity of purpose or agreement on goals, and they flounder. Through the vision development process, all school community members, not just a committee of teachers, articulate their dreams and meld them into a vision that all members can work toward. Cultural therapy, as currently designed, does not explicitly ask participants to develop shared goals. Lasting change through cultural therapy is more likely if participants see that they share goals with people of diverse cultural backgrounds and if they all agree that they will make the changes or accommodations necessary to achieving these goals.

In accelerating schools, the principle of empowerment coupled with responsibility relates to the concern that the entire school community has to be committed to changing its school culture. A faith in democratic governance (with all of its responsibilities) has to become integrated into the school culture or the school community members will become overwhelmed by demands on their time and expertise. This process is one of the hardest parts of the transformation because it requires that people act on their ideals. This principle also has relevance to cultural therapy. Changes made through cultural therapy will be superficial if the participants do not take responsibility to scrutinize their own attitudes and to change practices in the school that are not productive.

The third principle, building on strengths, guides accelerating schools' efforts to raise expectations for all members of the school community. People are more willing to embrace the project goals when they find that participants are not trying to find fault with others and do not tolerate finger pointing and blame passing.

Participants often find that they and other members of the school community have talents and skills that were previously untapped. Even the name of the project—Accelerated Schools—builds on the strengths of the children served by participating schools, because many people associate acceleration with programs for "gifted" children. For the process of cultural therapy to become an accepted activity within schools, a more positive label might be necessary, because most people associate "therapy" with the efforts to eliminate problems. The process of cultural therapy can build on the strengths of its participants. It is currently designed to provide a nonjudgmental examination of cultural assumptions held by participants. It is difficult to do this kind of exploration without making explicit the limitations of any cultural perspective. This process is often upsetting to participants because they feel that their entire value system is being challenged. Cultural therapy will have lasting effects if it encourages participants to build on the strengths within the diverse cultures represented in the school.

Notes

1. This study was funded by the Accelerated Schools Project through funds from the Chevron Corporation. Special thanks are extended to Henry Levin, director, and Wendy Hopfenberg, associate director, for their support, encouragement, and openness throughout the course of the research. See C. Finnan (1992), *Becoming an Accelerated Middle School: Initiating School Culture Change*, for a more complete account of this study.

2. The name of the school has been changed.

3. Larry Cuban (1992) recently examined the history of the junior high school and middle school movements and found that most middle schools resemble junior high schools.

4. The only deviation from a typical middle school schedule was a 2-hour language arts block designed to improve reading and

language arts skills for the students. The 2-hour block had been designed by Calhoun's language arts teachers the previous year. The decision to require 2 hours of language arts forced them to eliminate all but one semester of electives.

5. Sheltered classes were designed for students who were still not fully proficient in English. They were no longer in limited- or non-English-speaking classes, but their English language comprehension and vocabulary were not strong.

6. At the beginning of the 1990-1991 school year, the administrators decided to create an administrative team, primarily to better deal with discipline and guidance issues. The vice principal for discipline and guidance (new this year) worked as a team with a resource teacher and a community liaison worker. They each took a grade level and worked with all of the students in that grade level.

7. Of the seven departments, the language arts department was the largest and most influential. The other departments were math, science, social studies, special education, physical education, and electives.

8. Many of these students came from families that recently immigrated from rural communities in the Azores off the coast of Portugal. Their parents did not receive extensive formal education.

9. During spring 1990, the principal, vice principal for curriculum, and several teachers attended a focus group to review the Accelerated Schools Project's plans to expand the project into middle schools. When Stanford began looking for a pilot school, Calhoun expressed its interest. The Stanford middle school project director gave a presentation to the entire faculty at the end of the 1989-1990 school year, and they unanimously agreed to participate.

10. This is an acronym for "gifted and talented education."

11. This approach to cooperative learning was developed by faculty at Stanford University.

12. In addition to not receiving additional funding for the Accelerated Schools Project, overall funding cuts were imminent for the next year.

References

Bardach, E. (1980). *The implementation game: What happens after a bill becomes a law.* Cambridge: MIT Press.

Berman, P., & McLaughlin, M. (1977). *Federal programs supporting educational change: Vol. 7. Factors affecting implementation and continuation.* Santa Monica, CA: RAND.

Brunner, I., & Hopfenberg, W. (1992, April). *Growth and learning in accelerated schools: Big wheels and little wheels interacting.* Paper presented at the annual meeting of the American Educational Research Association, San Francisco.

Cuban, L. (1984). *How teachers taught: Consistency and change in American classrooms, 1890-1980.* White Plains, NY: Longman.

Cuban, L. (1992). What happens to reforms that last? The case of the junior high school. *American Educational Research Journal, 29*(2), 227-252.

Fine, M. (1991). *Framing dropouts.* Albany: State University of New York Press.

Finnan, C. (1992). *Becoming an accelerated middle school: Initiating school culture change* (Report prepared for the Accelerated Schools Project). Stanford, CA: Stanford University.

Geertz, C. (1973). *The interpretation of cultures.* New York: Basic Books.

Goodlad, J. I. (1984). *A place called school: Prospects for the future.* New York: McGraw-Hill.

Hopfenberg, W., Levin, H., Meister, G., & Rogers, J. (1990). *Toward accelerated middle schools* (Report prepared for the Project to Develop Accelerated Middle Schools for At-Risk Youth). New York: Edna McConnell Clark Foundation.

Hopfenberg, W., & Levin, H. (1993). *Resource guide on the accelerated school.* San Francisco: Jossey-Bass.

Levin, H. (1993). *Accelerated Schools after six years* (Paper prepared for the Accelerated Schools Project). Stanford, CA: Stanford University.

McCarthy, J., & Still, S. (1992, April 20). *Assessing the progress of an accelerated school: The Hollibrook Elementary School Project.* Paper presented at the annual meeting of the American Educational Research Association, San Francisco.

Page, R. (1987). Teachers' perceptions of students: A link between classrooms, school cultures, and the social order. *Anthropology and Education Quarterly, 18*(2), 77-99.

Peshkin, A. (1978). *Growing up American: Schooling and survival of community.* Chicago: University of Chicago Press.

Peshkin, A. (1986). *God's choice: The total world of a fundamentalist Christian school.* Chicago: University of Chicago Press.

Sarason, S. (1990). *The predictable failure of educational reform: Can we change before it's too late?* San Francisco: Jossey-Bass.

Schlechty, P. (1990). *Schools for the twenty-first century: Leadership imperatives for educational reform.* San Francisco: Jossey-Bass.

Sizer, T. (1992). *Horace's compromise: The dilemma of the American high school.* Boston: Houghton Mifflin.

Spindler, G., & Spindler, L. (1987). Issues and applications in ethnographic methods: Editorial introduction. In G. Spindler & L. Spindler (Eds.), *Interpretative ethnography of education: At home and abroad.* Hillsdale, NJ: Lawrence Erlbaum.

Spindler, G., & Spindler, L. (1989). Instrumental competence, self-efficacy, linguistic minorities, and cultural therapy: A preliminary attempt at integration. *Anthropology and Education Quarterly, 20*(1), 36-50.

Spindler, G., & Spindler, L. (1990). *The American cultural dialogue and its transmission.* New York: Falmer.

Spindler, G., & Spindler, L. (1991, October 4-6). *The processes of culture and person: Multicultural classrooms and cultural therapy.* Paper prepared for the Cultural Diversity Working Conference, Stanford University.

Wehlage, G., Smith, G., & Lipman, P. (1992). Restructuring urban schools: The new futures experience. *American Educational Research Journal, 29*(1), 51-96.

Ann Locke Davidson

5

Students' Situated Selves

Ethnographic Interviewing as Cultural Therapy

ANN LOCKE DAVIDSON

Ann Locke Davidson began her career in education in the People's Republic of China, teaching Western literature, composition, and conversation to university students. These and other experiences teaching in diverse U.S. classroom settings made her well aware that social differences can play a major role in classroom interactions. An interest in better understanding these issues led her to graduate work in education at Stanford University, where she received her Ph.D. in curriculum and teacher education and M.A. in anthropology in 1992. Her research focused on the social construction of ethnicity across two northern California high school settings. She was particularly interested in the role that school and classroom practices play in shaping students' sense of their ethnicity in relation to schooling. Today, she is working as a postdoctoral fellow at the Learning Research and Development Center at the University of Pittsburgh, and as an ethnographer for a portfolio-based assessment research effort associated with Harvard's School of Education. Her major research interests center on the relationship between school and classroom practices, school culture, and youths' construction of school self. She recently completed coediting (with Patricia Phelan) *Renegotiating Cultural Diversity in American Schools* and is coauthoring (with Patricia Phelan and Hanh Cao Yu) a second volume describing the ways in which cultural aspects of students' family, peer, and school worlds combine to affect youths' involvement in schooling.

*Being Black and going to school in St. Louis doesn't really
exist. . . . We even got sent to juvenile 'cause it was like, that was
back in the days when everything was just crazy and we didn't care.
And before we realized who we were, where we were going, we were
just, you know, out there, floating around.*

*But now [since I moved to California], it's changed. . . . I don't
tolerate that anymore. I just say forget it, you know. That was a
long time ago, that was the old me. (RA27STC: 696-697;
RA27STB: 139-151, 482-485)[1]*

Johnnie Betts, African American
sophomore at Huntington High School

I first met Johnnie Betts in 1990. The transcript above, compiled
from two of our interviews, represents part of our exploration
of Johnnie's transformation from an "old" to a "new me." Prior to
our conversation, Johnnie had been a D and F student and a
member of his neighborhood gang in an inner-city St. Louis neighborhood; when I met him in a California high school, he was on
the honor roll and had been named to his district's all-league
junior varsity football team. As detailed later in this chapter, I
came to see Johnnie's transformation as something that reflected
a change in the behaviors, norms, expectations, sanctions, and
values—the cultural worlds[2]—he encountered in St. Louis and
California. Johnnie had developed "situated selves" (Spindler &
Spindler, 1989) in response to the immediate realities of his day-to-
day life. Equally interesting to me, however, was that interviews
designed to encourage Johnnie to describe various aspects of these
cultural worlds led him to reflect upon and analyze his California

AUTHOR'S NOTE: The research reported here was supported by a Spencer
Dissertation-Year Fellowship and conducted under the auspices of the Center
for Research on the Context of Secondary School Teaching with funding from
the Office of Educational Research and Improvement, U.S. Department of
Education, Cooperative Agreement No. OERI-G0087C235. I gratefully
acknowledge the insightful comments and helpful suggestions of Patricia
Phelan, George Spindler, and Louise Spindler.

and St. Louis situated selves. Over the course of four conversations, Johnnie moved from making vague references to *his* tendency to get into "trouble" and "do bad" in St. Louis to analyzing some of the forces he was responding to when crafting a "gangbanging" versus pro-school self.

This chapter reveals some of the ways in which ethnographic interviews can function as a form of cultural therapy. Such conversations can encourage youths and the adults who work with them to examine the persona(s) the youth presents in light of the sociocultural worlds he or she navigates in diverse community and school settings. I use two brief case studies, first, to illustrate how youths' situated selves are played out in response to the cultural worlds in which they find themselves and, second, to show how interview questions can encourage students to reflect upon and analyze their behaviors and actions.

The data presented here were collected as part of my dissertation study, an inquiry concerned with understanding how youths' experience of their ethnicity shapes and is shaped by experiences in school and classroom contexts (Davidson, 1992). That study was not concerned with creating change but with exploring when and how ethnicity becomes relevant to youth and in understanding the role that school plays in this process. Nevertheless, when students were asked to think more consciously about their behavior and the messages they receive within family, peer, and school worlds, they began also to reflect upon the behaviors, norms, expectations, and values they and others associate with their ethnicity. In some cases, this also led to preliminary consideration of the social and institutional forces that cause youth and others to develop folk theories about what it means to be from a particular background.

Our conversations fell short of my ideal for cultural therapy: enabling youth to situate themselves in history in a way that assists them to understand and contest the cultural, economic, and political forces that constrain their lives. Nor did the conversations go far enough toward making unequal power relationships in the classroom, the school, and larger society explicit (Spindler & Spindler, this volume). Yet, in revealing how interview questions can lead students to reflect on and evaluate their behavior from a situated perspective, these conversations provide insight into how adults can lay the groundwork for such conversations.

The Study: Design and Methods

The data for this chapter were collected as part of the Students' Multiple Worlds study,[3] a project carried out at the Center for Research on the Context of Secondary School Teaching (CRC) at Stanford University. The study included 54 students from four urban, desegregated high schools in two California school districts. Through a series of interviews and observations, we sought to identify, from the student's perspective, factors that affect academic and social engagement with the school community. Four to six interviews, lasting from 45 minutes to 2½ hours, depending on the informant, were carried out over a 15-month period. These interviews asked youths to describe and reflect upon factors within their families, peer groups, and schools that affect their lives at school. The sequential nature of the interviews enabled us to build relationships and to explore changes in students' behavior and circumstances over time. In addition, we spent days with individual youths in their high schools—attending classes, going to lunch, and, in some cases, visiting homes. These observations helped us collect more material over which we could interact with students. In general, we found the youths hungry to talk to a "safe" adult: In many cases, our interviews ran longer than expected, and we continue to keep in touch with some of the youths by telephone. The extent to which a student responded varied, however, depending both on personal circumstances and on the relationships we developed.

While the interviews varied both in emphasis and in complexity, the general approach was similar. We began by asking broad, open-ended questions, allowing students to describe those aspects of their lives that they saw as most important. We then used a series of probes designed to encourage students to reflect upon topics they could have overlooked. We also encouraged them to elaborate on topics that seemed especially salient by using responses designed to encourage evaluation of our interpretations (e.g., So what I think I hear you saying is _____?) and to expand on their descriptions (e.g., Is there anything else? Um-hmm? Really? Can you help me understand what you mean by _____?).

In the following section, I briefly describe the interview foci. While methods sections are typically short, I include this brief description because of my emphasis on interviewing as a means to elicit students' perceptions and encourage reflection, that is, as a means of laying the groundwork for the "consciousness-raising" aspects of cultural therapy. In addition, I highlight interview questions especially relevant to this chapter. At the same time, these interviews are not a recipe. Similar interviews are co-constructed by both the interviewer and the interviewee; the differences in youths' lives and personalities shaped both the content and the rhythm of our conversations.

The Interviews and Their Foci

During our first meeting with students, most of whom were freshmen at the time, we invited youth to describe school factors that affect their engagement with learning, such as classroom organization, teacher attitudes, pedagogy, peer relations, and overall school climate. We asked general questions, for example, "Tell me about your school. What is it like to be here?" "Who are your friends?" "Tell me about the different groups here." "What do they think is important?" Many were tentative upon this first meeting, and in most cases we felt that we were receiving a very incomplete picture of students' feelings and perceptions. Nevertheless, the use of open-ended interview questions, particularly those concerning students' friends and other peer groups, gave students an opportunity to hint at what they thought was important. Comments about friends and family, cultural background, and ethnicity were common. This led to an explicit exploration of these issues in two later interviews, both of which generated the bedrock of information and understandings that enabled us and the youth we interviewed to reflect on their lives from a more situated perspective.

These two interviews centered on eliciting the behaviors, norms, expectations, sanctions, and values that students perceived as characterizing their family, peer, and school worlds. The first interview, shown in Table 5.1, provided a general picture of these issues.

The second interview, conducted during the second year of the study, provided a more specific understanding of the behaviors, norms, expectations, sanctions, and values students saw as reflective of their ethnic backgrounds. Questions concerning ethnicity in students' families and peer worlds were adapted from those shown in Table 5.1. (For example, we asked, "In what way(s) does your family's behavior reflect your cultural background?" "What do your friends expect for people of your ethnicity?") Additionally, we developed a set of questions that asked youths to consider how their school responds to their ethnic group in particular and ethnic diversity in general. (For example, "How is your heritage talked about by teachers? By other students?" "Does being _____ affect your life in school or particular classes?") During these interviews, students provided information that enabled us to identify potential areas of conflict between family, peer, and school worlds, reflect upon the cultural sources of their peers' and family's behavior, and reveal much about the meanings they receive about their ethnic background within different worlds. Our questions about others' expectations for members of a youth's ethnic group were particularly useful in this regard.

Two additional interviews were also conducted during the second year of the study. The first was largely concerned with identifying areas of overlap between students' family, peer, and school worlds. We asked questions concerning friends' and parents' involvement in school (e.g., "Are there things you do with your friends that have to do with school?" "In what ways are your parents involved in school?") and questions concerning the involvement of friends and family with each other (e.g., "How do your parents feel about your friends?" "How do your friends interact with your parents?"). This helped deepen our understanding of areas of cultural congruence and conflict in students' lives (that is, areas of match and mismatch between youths' family, peer, and school worlds).[4]

The second interview focused on eliciting students' perceptions of pressures in their family, peer, and school worlds. It proved helpful for deepening our and students' understanding of forces within their lives—both societal (e.g., poverty, community violence) and interpersonal—that structured the development of particular situated selves.[5] We also asked a series of questions about school practices, policies, and climate, two of which encouraged students to reflect on factors within schools that constrain their lives. First, we asked students to describe help they were receiving with regard to course decisions, college, goal setting, and personal problems. Second, we asked students how they felt about the pattern of classes they were taking. The latter question was especially salient for high-achieving youths of color from underrepresented ethnic groups, in that it gave them an opportunity to reflect on and critique their isolation in advanced classrooms.

Ethnographic Interviewing in Action

The following case studies focus on two sophomores, the first an African American male, the second a Latina female. These youths were chosen because they provide clear, vivid illustrations of the situated self as defined by the Spindlers (this volume), a self "linked to the attainment of ends defined within the framework of a lifeway or social context," the self "encompassing those aspects of a person as he or she copes with the everyday exigencies of life." The cases begin with a general description of the youths' social background and negotiation of varied sociocultural contexts. I follow each with excerpts from interviews that reveal how questions about behaviors, norms, expectations, sanctions, and values led these youths to reflect upon and perhaps deepen their understanding of the adaptations they made to varied sociocultural worlds.

The notion of situated self is helpful for making sense of the behavior of the youths I describe. Situated selves are not, however, always as neat and tidy as they appear in these case studies.[6] Students do not always display a coherent and consistent response to their cultural worlds but may alter over time or in response to the

TABLE 5.1 Students' Multiple Worlds Study: Core Interview

Sociocultural Components	Family	Peers	School	Self
Ways of behaving/ actions	What sort of things do you do with your family (e.g., vacations, movies, sit around and talk, chores)?	What things do you do with your friends (e.g., walk to school, hang out at lunch, talk in class, sports, after-school activities, movies, mall, hikes, dates, party)?	What sort of things do you do in school (e.g., cut classes, extracurricular sports, homework)? How do you behave in classes (e.g., clown, quiet, work, participate in discussions)?	What are your preferences in terms of how you spend your time?
Ways of behaving/ interactions	What do you talk about with your family (problems, when something good happens, relationships, future, family interactions, expectations, and so on)?	What do you talk about with your friends (teachers, other peers, relationships, marriage, weekend plans, opposite sex, parents)?	What do you talk about with your teachers (e.g., schoolwork, personal matters, other students, future plans)?	What things are important for you to talk about?
Expectations (past)	Has your family always expected the same things (e.g., when you were younger, before you came to the United States)?	Have your friends always expected the same things?	Have your teachers pretty much always expected the same things?	Feelings and thoughts about these expectations?

138

	Parents	Friends	Teachers	Self
Expectations (future)	What do your parents expect you to do in the future? How do they let you know? (e.g., talk to you, model, tell others)?	What do you think most of your friends will be doing after high school (e.g., working, college, married)? What do they think you'll be doing?	What do your teachers expect you will do in the future? (e.g., go to college, work, trade school, marry)? How do they let you know?	What do you see yourself doing in the future?
Rules	What sorts of things would your parents not let you do? What could you get in trouble for? What would your parents say no to?	What could you do to make your friends upset with you? What do your friends give you a hard time about? What sort of things have your friends done that have upset you?	What are the rules that you have to obey at this school? In classes? Are rules different in different classes?	Your feelings about these rules?
Sanctions	What would happen if you did the above?	What would they do if you did the above? What would you do if you were upset with them?	What would happen if you broke the rules (school or classroom)?	Your response in each situation?

shifting power relationships and changed meanings they encounter in a given setting (Davidson, Yu, & Phelan 1993).

Johnnie Betts: From "Gangbanging" to a "Cool" School Self

Johnnie, an African American sophomore, has moved five times between an African American inner-city neighborhood in St. Louis and a middle-class neighborhood in California. Johnnie's mother, a beautician, lives in St. Louis with Johnnie's two toddler brothers, 12 and 13 years his junior. Johnnie's uncle, his mother's younger brother, lives in a California suburb with his wife and three children. He works for the FBI. Upon Johnnie's most recent move to California, when he came into eighth grade under age, administrators advanced him to ninth-grade remedial classes, where he made his school's honor roll for two semesters. In tenth grade, Johnnie was moved to the general track, where he earned a 2.17 grade point average (GPA) during the first semester of his sophomore year and district honors for his participation on his school's junior varsity football team. This contrasts with his academic performance in middle school, where he earned Ds and Fs.

While in his California high school, Johnnie presents a situated self who combines academic achievement with street-stylized cultural behaviors he considers appropriate to a pro-African American male identity. Johnnie's situated self can be located in his visual presentation of self (saggy pants, dark sunglasses, gold chains, and gold-capped incisor go alongside an athletic duffle bag stuffed with textbooks), in the cool nods he sends to male friends in the hallway, and in the verbal jibes he casts at his African American friends while in classrooms: "Oh, you got *crowned* Jack!" "Hey, you're just about as dumb as you look, you know that?" "You don't know *none* of the answers, you just raise your hand every time." It can be seen as well in Johnnie's occasional switches to Black English grammatical patterns when engaged in social, as opposed to academic, conversation with teachers in the classroom: "Why come they're in the hall?" "I don't know, Ms. Ashton, if somebody did a murder you gonna' take everybody to jail?" "So, all we doin' is writin' out the word for word for simulate?" At lunchtime and while in the halls, Johnnie spends time with fellow African American males, using Black English almost exclusively.

Johnnie is aware of this stance; indeed, he cultivates his "cool" pro-school self:

> Things that I do, you can't tell that I'm kind of like a good—I get good grades. You straight out look at me you'd be like, "Oh God! Man, this kid is . . ." 'Cause if you see somebody that's trying to act cool or whatever, and you see somebody "What's up?" and you see somebody like that and you see them cat walking and you're like, "Look at that!" You can almost—you can tell by the character. (RA27STA: 629-633)

Moreover, Johnnie is proud of his heritage and does not want to do anything that might call his commitment into question:

> When I think about being Black, I'm happy, you know, I think about cool. . . . because we have a lot of, *lot* of famous Black people, Black stars. Black people dominate sports, Black people dominate the music industry. I like it because we have a lot of Black, intelligent, fearless leaders like Malcolm X, Martin Luther King, all those guys, and you know. And I just like it because our background, you know, some you can't be proud of them and some you can. I like it because you know—a lot of people think well there's only White queens and this and that, but there's a lot of Black, beautiful African queens, you know. I like that. . . . Queen Nefertiti and all those. I'm proud. I'm proud of my background and heritage and I could never sell out. That's what I'm proud of. . . . To me, I think Black people are just as strong as White people in a sense. (RA27STC: 1219-1221, 1229-1260)

Prior to his arrival in California, Johnnie cultivated a situated self that looked and behaved quite differently. For this "gangbanging" self, partying, hanging out on the street, and fighting were central. Below, Johnnie describes some of the behaviors and expectations that structured his life as a member of his neighborhood Crips gang:

Johnnie: We went to parties a lot. Stuff happened like . . . we even got sent to juvenile 'cause it was like, that was back in the days when everything was just crazy and we didn't care. And before we realized who we were, where we were going, we were just, you know, out there, floating around.

ALD: Really?

Johnnie: Yeah, just gangbanging and all that kind of stuff. We was downing colors and all this, but now, it's changed.

ALD: Can you describe to me—you know when you talk about gang-banging and colors and going down to juvenile—can you give me an incident or something to help me understand like what your life was like then?

Johnnie: Yeah, 'cause I never went to juvenile, that's the only place I stayed out of, but a lot of my friends, they always got caught and stuff. But like, when we talk about gangbanging, it's like you just sit around the block and all your boys and your friends be drinking and stuff and you might see some group of kids, group of other dudes that they don't like. Could be old, young, could be anybody except like girls. But they'd just be walking by and looking at you and even if they don't look at you, one of your partners says, "Let's get 'em man," and they already wasted and stuff so they just rush 'em and then they take out their little rags or whatever and throw them around. (RA27STB: 138-180)

For this self, school was irrelevant. Johnnie and his friends rejected academics, celebrating suspensions and ostracizing peers who tried academically:

When I was in sixth grade down there, the teachers was all—they were strict, man, they'll hit you, grab you. My teachers they hit me with a ruler and I said, I took the ruler and I broke it, and I left the class. And they were like going, "Suspend him," but I didn't care 'cause I didn't want to go no way. So it was really—when you got suspended in school in St. Louis it was like, "Yeahhh, I got suspended!" (laughter) It was like "Yeah, alright!" you know. (RA27STB: 1382-1400)

It ain't really cool, you know. Being Black and going to school in St. Louis really doesn't exist. . . . like in the city, the city. Nobody goes to school . . . I mean 'cause if you do, usually everybody will cop you off and all this other stuff. They don't really focus on school, and if they do it's just to get out of high school or whatever. (RA27STC: 695-697, 717-736)

In summarizing his school experiences up to his arrival in California, Johnnie states:

I was always getting in trouble in school. I mean, this is the best years I had ever! The best school years. I was, school, my mom used to say, "I'll be glad when you're out of school. Going up here every other week. Every school you go to you get kicked out of." (RA27STEN: 992-999)

Interviews: Toward an Understanding
of Johnnie's "Cool" School Self

My interviews with Johnnie focused on understanding factors that made it possible for him to combine academic achievement with a pro-African American identity in California and directed him toward rejecting pro-academic behavior and adopting a "gang-banging" self in St. Louis.

During our first meeting, Johnnie was cautious and hesitant. Before the interview, he asked me how many times he would have to talk to me; during the interview, he spent much of his time leaning back in his chair with his sunglasses on. He hinted vaguely at the "trouble" he'd had in St. Louis but did not go into detail:

ALD: And when did you move out here?

Johnnie: Like—see, I came out here in the summer, I went back to Missouri, and I didn't want to stay there 'cause, I was getting in too

much trouble there so, my mom wanted me to come out here and
live with my aunt, 'cause my uncle knew I'd do good out here. So I
came out here. (RA27STA: 45-53)

Later in the interview, I asked Johnnie to elaborate on his "trouble." Again, he was vague:

ALD: Your mom was worried like you were going to get in trouble with
your friends?

Johnnie: Well 'cause, OK, like in Missouri it's like down in L.A., there's
a lot of crime there and everything and youngsters get in a lot of
trouble with drugs and everything, gang violence, so she didn't
want me to get in that kind of trouble. And so she sent me out here
because my uncle—he works for the State, he's an FBI agent and so
she thought if I came out here and stayed with a police officer or
something like that, my uncle, I won't get into trouble. (RA27STA:
89-106)

While learning little specific about his situation, Johnnie's brief
references to the other world he navigated in St. Louis offered
hints about what might be important.

Johnnie's references to his tendency to get into trouble emerged
again during the interview focusing on family, peer, and school
worlds. The interview began with my asking Johnnie what kinds
of things he likes to do with friends. When I asked, "Do you go to
parties with your friends?," Johnnie replied:

I go to dances, but I'm not up on parties 'cause ahm, I had my share of
parties when I was in Missouri, 'cause that's like L.A.?

ALD: Um-hmm?

Johnnie: It's real bad there. And I got—when you go to parties it's always
going to be broke up, just by the cops because of fliers, or it's going
to be a lot of drinking and stuff, people are going to start fighting,
so. And then when I come home, I *know* I can't come home to my
aunt's house drunk so, I just say forget it, I just go to dances, where
I know I'm safe. But if it's someone like my cousin and he wanted
to go to this party I know he's legit so I'll go.

ALD: When you talk about your cousin being "legit"?

Johnnie: Yeah?

ALD: What do you mean he's "legit"?

Johnnie: 'Cause I know his moves, I know what—'cause I've been around him a long time and I know that he's going to know "Johnnie don't go to this party" and this and this—'cause he, 'cause he knows I get in trouble. I would get in trouble so bad if I go to a party or something and something happens. I don't go to party 'cause stuff happens and cop breaks it up and you got alcohol or something at a party and you're going down [downtown, to the police station]. (RA27STB: 56-74, 93-108)

I asked Johnnie to talk more about his tendency to "get in trouble" by asking whether partying was a personal inclination. In responding, Johnnie looked outside himself to consider the behaviors and norms structuring behavior in his St. Louis peer group:

ALD: Is it hard for you to resist temptation to like drink or get high or whatever?

Johnnie: Not really, 'cause . . . 'cause in Missouri, that's all your partners did, is just, you know, they sit out on the block—'cause we got neighborhoods—they just sit on the block drinking stuff and smoke, whatever. And I know it's addiction and I don't want to get addicted to none of that stuff and trouble me, so. I don't like to be felt like I'm being put in control and can't stand up straight, so I don't go to those kind of parties.

ALD: So with your friends in the past you guys would party a lot then?

Johnnie: Yeah, yeah we went to parties a lot. Stuff happened like . . . we even got sent to juvenile 'cause it was like, that was back in the days when everything was just crazy and we didn't care. And before we realized who we were, where we were going, we were just, you know, out there, floating around.

ALD: Really?

Johnnie: Yeah, just gangbanging all that kind of stuff. We was downing colors and all this, but now, it's changed. (RA27STB: 119-151)

As Johnnie elaborated on ways he spent time with friends, he also made comments that indicated his St. Louis situated self was not one with which he felt comfortable. For example, "It was pretty hard back then." "It's easier for me out here." "I like I just fit in better here." Nor did he seem particularly proud of his "gangbanging" behaviors:

> Yeah, they could be smart. But it's—it is just a bunch of stupid kids running around. Suckers, they're suckers, man. They sucker other people, like we'd get other kids, we'd get *little* kids like 6 years old, and somebody down there is not supposed to be down there, we'll go tell them, "Hey!" little kid'll walk up to them and go, "Hey! You got to leave," and if he try to tell the kid to go on about his business the little kid might shoot him.
>
> They know that we got, they know the little kid, he knows he can't go to jail 'cause he's only a juvenile, if he'll go to juvenile he going to get to blame his parents. But he knows he's not going to jail for nothing, so he'll just say, "Alright, I'll do it for you Johnnie, I'll do this for you." And that's how they get their colors and stuff by doing something stupid like that, going and robbing a store, little kids. (RA27STB: 504-555)

Knowing Johnnie's feelings, I was interested in understanding why Johnnie joined the Crips. I suspected, given the discomfort he expressed as well as his frequent, enthused references to the changes he had made, that matters were not so simple as a tendency to find trouble. Rather, I felt that trouble found Johnnie readily in his inner-city St. Louis neighborhood. When pressed to look more closely at his decision to join a neighborhood gang, Johnnie began to look at his behavior from a more situated perspective, referring to the expectations that permeated his St. Louis world:

ALD: Why did you claim blue [color of the Crips] as opposed to red?
Johnnie: Why did I claim blue instead of red?
ALD: Uh-huh.
Johnnie: 'Cause that's where my friends were going to school at, and like that's where my sister was living down there, and I used to always

go down there and I had a lot of friends down there, so it was like, "Alright man, I'm going to get in with you all," and he was like, "OK cool, you're in."

ALD: So it was sort of like they were there and you were there?

Johnnie: Yeah, they were like something happen I'd just call my homeboy. They were like always at your back.

ALD: Great protection.

Johnnie: Yeah.

ALD: It is! So it sounds like now things are kind of different for you here.

Johnnie: Yeah they are.

ALD: Are any of your friends in gangs, Johnnie?

Johnnie: After that I stayed . . . no, I don't tolerate that anymore. I just say forget it, you know. That was a long time ago, that was the *old* me. And that was the only way to get out, and it could have been a lot worse, I could have—I was only.[7] 'Cause now, if I go back nothing will happen, they'll just go like, "Yeah, you're out," and I'll just be like a loner because I'm out, I ain't down with their set [a block or blocks within a neighborhood associated with a particular gang] no more, I have to move to like a area instead of a neighborhood, 'cause in Missouri we got neighborhoods, we got hoods, north, south, east, west territories. And I would have to move to like a county and like an area instead of a neighborhood, 'cause in any neighborhood is a gang, gangs, something like that. They even have little kids down there carrying pistols and stuff. (RA27STB: 453-502)

Johnnie's reasons for joining the gang are similar to those given by East Los Angeles Chicano gang members (Vigil, 1988). His desire for the personal protection gang membership can provide and fear of social isolation are reflected in statements such as "they were like always at your back" and "I'll just be like a loner . . . I would have move to like a county and like an area instead of a neighborhood." Vigil (1993) points out that toughness affords gang members some relief from the fear omnipresent in street life, while gang camaraderie provides emotional support and a sense of responsibility as members work to earn that support. Such factors are particularly important for males, where "'being a man'—tough, unfeeling, courageous and daring—limits the role choices available to males forced to adjust and adapt to street realities" (p. 105).

I also wondered whether Johnnie had thought about factors that shaped his friends' rejection of school and acceptance of gang subculture. Some have argued that the degree of gang involvement depends on the effects of racial and cultural discrimination, poverty, and the failure of family and school authorities to influence and guide (see Klein, 1968; Vigil, 1988, 1993). Were Johnnie and his friends simply "suckers"? Or were there also environmental factors that pushed them toward gangbanging behavior? Questions about the behaviors and expectations at Johnnie's St. Louis middle school prompted Johnnie to address this issue:

ALD: Let's move to school and maybe you can talk a little bit about how things are different here as opposed to Missouri with like your teachers and your classes.

Johnnie: Oh, in Missouri teachers, teachers were rough too. They would beat down the students.

ALD: Were they from the neighborhood or were they—

Johnnie: They were from all around, they were strict though. They were the strict kind, "Do this work and if you don't do it you're going to be [inaudible]." They were the kind of teachers that, my teachers used to whup me, like they say in the old days how the teachers used to spank you. Well Missouri they never stopped that, until you get high school. . . .

Teachers, they were like, they didn't care, they didn't care what you do and how you do it or where you end up 'cause they be like—some our teachers they actually tell us you going to be nobody. And they'd—if somebody keeps telling you you're gonna' be nobody, you're going to take that in and you're going to say, "Well damn, I'm going to be nobody. Look at my grades, they're right." But, they don't tell you that you have a chance to make it, like they don't tell you that you have a chance to get yourself together and get on the good foot, and get on the right track. They tell you, "You going to be nothing, you going to the streets, you're going to be working at 7 ," you're going to be doing this and you're gonna be doing that. . . .

Teachers here, they do it too, but they'll tell you, they'll be like, "You can make something of yourself. You don't have to do this," you don't have to do that. In St. Louis, some of my teachers *bought* drugs off of us. Off of my, they bought drugs at the school. . . .

ALD: Wow, it just sounds totally different. So the difference here, teachers will tell you you're going to be nobody but they also tell you you can be somebody?

Johnnie: Yeah, they don't really—they don't stress on you can't be anything. Strict teachers in St. Louis that's their *main* object is to tell the student that you're lower than trash, you're nothin'. Teachers here, they help you. They help you a lot. There they just like, "Whatever . . . whatever you want to do." (RA27STB: 1357-1379, 1395-1422, 1441-1454)

As I reflected my understanding of Johnnie's situation, he then looked further, going beyond descriptions of his teachers' low expectations to a beginning analysis of the shared community understandings about the local economic situation and its implications for youths:

ALD: It sounds like the expectations are very, very different.

Johnnie: Yeah, 'cause they know in St. Louis growing up as a young teen you don't do nothing no way because that's really how it is. Can't get a job. No good jobs there.

ALD: How do you think that makes the students there feel toward school?

Johnnie: Like, "Ahh, the hell with it." They don't care. (RA27STB: 1456-1469)

In explaining his and his friends' disengagement, Johnnie had come from speaking simply about his tendency to find trouble to speaking adamantly about the reality of the local economy, the role his teachers played in communicating its hopelessness, and the realities of street life. Johnnie had moved not only physically but analytically outside of the subculture in which he had been situated to reflect on possible sources of the behaviors, norms, expectations, and values that governed his life in St. Louis.

Johnnie and I also discussed factors that underlay his ability to develop a new situated self in California. Questions about his new friends served as a starting point from which Johnnie began to analyze the factors that enabled him to adopt a new situated self:

ALD: Your friends now, what do they expect of you now in terms of the way you behave, the way you act?

Johnnie: My friends now, all my friends they be like, "Man!" 'cause when
I first came out here, when they, they all know—I know people back
here and back there and they all know me so when I come back they
don't—shit, they be like, "Oh yeah we're glad to have you back,"
and they take me out and stuff and we just kick it or something like
that. And they be like, 'cause when I come back, it was like, "Man
Johnnie, you changed man, you changed, I remember when we used
to go to school out here and you wasn't crazy like this and everything. Talking about all this crazy stuff." And it was like, my one,
my one, I got a friend here named Tommy, and he's really cool and
everything, he was telling me too, but I should have listened to him
early, he's all, "Man, I'm telling you dude, you go back there you're
just going to get into trouble, something's going to happen," and it
did. He's all, "Man, we don't want none of that gangs bothering us,
'cause all it is is brothers killing brothers and it's low man, why you
going to shoot another dude that's your own color?" (RA27STB:
559-598)

Johnnie's friend's point of view is clear. Gangbanging is beneath
a "brother's" standard of decency ("It's low").

Johnnie also described reading significantly different messages
about future possibilities in his new school world. One source of
these messages was located in teachers' actions:

ALD: In thinking about your teachers, the ones you have now, what do
they expect out of you?

Johnnie: Expect me to graduate, and to go to college, and to be something.

ALD: How do you know that?

Johnnie: 'Cause they tell us! Tell us, they say something like, "I want you
to do good this year so you can pass my class so you can go into a
higher class and so you won't be back here." . . . Miss Ashton, she'll
go all off on the board and she'll tell you, you know, "If you think
you can't even spell this word, think you're going to go in the English
class next year?" And then she'll say well, she'll talk to you. She
won't put you down. She'll talk to you and she'll go, "Yeah, you
know I love you. You know I want you to make something out of
yourself, so stop messing around in class." (RA27STB: 1493-1537)

Six months later, Johnnie expanded his description, going beyond teachers' attitudes to take his environmental situation into account. Here, issues of physical safety and better school conditions came to the fore:

ALD: Can you talk a little bit about what it's like to be a Black student here [California] as opposed to St. Louis?

Johnnie: Well, first of all you get to live. Second of all, the school is better and the teachers are better, people—you don't have to worry about walking down the street, getting shot, or walking down the street getting gangbanged, getting jumped, getting your clothes taken away—here, you're walking and you're cool with everybody. You either settle it yourself, usually it doesn't get in a fight, or you go to a teacher and they get suspended.

St. Louis, you're walking, you have a fight, you get jumped by the whole school. You walk up, they take your clothes and whoever comes to pick you up, your mom and dad, they'll beat them in the head, take their purse or money and run. (RA27STC: 627-650)

As Johnnie continued, he reflected on how these factors restructured his behavior, moving him toward a new situated self:

Johnnie: And here it's not like—it's better. You know? But when I first came here, it was like—'cause I was born out here. When I first came back, when I was a teen? I was—'cause I had been in St. Louis for a long time and I was gangbanging it, so I thought I was pretty bad. And I came here and I was like, "Why are all these people nice to me??!! Why?" I mean, I looked at them mean and everything, I was mugging them and everything, I'm like, "Why do you want to be my friend?" OK?

ALD: You were like trying to give them the evil eye?

Johnnie: Yeah, and so my one friend Jerome was a senior last year, and he goes, "Well you know, I want to be your friend, it's cool." So that's how I—if it wasn't for him, I'd probably be a loner, I wouldn't know nobody. 'Cause he introduced me to every—like 90 percent of everybody at Huntington. I mean he took me out at lunch like three days—for the three days I was here—every single day and introduced me to everybody. I mean everybody. And that's why everybody knows

me and . . . but at first it was like, "Why do you want to be my friend,
I don't like you." You know, "I'm from a different set, I'm cool."
(RA27STC: 650-688)

Johnnie is clear about the assumptions that were part of his St.
Louis worldview. Those from a different "set" (block or blocks
within a neighborhood) are one's enemy; to protect oneself (to
live), one has to adopt an aggressive and antagonistic posture
toward unfamiliar others ("mugging"); to be cool ("bad"), one
must be "gangbanging it" (belong to a gang). The culture shock
Johnnie experienced upon moving into his new California environment is also clear; indeed, Johnnie relied on a translator of sorts
(Jerome) to help him cope with and adjust to the norms of his new
environment. Johnnie had moved to the point where he was able
to discuss and reflect upon the adaptations he made to his St.
Louis and California schools from a situated perspective.

Carla Chávez: Classroom and Community Selves

Carla, born and raised in a working-class barrio, is an academically high-achieving sophomore of Mexican and Cuban descent.
Her mother, who works weekdays as an inspector in a paper
factory and weekends at a local taqueria, is the daughter of Cuban
immigrants who fled their home when Fidel Castro triumphed in
the early 1960s. Carla's mother and her family left behind a successful small retail store and a comfortable lifestyle to struggle to
make a living in the United States. While Carla's mother did not
finish high school, she eventually earned her GED at night school.
Carla's father immigrated to the United States from Mexico in his
early twenties to find work. While he dropped out of school at an
early age to work and speaks little English, he has succeeded in
establishing his living as a welder. Carla's oldest brother and best
friend have both dropped out of high school, and none of her close
friends—all of them Latina—is in her advanced classes. In contrast, Carla earned a 4.0 GPA as a freshman and a 3.5 GPA as a
sophomore with a challenging academic course load, including
accelerated English, accelerated world history, chemistry, and ge-
ometry. She is one of a handful of Latina students taking advanced

courses; during her sophomore year, she was often the *only* trans-ported Latina female enrolled in her classes.

The Spindlers (this volume) describe a bicultural adaptation in which an individual develops a degree of comfort in two cultural systems. While Carla is not comfortable in her advanced class-rooms, she fits this pattern in the sense that she adapts situation-ally and successfully to the demands of varied cultural worlds. Outside school, whether relaxing with friends and family at her father's large home in downtown Mostaza, working weekends selling "churros" at the local flea market, or sleeping and eating at her mother's apartment (Carla's parents were divorced when she was in middle school), Carla is surrounded by people who are familiar with her Latina heritage and supportive of her ethnic self. While with her friends from her community, Carla pushes a blended ethnic identity, what I refer to as her "community self," to the fore. Carla's community self talks of friends, boyfriends, and family: such as Carmen's date last Friday, Imelda's pregnancy and up-coming marriage, Carla's anger that her mother will not let her cruise in her barrio on the weekends. Carla's community self uses barrio English—inserting "Mexican words, if Spanish goes real well" (RA28STEN: 572-574) into English phrases: "Qué quieres comer?" "I ain't eatin'. Why you eatin' yogurt? It's sick!!" Carola and Marcelo Suarez-Orozco (1993) describe an emphasis on spiri-tual and interpersonal relationships and an emphasis on the here and now as cultural norms that cut across Latino ethnic groups. Carla and her friends fit this pattern. As she explains, Carla's peers focus on relationships, personal feelings, and concerns rather than school-related topics:

ALD: What kinds of things do you like to talk to your friends about at school?

Carla: The things that happen that day, or rumors or what's happening, what's going on with other people, different things. . . .

ALD: Do you talk to your friends about problems you might be having?

Carla: Yeah, sometimes I have to talk to someone, and see if they can help me.

ALD: School?

Carla: School? Yeah . . . no, not really. We really don't talk about school much. We're here enough. If we have like homework, we talk, "Oh I have so much homework!" or if we have a test, "Did you study for the test?" (RA28STB: 43-70)

I don't talk to them about school and all that. I talk to them more about my personal life and how I feel. It's different. (RA28STD: 1267-1270)

Over the 15 months that I knew Carla, lunchtime was the only time during the school day when she had the opportunity to spend time with her community peers and the only time when she revealed the linguistic aspects of her cultural background or talked about her home life and personal concerns.

During most of the school day, Carla's classroom self emerged. For this self, the dominant topic of concern was school. It was present in what Carla talked about during the days I spent with her in chemistry, the only course where she had an opportunity to chat with class friends because she sat in a group: "I finished the rough draft of my essay for English." "How much did you write down for the first one?" "Mrs. Cook, she's messed up. She tests different classes on different days!" Nonacademic conversations with classroom friends were light and nonpersonal, despite the fact that Carla identified an Asian American woman in her work group as one of her best classroom friends. "I had toast and orange juice for breakfast." "Your hair looks good like that, Carla." "I hate my feet." During the 7 days I observed Carla in chemistry, personal topics came up only 10 times. The closest a conversation came to home was when Carla displayed photos of her Latina friends after I, spying the pictures in her wallet, asked to see them. According to Carla, such school-dominated conversations are typical both inside and outside of class. For, as she explains:

You don't really share your personal life with them, 'cause you really aren't, you know, the culture isn't quite [the same]. We don't talk about that. We just talk about school or school things. We just talk about school. (RA28STD: 1248-1259)

Carla's classroom self is also characterized by her clandestine efforts to stay abreast of classmates who often seem to know things that she does not. For example, Carla learned that a PSAT practice test booklet existed during a casual passing period conversation with a classroom friend. This friend also told Carla that she was practicing and doing well on the test. Carla revealed only curiosity rather than concern during the conversation. Upon arriving at her next class, however, she told her teacher that she needed a pass to the bathroom and then went to the office instead to get a PSAT practice booklet. Carla told me later that she felt an immediate need to get information on a test that she was in fact quite worried about.

Finally, Carla's classroom self is silent. Of five teachers interviewed about Carla, three noted her tendency to disappear quietly in the crowd: "She'll raise her hand, but not very often . . . I don't see her as a leader" [RA031ST1: 27-28, 34]. "She's the type that teachers will overlook because she doesn't stand out—either as a nuisance or as a top student. So she'll get overlooked because of the sheer number of students that teachers deal with" [RA076ST1: 38-43]. "She'd get a little bit more attention if she'd turn around and raise a fuss. She's kind of a model student. *Too* much so, I would say" [RA28ST08: 8].

Interviews: Toward an Understanding
of Carla's Silent Classroom Self

My interviews with Carla focused on understanding the community and school experiences that underlay her inclination to leave the outward markers of her ethnicity behind when she moved into her high-track classrooms. In addition, I was interested in understanding her silence in these courses.

One of the first things I learned from Carla was that her older brother had left school:

ALD: Can you tell me a little bit about yourself and your family?
Carla: Well, like what, my age?
ALD: Yeah, you can start with that.

Carla: I'm 14, going to be 15 during the summer. I live with my dad right now, but I'm supposed to be moving in with my mom because they're getting a divorce. And I have three brothers, two which are older and one which is younger. One has dropped out of school and the other goes to Explorer and my little brother goes to middle school. (ES28STA: 1-30)

During our second interview a few months later, Carla told me that her close friends also did not do well in school. Carla's readiness to divulge this information indicated its potential salience. In addition, I was interested in understanding what motivated Carla to expend the extra energy it would require to maintain friendships with students outside her classes:

ALD: So you've always kind of done real well with school, and your friends have done just kinda medium in school?

Carla: Yeah.

ALD: That's interesting because a lot of times kids who do well in school have all friends who do well in school.

Carla: That's true. (laughs) Not with me.

ALD: Not with you. Tell me about your very best friends—why don't you describe them to me—and tell me why you like them.

Carla: Mmm, I don't know. 'Cause they're nice. They talk to me, about their problems, we talk about things. We have a lot of things in common. And there are some things that are not in common that we have. We have a lot of things in common, but we're also different. And we just talk. We talk to each other without being uncomfortable, we're comfortable with each other so we talk to each other about things. (RA28STB: 103-127)

Clearly, issues of "comfort" and "having things in common" were central for Carla. As I began to spend time with Carla during her sophomore year, however, I learned that she found it difficult to *clarify* the source of the discomfort she experienced with friends from advanced classes:

ALD: I'm trying to figure out what it is for you that makes being with [names friends] different and nicer for you at lunch than being with your other friends. You mentioned that maybe it was that the values were different?

Carla: Yeah, different. I don't know. Different. I don't know.

ALD: Do you know the differences in the values?

Carla: I feel more comfortable with them. That I don't feel with my friends from class.

ALD: Do you have any sense of what it is that makes you feel more comfortable?

Carla: I don't know, I just feel more comfortable. . . .

ALD: You said that you guys had similar values?

Carla: We listen to the same music, you know, we talk about the same things, like on a similar subject kind of. But with my classroom friends, they like different things, they're into probably different music, they have like a different life than I do. . . . in music and how we live, and where we live. . . .

ALD: And when you say how you live, what's the difference in how you live?

Carla: I don't know, I guess how our parents, you know, had brought you up.

ALD: I see.

Carla: Different. . . . I don't know, they're just like. . . . I really can't explain it. I don't know. (RA28STC: 844-914)

As Carla described her family's and friends' values and the way she lived, I was able to identify some of the ways in which the behavior and expectations in her family differed from those in the stereotypical European American family. For example, Carla's parents place a great importance on the extended family and have supported various extended family members financially over the years. In addition, Carla faced certain restrictions on her freedom of movement because of her parents' beliefs about appropriate Latina behavior. Finally, Carla described an emphasis on generosity and putting the group's needs before the individual as a value held by both close friends and family. In contrast to many of the other youths I interviewed, however, the *specifics* of these differences were not at the forefront of Carla's mind. Rather, while sure of her discomfort, she seemed less certain about differences between herself and her classroom friends.

A second theme also emerged during our conversations. As Carla and I spoke about her ethnicity, she revealed that she perceived low expectations for Latino youth from almost everyone around her. Below are three separate segments from an hour-long interview focusing on ethnicity in Carla's family, peer, and school worlds:

Segment 1: *How do you feel about your heritage?*

Well, I'm proud of it. I feel that, you know, that Latins aren't stupid. I'd like to be one of them that could achieve something. 'Cause most people think that Latins aren't—you know, that they can't do nothing, that they're just going to become like in the lower class. And, I think that's not true. I think that everybody's the same. You can do anything you want to. (RA28STEN: 124-136)

Segment 2: *What about, not thinking about you and your grades, but when your friends talk about other Mexican people, what are their expectations of them in terms of their grades?*

They probably don't think they do good. You know, they expect that like most Mexicans get Fs. So they, you know, they're surprised, because Mexicans don't do good. Most of them are dropouts. They expect most of them to get pregnant when they turn 18 or something. (RA28STEN: 742-756)

Segment 3: *In terms of people here at school, what kinds of expectations do teachers and administrators have of people of your background?*

They probably don't expect us to get as high. They probably expect us a lot of us to drop out, not to graduate. I think they expect more of us to have babies.

Have people said or done anything that makes you feel that way?

No . . . but, no, I don't know. You just feel it. Feel it.

Do teachers appear surprised that you do as well as you do?

Ahm, they might be thinking it, but they don't say it. (RA28STEN: 868-886)

The same theme emerged during a special interview I conducted a month later on Carla's life history, as Carla talked about her transition to advanced track classrooms:

Carla: . . . then in eighth grade that was when I got all accelerated courses so . . .

ALD: They moved you up?

Carla: Yeah. Even science. Uugh . . . 'Cause I was like in regular science. But I think Mr. White, my teacher, I think he didn't expect much from me because I was Hispanic, I was like the only—like Anita was in there too, it was like me and her was the only ones in that class. But then I was like the first one to get like the best score in the class, so he was really surprised! And I got it like a couple of times, and so, we had like, we got a champion's chair. You could choose where you sat and the seat, your seat would move around and it would be soft and everything. So I got that. But after that I retired, 'cause my name was up there too many times. After three times you retired.

ALD: So you really challenged his expectations, didn't you.

Carla: Yeah. I don't think he expected that. I don't think he expected that much for me.

ALD: What made you think that?

Carla: It didn't seem like—it seemed like he was surprised . . . surprised. (RA28STAB: 1585-1621)

Carla also described her transition from general to advanced classes:

ALD: Do you remember—how was the transition to the accelerated classes?

Carla: It was different. It was yeah—'cause it was like more challenging. Different people . . . mostly White people. (RA28STAB: 1521-1530)

Carla's comments about others' expectations and her references to isolation stood out as important themes, seemingly as important as the value differences she felt but could not describe between herself and her classmates.

During our last interview, when I asked Carla how she felt about being in her high school's advanced classes, these themes came together. Again, Carla talked about her discomfort. This time, however, she looked to a new source to explain it. Rather than value differences, Carla emphasized her fear that her classmates might not think she belongs and her perceptions of their low expectations:

ALD: Can you talk a little bit about how you feel about being in the accelerated track?

Carla: Well, I kind of feel uncomfortable. Not many Mexicans and Hispanics are in those classes. And so it kind of makes me feel uncomfortable.

ALD: I want to push you a little bit about that. Can you think—I know it's a hard question, but—what about that makes you feel uncomfortable?

Carla: Because . . . they probably think of me as weird, because they think Hispanics, probably they have this view that most Hispanics are dumb or something. Have that opinion, you know, get bad grades. So, I don't know why I feel uncomfortable, I just . . . means you're not really with any other . . . many people.

ALD: You feel that they might be looking at you and wondering what are you doing here kind of a thing?

Carla: Maybe at the beginning of the school year, yeah. But probably by the end they might realize that I belong. (RA28STD: 540-570)

More fully aware of Carla's feelings about her isolation, I interceded at this point with a hypothesis about her silent classroom persona:

ALD: And it's the peers in the high-track classes that make you feel uncomfortable, not your friends who aren't in those classes?

Carla: Yeah.

ALD: In another interview that I had with a person in Adobe Viejo, she said exactly the same thing. And she said that sometimes she feels like . . . she's really afraid of like raising her hand to ask questions because she's afraid that they're going to—she's Black—she's afraid that they're going to think she's stupid and doesn't belong there.

Carla: And she'd probably say the wrong thing.

ALD: Um-hmm. Do you ever feel that way?

Carla: Yeah! If I raise my hand and say the wrong thing, I feel dumb.

ALD: And because you're Latino?

Carla: Yeah.

ALD: You feel like you would stand out more or something?

Carla: Maybe. Then again, everybody's different, nobody would notice.

ALD: Would it be easier for you if there were more Hispanic kids?

Carla: Yeah. Yeah, it probably would be. (RA28STD: 572-605)

Carla is not certain of her conclusions. Situated, on the one hand, in a sociocultural context where the academic failure of Latino youth seems an unwritten rule and, on the other, in classrooms where issues of race and social stratification are never discussed, she has strong suspicions about her classmates' and teachers' attitudes. Carla cannot, however, determine whether her suspicions are true. As such, she is left with a feeling of uneasiness and discomfort, an uncertainty about whether she is truly accepted. I realized that the discomfort Carla felt and her tendency to hide her community self while with classroom friends might stem as much from feelings that these peers look down on her friends and family as from value conflicts and cultural differences.

Carla moved from speaking vaguely about different values to describing and reflecting upon the messages she receives from the sociocultural context in which she finds herself. She continues to voice this analysis of her bicultural adaptation strategy. Whether Carla's ability to reflect on the implications of her isolation developed with our conversations, or simply reflects her decision to allow me to share this aspect of her life, is open to question. At the very least, however, Carla began to voice her feelings to someone outside her ethnic group—arguably a first step toward critiquing and contesting the stratification she observes. Moreover, in publicly considering whether her quiet and reserve stem out of a fear that her classmates will discount her, she also examined the assumptions that guide her behavior.

One other aspect of these conversations is also notable. I initially assumed that Carla's "instrumental competencies" (Spindler & Spindler, this volume) extended to most realms of academic achievement. When I asked Carla how she found information on achievement tests and colleges, however, she explained that she turns to European American and Asian American peers because she has no adult in her school environment with whom she can discuss her goals and ask questions. (Carla's high school does not have counselors.) Carla and I educated one another about the implications of this when I suggested that she consider applying to a prestigious local university, not doubting that she would do so if interested, and Carla told me that while she wanted to attend she thought she would not qualify for admission because she did not participate in student government or sports—activities defined by her classmates as essential for admission. She was extremely surprised when I told her that the university would look favorably upon her work and volunteer experiences. (Carla volunteers 4 hours per week in the geriatric ward of a hospital in her community and works 20 hours per week at a local restaurant.) Moreover, she did not realize that scholarships are available and had taken a teacher's sarcastic comment that "one would automatically gain admission with payment prior to admission" quite seriously. In later conversations, Carla and I discussed some of the reasons that she lacked information relative to her friends—such as her school's lack of information, her parents' lack of experience with the U.S. system of higher education. In this sense, she was able to stop blaming herself for her lack of information and we developed a plan whereby she could gain the assistance that she wanted with the college application process.

Conclusion: Ethnographic Interviewing and Cultural Therapy

While I entered my fieldwork with a descriptive rather than interventionist agenda, I believe that the conversations I had with youths created opportunities for both me and them to look at their lives from an expanded and more situated perspective. As the young people tried to help me understand their worlds, they appeared to evaluate the adaptations they made from new points of view, analyzing some of the forces they responded to when constructing their situated selves.

Conversations with Carla and Johnnie indicate that it is necessary for those concerned with cultural therapy to create situations conducive to enabling youths to reflect on the shifting worlds they navigate when constructing their adolescent selves.[8] For example, Carla, like many academically high-achieving youths of color, was quite conscious of the discomfort and anxiety she experienced with friends from high-track classrooms.[9] She seemed less confident about the source of this discomfort, however. Realizing that her feelings stemmed partially from isolation within a stratified academic system was a first step toward thinking more politically about her situation.

Ethnographic interviews can help create conversational spaces where youths can examine (and ideally critique) messages they receive within local and national sociocultural realms. These messages often stem from political and economic differences and are reflected in mainstream cultural assumptions about who is and who is not capable of what. The Spindlers (personal communication) state: "It is the culture of interaction as related to cultural differences that we think cultural therapy should be directed at, plus attention to skewed perceptions, stereotypes, and prejudgments." In offering space for youths to examine and analyze the culture(s) of interaction they navigate, ethnographic interviews appear promising, both for making familiar assumptions strange and for making unequal power relationships in the classroom, the school, and society more explicit.

Notes

1. Here and elsewhere in this chapter, quotations are identified by file code (e.g., RA27STC) and line numbers. These interviews are part of a public-use file that will eventually be made available to interested researchers through Stanford's Center for Research on the Context of Secondary School Teaching (CRC). Also, brackets [] indicate text inserted for clarification. Three ellipses (. . .) indicate a *pause* in the dialogue, four ellipses (. . . .) indicate that a segment of interview text has been *omitted*.

2. I use the term *world* to refer to cultural knowledge and behavior found within the boundaries of a particular social context. Each world contains values and beliefs, expectations, actions, and emotional responses familiar to insiders (Phelan, Davidson, & Yu, 1993).

3. The Students' Multiple Worlds study is headed by Patricia
Phelan, formerly senior research scholar at CRC and now associate professor of education at the University of Washington at
Bothell. Participating students varied along a number of dimensions, including gender, ethnicity, achievement level, immigration
history, and transportation status. An equal number of high- and
low-achieving students were selected from each school and both
students of color and European American students were included in
the two achievement categories. The majority were in their first year
of high school and were invited to participate by school personnel.
The study and its participants are described more fully in other
publications (Phelan, Davidson, & Cao, 1991; Phelan et al., 1993).

4. While much of the literature on culturally diverse youth and
schooling emphasizes the importance of cultural differences between home and school in generating interaction difficulties and
inequitable treatment in classrooms (see Erickson & Mohatt, 1982;
Heath, 1982; Vogt, Jordan, & Tharp, 1987), we did not assume that
such differences were necessarily important. Rather, we gave students an opportunity to describe whether, when, and how such
differences matter.

5. The relationships we developed with youths over previous
months were particularly important for this interview; youths
were forthcoming about issues they were hesitant to discuss with
either friends or family, including concerns about peer pressure,
family violence, failure in school, and so on. (See Phelan, Cao, &
Davidson, 1992, for a complete description.)

6. Moreover, patterns of adaptation to cultural contact vary
among individuals (Spindler & Spindler, this volume). In some
cases, for example, youths may adopt a blended identity, in which
case presentation of self may vary much less dramatically across
cultural contexts (Rosaldo, 1989).

7. Here, Johnnie is referring to an incident where he was beaten
badly by fellow gang members when they learned that he was
leaving the gang because of his impending move to California.

8. At the same time, as the Spindlers point out, increased
awareness of cultural assumptions and their effect on behavior
and interactions may be important for some students as well as

their teachers. I was struck by the number of European American youth with little or no understanding of culture. Many were baffled by a brief written protocol that asked, "When I think about my cultural background, I . . .," explaining that there was nothing cultural in their or their family's behaviors. This is significant in the sense that, if those from the majority culture see their behavior as normal, it is more likely that they will see and treat the behavior of others as deviant. Indeed, misinterpretations of students' culturally based behaviors and actions can result in misunderstandings and inequitable treatment in the classroom (see Erickson & Mohatt, 1982; Heath, 1982; Spindler & Spindler, 1982).

9. Of 16 high-achieving youth of color interviewed as part of the Students' Multiple Worlds study, 8 described their isolation as a significant source of stress and 6 felt pressure to hide their ethnic selves (Phelan et al., 1992). Academically successful authors of color express similar feelings (see Cary, 1991; Gray, 1985; Monroe, 1987; Neira, 1988).

References

Cary, L. (1991). *Black ice*. New York: Knopf.

Davidson, A. L. (1992). *The politics and aesthetics of ethnicity: Making and molding identity in varied curricular settings*. Unpublished doctoral dissertation, Stanford University.

Davidson, A. L., Yu, H. C., & Phelan, P. K. (1993). The ebb and flow of ethnicity: Constructing identity in varied school settings. *Educational Foundations, 7*(1), 65-87.

Erickson, F. D., & Mohatt, G. (1982). Cultural organization of participation structures in two classrooms of Indian students. In G. D. Spindler (Ed.), *Doing the ethnography of schooling: Educational anthropology in action* (pp. 132-175). New York: Holt, Rinehart & Winston.

Gray, J. (1985, March 17). A black American princess: New game, new rules. *The Washington Post*, pp. E1, E5.

Heath, S. B. (1982). Questioning at school and at home: A comparative study. In G. D. Spindler (Ed.), *Doing the ethnography of schooling: Educational anthropology in action* (pp. 102-131). New York: Holt, Rinehart & Winston.

Klein, M. W. (1968). Impressions of juvenile gang members. *Adolescence, 3*(9), 53-78.

Monroe, S. (1987). Brothers: A vivid portrait of black men in America. *Newsweek, 109*(12), 53-86.

Neira, C. (1988). Building 860. *Harvard Educational Review, 58*(2), 337-342.

Phelan, P. K., Cao, H. T., & Davidson, A. L. (1992). *Navigating the psychosocial pressures of adolescence: Voices and experiences of high school youth* (P92-138). Stanford, CA: Center for Research on the Context of Secondary School Teaching.

Phelan, P. K., Davidson, A. L., & Cao, H. T. (1991). *Students' multiple worlds: Study design, sample description and summary of student record data* (WP-1005). Stanford, CA: Center for Research on the Context of Secondary School Teaching.

Phelan, P. K., Davidson, A. L., & Yu, H. C. (1993). Students' multiple worlds: Navigating the borders of family, peer and school cultures. In P. Phelan & A. L. Davidson (Eds.), *Renegotiating cultural diversity in American schools* (pp. 64-100). New York: Teachers College Press.

Rosaldo, R. (1989). *Culture and truth: The remaking of social analysis.* Boston: Beacon.

Spindler, G., & Spindler, L. (1982). Roger Harker and Schonhausen: From familiar to strange and back again. In G. D. Spindler (Ed.), *Doing the ethnography of schooling: Educational anthropology in action* (pp. 20-46). New York: Holt, Rinehart & Winston.

Spindler, G., & Spindler, L. (1989). Instrumental competence, self-efficacy, linguistic minorities, and cultural therapy: A preliminary attempt at integration. *Anthropology and Education Quarterly, 20*(1), 36-50.

Suarez-Orozco, M. M., & Suarez-Orozco, C. M. (1993). The cultural psychology of Hispanic immigrants: Implications for educational research. In P. Phelan & A. L. Davidson (Eds.), *Renegotiating cultural diversity in American schools* (pp. 118-148). New York: Teachers College Press.

Vigil, J. D. (1988). Group process and street identity: Chicano gangs. *Ethos, 16*(4), 421-445.

Vigil, J. D. (1993). Gangs, social control and ethnicity. In S. B. Heath & M. W. McLaughlin (Eds.), *Identity and inner-city youth: Beyond ethnicity and gender* (pp. 94-119). New York: Teachers College Press.

Vogt, L. A., Jordan, C., & Tharp, R. G. (1987). Explaining school failure, producing school success. *Anthropology and Education Quarterly, 18*(4), 276-286.

Mary E. Hauser

6

Working With School Staff

"Reflective Cultural Analysis" in Groups

MARY E. HAUSER

Mary E. Hauser has had only one September in which she was not in a classroom either as a student or a teacher since she was 4 years old. So it seems quite natural that her research should center on schools and classrooms. She has experience working with preschool, elementary, middle school, and college age students (she never taught high school), but her focus (and passion) is early childhood education. As a result of a year spent working in China at two Normal Schools (that term is commonly used in the PRC), her professional focus has broadened to include a strong emphasis on the role of the social and cultural context in determining what goes on in classrooms. She was able to pursue this interest in the Graduate School of Education at the University of California, Santa Barbara. Her Ph.D. was awarded by the University of California, Santa Barbara, in 1990. Even though she is now Assistant Professor in Early Childhood Education at Carroll College in Waukesha, WI, she has maintained close ties with the elementary school in California where she did her dissertation research (the site of the events discussed in this chapter). She and a first-grade teacher have established a close collaborative relationship, which has resulted in coauthoring a chapter in a soon to be published volume that provides a critical analysis of the "at-risk" construct and proposes an alternative paradigm for viewing children and their families as "at promise."

This chapter tells the story of how the concept of cultural therapy was adapted and used in a group process. It provided a means of structuring a series of meetings to share information from an ethnographic study with staff members of a culturally diverse elementary school. In reviewing the series of meetings, which were termed *reflective cultural analysis*,[1] the reactions of the participants were reframed according to a variation of the concept of the enduring self. Through their responses to the content of the sessions, an identity defined by the culture of teaching and learning that the staff members constructed and valued over time emerged that was interpreted as an enduring professional self.

Brand School,[2] in a small city adjacent to a northern California metropolis, contains a heterogeneous student population being taught by a majority of Euro-American teachers who represent a mainstream American sociocultural orientation.[3] Of the student body of 300, 44% were considered non- or limited-English speaking (NEP, LEP) and included students who spoke Lao, Hmong, Khmer, Spanish, Russian, Punjabi, or Chinese as their home language. When the school opened (the year before the study began) in response to rapid population growth in the district, Brand received more Cambodian, Hmong, and Lao students than anticipated. These students made up about one third of the total school population.

This volume is intended to explore the concept of cultural therapy and its applications to multicultural education. It is necessary to first explain my views in this regard. The sense of cultural therapy that I applied is one that includes cultural consciousness-raising as the primary component. This view is contained in the ideas about cultural therapy that the Spindlers have advanced: "This process involves a kind of consciousness raising similar to Freire's 'conscientizacion' " (Spindler & Spindler, 1989, p. 41). It is elaborated by Trueba (1989, p. 43) in the statement, "a process of bringing to the surface of our awareness of our own cultural identity in its historical, sociocultural and political context." I felt that increasing the awareness of the school staff about the nature of the cultural transmission taking place in the school could be done effectively by adapting these ideas. I do not, however, see the process as having the necessarily remedial focus that I feel is part of the association we generally have with the *therapy* part of the term *cultural therapy*. *Therapy* implies that there is a problem to be solved, a change that has to be made. While people who are comfortable with the value of therapy processes may see no problem with the use of this term, more commonly the connotation attached is a negative one, implying that people are not able to solve their own problems and that someone has to get inside their head to help. I see this connotation of the use of *therapy* limiting the effectiveness of the tool and as one of the problems that I encountered in my application. The Spindlers also expressed the opinion that *cultural therapy* may be an unfortunate term (Spindler & Spindler, 1990, p. 68), but they felt that, in the cases where they have used it, the mismatch between the teachers' beliefs and practices was so great that *therapy* seemed appropriate. Admittedly, a value of the use of *cultural therapy* has been to provide a somewhat depersonalized way to get people to be able to change their minds about what they do or think, but I also see it as an instructive technique that enables people to understand how our cultural system determines our perceptions of other people's competencies (Trueba, 1989). Because my primary purpose was to instruct (in the context of group process), I used the term *reflective cultural analysis*. In the third section of the chapter, I address one of the pitfalls that I encountered through a negative association with the term cultural *therapy*.

The enduring self that the Spindlers (1989, p. 37) describe has historical and traditional depth. It is an identity of self based on connections with an idealized version of traditional values, of how things "should be." The situated self is more pragmatic and responds to the exigencies of everyday life. It is the coping self. If the enduring self is defined by deep-seated traditional values and behaviors, then the situated self can be defined by reactions to changing contemporary experience.

Organization of This Chapter

The story of my experience with reflective cultural analysis has been divided into four sections. The first part will provide the statement and elaboration of the problem I faced in preparing the reflective cultural analysis sessions. Next, I will present background information on the school and the study for the reader to understand the context in which the meetings were held. The third section will describe the meetings themselves and how I have made the connection between the responses of the participants and the concept of the enduring and situated selves. Finally, I will provide some caveats for the use of reflective cultural analysis (or cultural therapy) in group situations.

The Problem

I began my work at Brand with an interest in exploring some of the challenges teachers face in a learning environment in an elementary school that has a culturally diverse student population and a staff that is largely mainstream American.[3] My research was guided by questions designed to help me understand the way in which teachers work with students whose home language and culture are different than theirs, and how teachers organize their instruction and their classrooms to accommodate the needs of their students. I was also interested in how general school events and practices demonstrate an acknowledgment of the diversity of the student population.

To learn about the school and understand the meaning of the events and practices, several levels of participant observation described by Spradley (1980) and Sevigny (1981) were employed over a period of more than 6 months. I became a familiar face to students and teachers as I observed, helped, and taught in classrooms and interacted in as many other contexts as possible. Interviews were also conducted with staff, teachers, parents, and district administrators, and documents relating to the school and the community were collected and analyzed.

Interpretation of the data collected was grounded in the model of cultural transmission that George and Louise Spindler advanced (for example, G. Spindler, 1963, 1987) and that has been widely applied by other educational ethnographers (see, for example, Henry, 1963; Lubeck, 1985; Macias, 1987; Warren, 1982). In this view, schooling is seen primarily as an agent of cultural transmission, the core of which is the teaching and learning of social and cultural values. Such values are the essence of schooling and are more important than academics as a component of cultural survival. Learning is accomplished not only through the explicit curriculum, that which is presented consciously by teachers, but also by the implicit or hidden curriculum, which comprises all of the knowledge not directly taught that is acquired by students.

In a school in which the student and teacher population is homogeneous, the process of cultural transmission is fairly uncomplicated. Teachers impart the rules and values of a shared culture in the context of their teaching content. The assumptions that the teachers make about the knowledge and experiences that students bring to a school are generally accurate because they are largely congruent with those of the teachers. But in a school in which the students speak many different home languages, the issue of cultural transmission becomes complex. Not only is the process complicated by language differences, but teachers must also consider religious, social, and institutional constraints on learning both the explicit and the implicit curriculum. How the process of cultural transmission occurred in such an environment was the interpretive focus of my research project.

At Brand, classroom environments that had an informal structure (not without standards of behavior, however) more closely approximated the kind of environment with which the students from Laos and Cambodia are familiar. Teaching practices were observed that fostered student collaboration, validated and built on students' past experiences, and afforded a variety of opportunities to learn in an environment that develops self-confidence as well as language and academic skills.

There were also a number of schoolwide events and practices that demonstrated recognition of the Cambodian, Lao, and Hmong cultures as well as accommodation to their needs as learners of a new language and social system.

The analysis indicated, however, that, overlaying the accommodations described above, the inculcation of American culture (knowledge, values, practices) is of paramount importance. Behavioral expectations in most classrooms emphasize working independently and quietly. The emphasis on the established curriculum did not allow for lessons to draw upon the past experiences of the students. The weekly sing-along focused on songs of American origin; only 11% of the library books contained themes or characters that were non-Euro-American; there was an absence of visual reminders of the cultural diversity in most classrooms. For a variety of reasons, interpreters were not provided at some of the important school events.

In summary, data indicated that, while educational practices occur that transmit cultural values to validate the ethnic backgrounds of students, some messages that the students receive with the lessons they learn devalue them and their cultural background by not recognizing the unique perspectives that are part of each culture. If a child becomes disconnected from what is personally significant, his or her ability to construct a positive and coherent cultural identity will be weakened (Ferdman, 1990). Strong ties to the home culture provide moral and social support that can facilitate positive school adjustment.

Teacher/Ethnographer Interaction

Despite my repeated use of the expression, "I'm just here finding out what is happening," and a host of variations on that theme, the teachers at Brand had a hard time coming to terms with the idea that I was *describing* a process and attempting to understand what went on in the school according to their perspective. They were accustomed to seeing other adults in the school as *evaluators* of some sort—especially people walking around with yellow tablets. I commonly fielded the question: "How are we doing?" I was encouraged to visit other schools in the district so that I could compare this school (the assumption was favorably) with the others.

This perception of the evaluative nature of my research caused me to ponder at length the best strategy for sharing information with the staff of this school so that it would not be seen as evaluative. In addition to the fact that this ethnography was designed to be descriptive and interpretive rather than evaluative, there were other considerations that made it important that this sharing process be done in such a way that the perception of evaluation would be counteracted. One was the practicality of the fact that I wanted to come back to the school the next year. It is a rich multicultural environment and the 6 months that I spent at the school generated a number of questions that I was eager to return to investigate. If I was considered an evaluator, my days as an educational ethnographer in this school were over.

Personal Bias

The subjectivity that defined my lens of analysis also shaped my thinking about designing a way to report to the staff. In framing my analysis of the ethnography, I had discussed my personal perspectives in terms of the "I's" that Peshkin (1988) has described. One I defined as the "activist I," the one that carried a concern for equal educational opportunities for ethnically and linguistically different students despite their limitations in language (Hauser, 1990). The "activist I" had made observations that I certainly felt were problematic for the success of the students. I kept in mind the necessity of understanding the data for myself, however, and presenting the information in such a way that it would not be perceived as negative. I was not a member of this culture, although I knew it well. If what I presented led to change, that had to be decided by the insiders, not by me, a marginal member. My goal was to present my ethnography so that it could serve as a basis for an informed decision about changes that may have been desired (Chilcott, 1987). I needed to bear in mind for myself the same thing I had told staff members who wanted to view me as an evaluator: "This is your school and if these observations lead to some changes, it will be up to you to make those decisions."

In summary, it was my intent to share the information I gathered and the interpretations that emerged from analysis of the patterns of events and activities in the school to demonstrate the descriptive nature of the ethnography. If changes were indicated as a result of what I reported, it would be because the ethnography formed the basis for an informed decision.

The Context

The community of West Bank, in which Brand School was located, had attracted the Lao, Hmong, and Cambodian immigrants from other areas of the state and the country because of the relatively low cost of housing, the availability of social services, and the favorable climate. The families are political refugees who were forced to leave their rural villages. For the most part, they had earned their living by farming before coming here. The Brand staff had a limited amount of time and opportunity to prepare themselves and their curricula to meet the needs of such a diverse and "exotic" (i.e., non-Euro-American) population.

Connie Claymore, the principal, is a dynamic woman with a "can-do" attitude, a commitment to children, and a strong desire to have her school be a harmonious environment. Despite the general satisfaction felt by the staff about the school, she reported in an interview that "my biggest problem is to keep everyone happy so they won't leave Brand School," (Hauser, 1990). On another occasion, she related, "That's really my goal for this school, for the staff to stay together, to stay committed together to moving these kids forward."

The staff (13 teachers at the time of the study) represented a range of years of experience (from 1 to 23). They felt proud of this small school, freshly painted and remodeled for its reopening. They and the principal regarded themselves as professionals and pointed out that six have master's degrees and two others are enrolled in master's programs. Six teachers have or are currently taking training to hold the California language development specialist certificate. Three teachers also have had ESL training. Two teachers serve as mentors in the district. To describe themselves to me, staff members used these words: *dedicated, hardworking, great, quality staff,* and *good communication.*

The Process of Reflective Cultural Analysis

The decision to use an adaptation of reflective cultural analysis as the vehicle for reporting to the staff was based on two considerations. The first had to do with my desire to place the emphasis on the school as a conduit of cultural transmission, thus providing an opportunity for the staff to increase their awareness of the role culture plays in schooling. As described in the previous section, my study had documented a preponderance of school events and practices that indicated the staff placed importance on the ideas of cultural assimilation, on Americanizing the students. I wanted to provide a way to make this implicit agenda explicit so that it could be examined in light of the fact that the staff considered this to be a multicultural elementary school. Increasing the awareness of the role culture plays in schooling requires that teachers come to this issue with personal knowledge about their past experiences and the meaning of those experiences as well as professional knowledge. According to Aronowitz and Giroux (1985): "Teachers need to examine their own histories—those connections with the past which in part define who they are and how they mediate and function in the world" (p. 160).

The second consideration was one that I hoped would balance possible excessive personalization of the issues resulting from the self-reflection that I planned. The observations of George Spindler and Louise Spindler (1989) are relevant here: "This [cultural therapy] process can be effective because it distances the individual somewhat from his or her own problems and makes objective reflection possible" (p. 42). So on one hand members of the group needed to be personal about their own histories and the role they played in shaping individual views, yet it was necessary to acquire sufficient distance that would allow them to make the familiar strange as they attempted to understand the meaning of the events of the school.

The Plan

My plan for reflective cultural analysis was proposed to the principal (Figure 6.1). The outline of the seven sessions I envisioned was attached to the proposal (Figure 6.2). Several sessions had a personal focus: individual's definitions of culture, personal educational history, personal cross-cultural experiences, personal reactions to culturally different classrooms. The principal agreed to this process, but institutional constraints, in this case in the form of the union contract, limited her endorsement. She could not require attendance. She could not give released time for the sessions. She could not completely give up the time designated for weekly after-school staff meetings. Because she didn't have staff meetings every Monday, however, I could begin some sessions at 2:30 p.m. On the Mondays that she held meetings, I could hold the sessions at the conclusion of the meeting (usually about 3:30 p.m.). Other after-school time was completely scheduled with tutoring sessions, district-level meetings, and so on, limiting full participation of the staff.

Despite the unfortunate timing, I was prepared to implement my plan. I reduced the number of sessions from seven to six. Further events caused me to rethink completely what I was going to do, however. Because of one staff member's inadvertent coloring of the situation by asking a question about the "sensitivity training sessions," a definite level of discomfort was evidenced by several teachers in preliminary discussions with me about what we were going to be doing. It is quite possible that this was her reading of the idea of cultural consciousness-raising that I described. In response, I distributed a memo to the staff (Figure 6.3). I wanted very much for the staff members to participate, so I deemphasized the role of personal teacher experience in determining the cultural transmission practices of the school and reframed the sessions to be more direct discussions of the data I collected. The effect of this decision will be discussed in the final section of this chapter.

RCA Summaries

Session 1. Using the more direct approach described above, I introduced the first session to the teachers by describing the purpose of considering the social context of Brand School. I underlined its importance with the growing heterogeneity of the

(text continues on page 183)

Reflective Cultural Analysis

"Reflective cultural analysis" is a process of bringing to the surface of our awareness our own cultural identity and its historical, sociocultural, and political origins. The purpose of this process is to explore and internalize the nature of our personal interpretation of American culture and the place minority cultures occupy within it. Reflective cultural analysis is not designed to change teachers or students but to help understand cultural differences and the judgments made on the basis of our cultural values.

A series of meetings will be held to engage in the process of reflective cultural analysis (RCA) using thoughtful, interesting, and stimulating activities. Keeping a personal journal will be a part of this process.

The in-service project is based on the following assumptions about how learning takes place:

- Learning of new information is based on past experience.
- Learning occurs in a social context and requires interaction with others as well as individual reflection.
- Learning is a constructivist process; that is, the individual constructs his or her own knowledge rather than receiving it from someone else.

Our experience with [this process] suggests that it can be effective because it distances [an] individual somewhat from his or her own problems and makes objective reflection possible. Some evidence exists that such reflection is essential to development and maintenance of self-esteem and positive self image.

—George & Louise Spindler (1989, p. 42)

NOTE: George and Louise Spindler of Stanford University developed the reflective cultural analysis technique. This in-service project is an adaptation of their work.

Figure 6.1. Brand School, Staff In-Service Project

Seven Sessions (1 hour each)

Each session will include time for personal journal writing.

Session 1

Conscious and reflective analysis of cultural differences presupposes a thorough understanding of one's own culture and its role in establishing the perceptions of others of different cultures. Therefore the initial meeting will address the topic of what our own culture is.

We will use a variety of strategies to construct our knowledge of culture and then consider the Spindlers' concept of the American culture as dialogue.

Session 2

We will review the ideas of the first session and then look for the relationship of our own personal educational history to our views of culture. How do our own educational histories fit into our concepts of culture? The construction of an educational time line will facilitate this process.

Session 3

Recalling and discussing personal cross-cultural experiences, including those related to education, will be the focus of this session. We will explore cultural knowledge in these experiences and how it was acquired. How did this shape our personal concepts of culture?

Session 4

Slides and photographs will be used to identify cultural differences in various kinds of classrooms. The values apparent in these classrooms will be discussed and compared with ours. How would we function as teachers in these

---

Figure 6.2. Outline for Reflective Cultural Analysis

schools? How would our school population learn in these classrooms?

Session 5

Based on the information in the previous session, we will consider possible areas of cultural conflicts within Brand School. (Note: Cultural conflict should not be confused with racial conflict.)

Session 6

We will focus on developing strategies to strengthen the cultural congruence that exists and to lesson the cultural conflicts within the school environment.

Session 7

We will explore a variety of methods for getting information that could apply to any population of students. This method is preferable to accumulating lists of cultural characteristics, which often leads to inaccurate stereotyping.

Summation and evaluation activities.

Researcher's Role

I will be the facilitator for each of the sessions described above. My purposes in participating in this project are the following:

- To provide information for Brand staff members about the importance of the role of the cultural context in education
- To provide a vehicle to find out more about the backgrounds of the students at the school
- To observe and participate in the process of reflective cultural analysis
- To analyze attitude identification and change from the journal writing

Figure 6.2. Continued

To: Brand Staff

From: Mary Hauser

Date: September 20, 1990

Re: Reflective Cultural Analysis

Are you wondering . . .

What is *reflective cultural analysis* anyway?

What am I getting into for the next 7 weeks?

Why are we doing this, anyway?

This memo is an attempt to address some of the questions that you have. This process is *not* designed to change us, only to give us an opportunity to talk and think about some of the ideas we have about cultural values. This is pretty important stuff because we have a school full of students whose cultural and linguistic backgrounds are very different than ours. We are mainstream, middle class—how does that affect what we do in our classrooms?

I think it will be fascinating to explore these ideas together. We are a very closely knit group; we have wonderful sense of the special environment that has been created at Brand School. We each possess the requirements to contribute greatly to this process: *ideas and past experiences.*

I'll provide the notebooks to write in and the food for body and mind that is necessary. I look forward to seeing you for an hour on Mondays after school beginning October 1, 1990, at 3:30 for the next 7 weeks. (Meetings will begin at 2:30 when L. does not have staff business to conduct.) So I can get the right number of notebooks and prepare the proper amount of food, please put a note in my mailbox with your name on it. Thanks!

Figure 6.3. Memo to Staff

student population at Brand and many other schools in the area. The idea of using a more holistic lens to view the school was contrasted with some of the more traditional lenses such as curriculum sequence, student/teacher ratios, or materials and equipment available. We talked about some of the things that made the school special, that defined it in contrast to others in the district. The small size, special programs, mission statement, and clear goals were mentioned. The teachers believe that Brand is unique, a position that I had recorded in my role as participant observer during the last 6 months. They agreed with one teacher's proud declaration, "The best school in the district is right here, I know." From another, "You don't need an Effective Schools checklist to know that the climate at Brand is good."

I explained that I had organized the data that I had been collecting into a series of chapters and that my dissertation was in effect the story of Brand School. The purpose of these sessions, then, was to "read" this story together. To demonstrate that the story I wrote was really theirs, I asked what they would write if they were asked to tell the story of Brand School. A brainstorming session yielded possible chapter content and the teachers conceptualized a book with five chapters: (a) History, (b) Goals, (c) Special Programs, (d) People at the School (staff and students), and (e) Look to the Future. This chapter outline was contrasted with the table of contents that I had made for my story about Brand. We saw that there were lots of similarities, especially in the subheads of my chapters, which included sections on the school district (early history, administrative reorganization, and the district today), creation of the learning environment, schoolwide events and practices, the research setting (including sections on staff and students), and summary and implications for practice. Actually, they had neglected to include only one part of Brand School that I had described: the influence of parents. When that discrepancy was pointed out, there was considerable embarrassment on the part of the teachers. "I wonder what that means?" questioned one teacher. They quickly pointed out that it must have been an oversight because they felt that in practice they demon-strated many positive connections with parents.

Nine teachers and the principal participated in this first ses-sion. I reported in my field notes, "It was an interactive experi-ence, which I wanted. I probably shied away from controversy, but I didn't want people to come away feeling threatened."

Session 2. Each successive session was planned to look at an-other "chapter" of the Brand School story. The second one, de-voted to goals, began by exploring the learning environment of the school. In my story, I had characterized the learning environ-ment as the sum total of the implicit and explicit events that occur in a specified area, an atmosphere was well as series of events and an assemblage of materials. It is not static but can be thought of as a dynamic entity being created and re-created in the interac-tions of teachers and students (Hauser, 1990). We first looked at the key elements of a good learning environment that had been synthesized from interviews with all of the teachers that I had prepared on an overhead. It included the following:

- Consistency. Clear and concise objectives. Student and teacher directed.
- A safe and secure place where individual dignity is respected.
- Quiet. Having children behave in a certain way. New things in the room.
- Kids and teacher feel comfortable in the room. Ownership (in the sense of responsibility for) of the children.
- A positive attitude. Nonthreatening.
- An atmosphere that dignifies kids. Lots of materials. A feel-ing of freedom from structure.
- "You just teach them the system."
- Clean appearance, not too busy.
- Opportunities for social development.

The kinds of values that the students got from a learning environment were then discussed and the issue of teacher power came to the fore. The powerful influence that teachers have on student learning occupied the majority of this session. My comments after the session included the following:

> This session was not at all the one I thought it would be. We really got into teacher power. Actually, I probably reinforced it because when it came up I know what I wanted to have happen. Teachers really control everything (by the atmosphere that they create in their classrooms) I think. I feel really nervous talking about people being white and middle class. It isn't wrong to be, but we should know that if we are (white and middle class), we need even more awareness of what we are doing with and for kids.

Session 3. This meeting, to consider Special Programs, stressed examination of what had been defined as schoolwide events and practices. These were frequently occurring events that were deemed important by the staff (determined through frequency of mention in interviews and general discussions throughout the semester). Examples of these were the weekly sing-along, the multicultural dance festival, the open house, and the daily morning announcements. We talked about what each event consisted of and what messages were transmitted to the students and community by each event. For example, did an event or practice demonstrate the importance of a culturally pluralistic perspective or the value of assimilation into mainstream American culture or both? An illustration from the open house event can demonstrate the nature of the discussion.

Open house, an event held each spring in many American schools, is organized to show parents something of what has been going on in each classroom during the school year. In Brand's district, open house is a time for teachers to go "all out." In the words of one teacher, new to the district, "If I knew that people went all out like this, I would have also. Next year I will know what to do." The superintendent, district office administrators, and school board members show up at each school's open house. Teachers (often with the help of students) spend a great deal of time to prepare displays of curriculum topics and post examples of work done throughout the year. It is viewed as an important event, an example of the best efforts of each classroom. Some teachers spend personal funds as well as extra evening or weekend hours to prepare their classrooms. On the evening of open house, parents are encouraged not only to visit the current classrooms of their children but also to take a look into the classrooms of the next grade level to see what their children may be doing the following year.

In discussing the kinds of messages that open house can send about the school, I reported an observation about one classroom. In that room, the decorations and examples of student work were not nearly as elaborate as those of many of the rooms. But when the students and their families came to visit, the teacher took a photograph of each family group. One interpretation of this act could be that the children were the center of her curriculum. Another is that it was a way for her to validate the participation of the family. Another is that it calls attention to the diversity of the student population. Many other rooms were decorated very elaborately based on themes—a carnival and cows being two examples. The messages sent by these rooms were quite different. The room environments emphasized curricular content. They were also teacher centered to the degree that the student work was placed against a backdrop of teacher-prepared materials. American affluence, not readily obvious to people who have not spent time in classrooms in other countries, was also evident. A main point of the discussion was that neither perspective was right or wrong. We merely theorized what information was transmitted by the appearance and events in each classroom.

Session 4. In keeping with the "chapters" the teachers had conceptualized, the topic of this meeting was the student population. One activity was to brainstorm characteristics of the students at the school to highlight the diversity of the population. A possible goal of this activity was to focus on making the student the center of the curriculum and to think about how one finds out about the variety of cultures represented in each classroom to plan lessons that will take into consideration the diversity they had described. My notes indicated the following:

> The brainstorming listed lots of affective and a few cultural characteristics—not achievement (characteristics). The teachers felt that affective (characteristics) were necessary to be in place before achievement could occur. We also talked about how these characteristics did not apply to any one group and brought up the notion that stereotypes can be helpful if they are informative and not negative. Then I talked about some characteristics of the various groups and we got into the idea of, "Is it ethnicity or personality that determines your behavior?"

My recollection was that this tack of the conversation was a way to deemphasize the ethnicity of the student population so that it would not have to be addressed.

Session 5. This meeting, focusing on parents, began with an assessment of the participation, both formal (such as coming to conferences) and informal (such as dropping the teacher a note or exchanging small talk with the teacher when children were picked up after school). Despite the general feeling that parents of the students at Brand were not involved (and the consequent implication that they didn't care), the staff was able to list many examples of participation such as a high conference attendance percentage, attendance at the multicultural dance program, and classroom helpers in several rooms. It is important to note that these examples were found to be true of parents from all of the ethnic backgrounds represented at the school.

Another discussion in the session had to do with what educational goals parents hold for their children. In my research, I documented that there was no essential difference in goals between cultural groups. I also documented that they were largely nonacademic goals, centering on qualities such as respect for authority, politeness, and respect for elders. The parents of limited-English-speaking students also emphasized the learning of English as a major goal.

Session 6. The final session was to focus on Brand School in the future and consider whether the school could be considered one that has *multicultural education* or *education that is multicultural* (the reader is referred to work Gibson, 1984, or by Sleeter & Grant, 1987, for a full discussion of these concepts). Unfortunately, I was called away from the area and plans for this session were left with the principal. I never got feedback about whether or not she held the session. Because she never volunteered any information, I assumed it was not held.

Reflections

My field notes indicated that the attendance dwindled:

> What does it mean that the priority is not RCA? People don't think this is important, people don't think there is a need to change, people are overloaded and have other duties? If the school is almost 40% SE Asian, then it seems that these are fundamental things to talk about. How does one deal with this? *All* things that teachers do are important, but it is easier to do those things that don't require emotional investment. M[4] talked about teachers avoiding conflict. I believe that is true. I think it is true of me, too. I'm wondering how to get it behind me, so to speak. There are lots of excuses.

The teachers whose attendance at the RCA sessions was the most consistent were those who seemed to be the most knowledgeable about the cultural basis of schooling. And so I worried that I was "preaching to the converted," so to speak. I was also concerned about my skills in leading the sessions, as reflected in this entry:

> I think I talk too fast, I think maybe I don't give teachers a chance to think. The silences are hard for me to handle. But,

as I reread these notes and think about these ideas I wonder about my reaction to those silences. The members of this group are probably not used to reflecting. They are expecting me, the "expert," to tell them things. So the silences are not for them to use . . . but for me to fill.

I also wrote, "I want people to discover the knowledge for themselves. But it is hard not to give them what I think is important. Very hard."

The Self in Cultural Process

Rethinking the ideas of the enduring and the situated self, almost 2 years after the RCA sessions were held, provides a previously unconsidered perspective to explain why attendance was low and interaction at the sessions was often less than enthusiastic. When the school opened the year before the study, half of the teachers transferred from other schools in the district. There were a number of reasons given for their willingness to transfer to a school in one of the less desirable neighborhoods in the community. The appealing, newly remodeled facility was definitely an attraction but so was a sense of creating an environment where their professionalism could be demonstrated. As Ms. Boxman recalled the month of preparation before school opened, "The principal relied on senior teachers, all self-starters. We were left to do our own thing, which was wonderful."

Using the ideas of self to think about this event, Brand School would be a place where the enduring professional self of each one of the teachers could be validated through reproduction in a new context. While the enduring self is generally considered to be a way of thinking about the total person, I can easily see it as defining a professional self, especially in light of these teachers with many years of experience. For those teachers who found it difficult (or impossible) to participate in the RCA sessions, the historical and traditional depth that the Spindlers see characterizing the enduring self (Spindler & Spindler, 1989, p. 37) can be likened to a strongly established set of professional values. Traditional views of teaching, such as the importance of the teacher as an imparter of information, of classroom organization and management associated with this view, of emphasis on content in the curriculum, and the perception of the student population as generally having homogeneous needs for instruction and knowledge, are manifestations of these values. The enduring professional self of the teachers had been shaped through their years of immersion in the system, first as students and then as professionals in the institutions of education. They had the belief that their experience and skills would enable them to be successful. These beliefs are demonstrations of strong senses of self-efficacy. They looked forward to shaping the curriculum and mentoring the first-year teachers who rounded out the staff. At the end of the first year, the school's test scores were higher than expected and so their sense of self-efficacy was validated.

In the second year of the school's operation, the student population increased (from 180 to 322) and it was necessary to have two classrooms at each grade level. More teachers were hired, including several that time revealed held enduring professional identities that were not in concert with those who held more traditional views. This unbalanced the existing structure of the school and served as a threat to the enduring professional selves of the strong, experienced teachers. Their dominant professional culture was threatened not only by the values of the new teachers but also by a student population whose home language and culture were very different. The ability of the experienced teachers to demonstrate success using their traditional skills was (implicitly for the most part) called into question.

The degree of difference in the cultures was also an important part of the context at Brand. If people look like us and the culture can be considered "Western," less discomfort is present and the interactions are easier. The students who spoke Lao, Hmong, and Khmer looked different and came from a non-Western, non-Christian, nonindustrialized culture. These conditions made it very different than the personal and professional culture that the teachers represent and have been transmitting in their classrooms. A case in point is the fact that the Russian students at the school were more accepted by some of the teachers who seemed to be the least comfortable with the students from Cambodia and Laos. They held the view that these students were smarter and had more potential. One student from Russia, blonde, blue eyed, and obedient, was described to me in this way: "That little H— is smart as a whip. She has learned English so fast." Another teacher engaged a volunteer Russian-speaking tutor for M—, a boy in her class. The tutor worked at a small table in the back of the classroom. This same teacher didn't want a Lao interpreter in her class because "I just don't like the sound of that language." The fact that these Russian students came from a culture that was more compatible with the teachers' personal and professional experience was never explicitly considered, however.

The students from Laos and Cambodia as well as the newer colleagues on the staff represented an incompatibility and a challenge to the values that had been internalized as an enduring professional self. A situated self did not emerge to respond to these challenges. So a strategy of reaffirmation was adopted. The teachers held firmly to the values they had developed.

Certainly this construct is helpful in understanding the reactions of some of the participants to the reflective cultural analysis sessions, especially those who only attended the first session. It removes some of the personality clash concerns and lets me understand that not feeling very successful in carrying out this process was not necessarily based on my poor teaching or on their pedagogical rigidity. Rather, it was based on the teachers' strong need to reaffirm their professional culture by resistance to the ideas made available through RCA. In contrast, for those teachers who found that the ideas we discussed matched a definition of their enduring professional selves, the sessions reaffirmed and elaborated their values.

Caveats

Reviewing this experience has allowed me to consider carefully how I would apply the ideas of reflective cultural analysis in group process in the future. First of all, the idea of cultural consciousness-raising must be carefully explained. As I wrote describing my sense of the nature of cultural therapy, the use of the word *therapy* carries a distinct problem and I feel uncomfortable with it. This is partially a personal perspective: I do not identify myself as a therapist but as a teacher and I view this process as facilitating construction of cultural knowledge rather than as therapy. Even the use of the term *reflective cultural analysis* was problematic, as I described. In considering future applications of RCA, I would first emphasize the idea of using the lens of culture to describe classroom environments and events. Once the focus of culture is defined and understood, critical connections to personal values and experience can be dealt with.

I also considered the use of RCA in group settings. My feeling at first was that RCA really only lent itself to one-to-one application. It seemed that the context of a group meeting wasn't effective because it was too formal, no matter what one might do (I even had food) to make participants comfortable. It seemed to me that, to be able to understand the influence of a person's culture on his or her teaching, it would be necessary to have more of a dialogue than the group process allows. The kinds of activities that I originally envisioned (refer to Figure 6.2) would have been especially difficult to implement in a group context. Even though I knew these teachers well, it was not possible to have the necessary background and rapport to accomplish what was implied by the ideas of a therapeutic session. I reasoned also that the variety of teacher perceptions would be difficult to accommodate. The group I worked with demonstrated clearly that some of the teachers were not convinced that anything needed to be changed.

My not understanding the power of the enduring professional self and the resistance to assuming a different identity for that self, however, probably had the most instrumental effect on the interactions in the sessions. This most probably was responsible for the inability to establish a level of comfort that would have lent itself to exploration of the effect of the enduring self on the daily practices of the teachers. Had this been possible, the fact that we were working in a group may not have been as much of a problem as I envisioned.

A final caveat has to do with personal involvement. In my case, the field notes I collected expressed a level of discomfort with presenting situations that would make the participants uncomfortable. I didn't want to have to deal with the ramifications of that issue: threatening the good communication I had established with the teachers, violating the harmonious atmosphere that the principal worked so hard to maintain, losing trust, losing my research site in the future. Once again, had I realized the power of the enduring professional self, I would have interpreted the events differently.

Summary

In this chapter, I have described how cultural therapy was adapted to a group process to report the results of an ethnographic study of cultural transmission in an elementary school. I considered the resistant reactions of some of the participants as expressions of an enduring professional self that was threatened by the changing nature of the school and the resultant changing nature of teaching. I saw this resistance manifested in nonparticipation and less than enthusiastic responses to the content of the sessions. Initially, my view had been that the sessions were not successful because there were not enough people there, because I did not lead the sessions effectively, because the teachers were exhibiting racism (one of the more flagrant ideas that I had in my desperation to understand the problems I seemed to be encountering). The Spindlers' viewpoint, that one can objectify and depersonalize problems by seeing them through a cultural framework, was, however, instructive in this regard. Using the ideas of the enduring self, seeing the events from a cultural perspective, helped me to understand the value of this process. I have a clearer understanding of the power of the enduring self that teachers construct. I feel that applying cultural therapy principles to a group process requires some special considerations because of the individual nature of that very powerful force.

And I still want to change the title!

Notes

1. The term RCA was also used by Henry Trueba (1989) to describe processes of cultural therapy. My definition and application of RCA are a synthesis of the work of the Spindlers and of Trueba.

2. All names used in this chapter have been changed to protect the anonymity of the participants.

3. The reader is referred to the ideas of American mainstream culture described by G. Spindler and L. Spindler in *American Cultural Dialogue and Its Transmission* (1990, chap. 3).

4. This refers to a conversation with a researcher at UC Davis who was discussing a literature workshop she had conducted based on *The Color Purple* by Alice Walker. She was amazed at how the students—classroom teachers in the area—avoided talking about the issue of homosexuality that was strongly implied in the novel, and she reasoned that it was because teachers don't want to deal with conflict and with "messy issues."

References

Aronowitz, S., & Giroux, H. (1985). *Education under siege.* South Hadley, MA: Bergin and Garvey.

Chilcott, J. (1987). Where are you coming from and where are you going? *American Educational Research Journal, 24*(2), 199-218.

Ferdman, B. (1990). Literacy and cultural identity. *Harvard Educational Review, 60*(2), 181-204.

Gibson, M. (1984). Approaches to multicultural education in the U.S.: Some concepts and assumptions. *Anthropology and Education Quarterly, 15*(1), 54-62.

Hauser, M. (1990). *Cultural transmission in a multicultural elementary school.* Unpublished doctoral dissertation, University of California, Santa Barbara.

Henry, J. (1963). *Culture against man.* New York: Random House.

Lubeck, S. (1985). *Sandbox society: Early education in black and white America.* Philadelphia: Falmer.

Macias, J. (1987). The hidden curriculum of Papago teachers: American Indian strategies for mitigating cultural discontinuity in early schooling. In G. Spindler & L. Spindler (Eds.), *Interpretive ethnography at home and abroad* (pp. 363-380). Hillsdale, NJ: Lawrence Erlbaum.

Peshkin, A. (1988). In search of subjectivity: One's own. *Educational Researcher, 17*(7), 17-21.

Sevigny, M. (1981). Triangulated inquiry: A methodology for the analysis of classroom interaction. In J. Green & C. Wallett (Eds.), *Ethnography and language in educational settings.* Norwood, NJ: Ablex.

Sleeter, C., & Grant, C. (1987). An analysis of multicultural education in the United States. *Harvard Educational Review, 57*(4), 421-444.

Spindler, G. (1963). The transmission of American culture. In G. Spindler (Ed.), *Education and culture* (pp. 148-172). New York: Holt, Rinehart & Winston.

Spindler, G. (1987). The transmission of culture. In G. Spindler (Ed.), *Education and cultural process: Anthropological approaches* (pp. 303-334). Prospect Heights, IL: Waveland.

Spindler, G., & Spindler, L. (1989). Instrumental competence, self-efficacy, linguistic minorities and cultural therapy: A preliminary attempt at integration. *Anthropology and Education Quarterly, 20*(1), 36-50.

Spindler, G., & Spindler, L. (1990). *American cultural dialogue and its transmission.* New York: Falmer.

Spradley, J. (1980). *Participant observation.* New York: Holt, Rinehart & Winston.

Trueba, H. (1989). *Raising silent voices: Educating the linguistic minorities for the 21st century.* New York: Newbury House.

Warren, R. (1982). Schooling, biculturalism, and ethnic identity: A case study. In G. Spindler (Ed.), *Doing the ethnography of schooling* (pp. 382-409). New York: Holt, Rinehart & Winston.

Juan García-Castañón

7

Training Hmong Refugee Students

Chicano Anthropologist as Cultural Therapist

JUAN GARCÍA-CASTAÑÓN

Juan García-Castañón received his Ph.D. in anthropology from Stanford University, where the Spindlers were his mentors. His doctoral dissertation topic led to an interest in the cultural and psychological treatment of mental disorders. He found that anthropology was not being used as a frame of reference when providing "culturally sensitive" treatment. Consequently, he pursued an M.S. in clinical psychology from San Jose State University and currently is a licensed Marriage, Family, and Child Counselor in the state of California. From 1978 through 1987, he worked as a mental health preventive specialist, mental health clinician, and child custody mediator. He believes that cross-cultural mental health treatment requires a thorough understanding of social and cultural processes. Currently, with Ignacio Aguilar, he is writing a book of cultural therapy techniques to provide culturally appropriate mental health services to Latinos. He is the Coordinator of the Counseling Education Program in the Department of Counseling and Special Education in the School of Education & Human Development, California State University, Fresno.

This chapter describes how the principles of cultural therapy were applied in a classroom with Southeast Asian refugees. We had set up a program to train several students—who were mostly Hmong but also some Mien and lowland Lao—as nursing assistants. The purpose of the program was twofold: (a) On a direct level, it was to help these refugees acculturate constructively and gain training for specific jobs; (b) on an indirect level, it was to establish a group of paraprofessionals in the refugee

197

community who could then help us serve the mental health needs of that larger community.

It was in the early 1980s in the San Joaquin Valley of central California that Southeast Asian clients were being referred to mental health services by local family physicians and other medical practitioners. The clients referred complained about physical problems but the medics were not finding underlying physical causes. The local mental health director asked for volunteers to work with this special population, but most professionals on the staff did not feel adequately trained to do so. As an anthropologist, employed as a mental health clinician, I was intrigued by the newcomers and their mental health needs and soon was able to arrange a transfer to the appropriate mental health services unit. Another mental health clinician, Joe Torres, and I found ourselves brainstorming about how to approach the issue at hand.

One problem we quickly became aware of was the fear expressed by Southeast Asian mothers and fathers that their children no longer respected them, that they were losing control of their children, that their children were no longer faithful to them as parents, or to their language, beliefs, and background. On the other hand, the children and younger people felt that the ways of their parents and grandparents were no longer relevant, that they were embarrassing and something they wanted to leave behind as old-fashioned. The problem was not so much that the perceptions expressed by the adults and the younger members of the Southeast Asian community were wrong or erroneous. The perceptions of each generational cohort were equally valid. We saw, however, that the negative valuation by the youngsters was not only damaging to the honor of the parents but also damaging to the children's self-concept as Asians in American society. That is, they were rejecting their ethnicity as detrimental and deficient (see Sue & Sue, 1990), and in George and Louise Spindler's terms, the end result was the undermining of the enduring self in favor of the "situated self." When "the enduring self" is battered "too often and too strongly by the requirements of the situated self . . . the enduring self will be . . . endangered" (see Chapter 1 in this volume; also Spindler & Spindler, 1992). In the case of the Southeast Asian youth, their rejection was observed as being severe, which could lead to no other effect than to undermine their sense of self. This severe rejection of one's own ethnic background at this point in their ethnic identity development could lead to psychopathology or other forms of family dysfunction (see Cappelletty, 1986). The end would preclude any return to an intact sense of enduring self once the assimilation strategy is perceived for what it is, "a process of the promise" (Shaef, 1987).

It was an eerie moment when my coworker and I realized that what was going on in the Southeast Asian community in the 1980s was the same thing that had been happening in the Mexican immigrant communities of the 1950s, the years when my coworker and I were growing up, trying to make our adjustment to American society, and the same thing that had been happening to Mexican children since the 1920s and 1930s, during and after the first wave of Mexican immigration circa the 1910 revolution (Saragoza, 1989). What we saw was that traditional social forms such as the family and the clan were being undermined and changed in ways that were not conducive to a smooth transition. The host culture was not culturally consonant to the newcomers' culture (see Sluzki, 1979).

Our perception was that the younger newcomers were being given conflicting messages in the schools about their parents' culture. It was not an explicit message but more of an insidious one, where children and adolescents have to reason for themselves, and arrive at the same conclusion, that there is something intrinsically wrong or bad about their culture, their parents' culture, when contrasted with mainstream American culture. As Chicano children, offspring of Mexican immigrants, we received the same negative message about our very spirit, and the only alternative offered by the American school system was translated in our unsophisticated little minds to "be white." This is the alternative I chose, and I was sure that Joe did too. And it cost us psychologically. I had managed to lose my identity and most of my respect for my Mexican heritage. I was thrown into a decade or two of confusion, as were many others from our generation and the subsequent ones, as we strove for blind acceptance. If it wasn't for genuine cultural heros such as Cesar Chavez, we would have been lost for sure, forever. But later we found out that we had been betrayed by pursuing the "process of the promise": that we would become fully accepted, and that we would reap our everlasting reward, if only we would become "American" (see Shaef, 1987). After many years of trying to shake off my "culture of origin," including the Mexican version of the Spanish language, the first thing asked by a potential employer as I was seeking gainful employment was whether I could speak Spanish. Luckily, Richard Rodriguez's book *Hunger of Memory* had not influenced my generation, otherwise I would not have written this chapter. This realization bears on George and Louise Spindler's elaboration of their conceptions of the enduring, the situated, and the endangered self, which has allowed me to rethink that period of time when we developed not only the training program but also a series of services for the Southeast Asian refugee community in the San Joaquin Valley.

The anthropological thought that helped guide my thinking and that I shared with my mental health coworkers was the idea that there were many ways of acculturating, some of which were not disparaging of the culture or heritage of origin. One could acculturate to the host culture without having to shed one's past cultural bearings. To do the latter was impossible without severe psychological costs. This idea is clearer to me now than it was then because of the Spindlers' recent work (1991, 1992; compare with 1957).

Based on what we were able to learn about how Southeast Asian refugees perceived their adjustment to the United States, we innovated several interventions and provided a climate to develop approaches to help them adjust in ways that minimized their stressors, at least by putting labels on what was happening to them as individuals, as families, and as a community. We assumed that they were like many immigrant groups to the United States—ready and eager to be part of American society. We also knew, however, what they were to face as the latest set of ethnic groups in American society. Some of their experiences, as related to me by Hmong coworkers and as described in the Southeast Asian mental health literature (Bliatout, 1984; Cappelletty, Kenkel, & García, 1986; "The Hmong," 1984; Lee, 1988; Owan, 1985; Quesada, 1987; Special Service for Groups, 1983; Trueba, Jacobs, & Kirton, 1990), will be presented here.

The Training Program

As we had speculated, developing programs for the Southeast Asian refugee community was going to be difficult, or impossible, without trained paraprofessionals to help us. But bridging the immense dissimilarity between the general Southeast Asian worldview and the American counseling worldview was also monumental. It appears hilarious in retrospect, and it was. Imagine trying to explain the id, ego, and superego to Southeast Asian newcomers to America. I wasn't sure after a while that I believed what I was trying to teach them. It was hard enough trying to teach them the concepts of "social" and "culture." One classroom translator expounded on the concept of "social" for several minutes (hours, it seemed to me). The class engaged in discussion and debate. The class finally agreed that "family" and "culture" were equivalent to "social." The concept of culture in their terms was equated with the practice of traditional rituals. The family concept was equated with "clan" (García, 1984-1985).

Somewhat early on, we knew that our Mexican/Chicano immigrant background was to be an important factor in helping us think through the strategies to be developed and implemented. We were not sure, however, just *which* elements were going to prove useful in making a cross-cultural connection, to establish rapport, trust, and understanding (see Martin, 1983/1989; Sue & Sue, 1990). As it turned out, my familiarity with Mexican folk healing traditions was sufficient to create the right kind of interest in the Southeast Asian trainees to develop a collaborative relationship. The available literature about the Hmong people and their medical worldview indicated that the belief and influence of spirits was parallel to many Mexican and other Hispanic folk beliefs. We hoped that this would provide a starting point and we were rewarded when we verified that we had found a common reference point (Bliatout, 1982).

Further, we realized that certain skills would be required to establish the necessary conditions for creating a genuine relationship between us, the professionals, and them, the students. They would help us establish a parallel relationship with the Southeast Asian clients being referred to us by the medical professionals and the Southeast Asian community at large. We had to make a cross-cultural connection among the Hmong, Mien, and lowland Lao students and to establish rapport, trust, and understanding between myself, as the trainer, and the students. I relied on the core conditions of counseling, such as empathic understanding, and respect, by conveying warmth, conveying genuineness, and being able to bridge the chasm between our worldviews through concreteness of content and affect (see Martin, 1983/1989). We also developed another as yet unevolved core condition, "cultural empathy."[1] Of course, it was important to be able to self-disclose, that is, to share personal experiences to facilitate the cross-cultural connection. This also meant exploring our relationship as teachers and students, as cultural brokers between the culturally different, as mental health professionals, and as students of American society and culture (Martin, 1983/1989). Our basic underlying assumption was humanistic, that as members of the same human species we would find more in common than not. This proved to be more challenging than we believed at that time. Yet the fact that we were Chicanos and that we had worn the same shoes before them made the challenge worth risking. It brought us full circle to the beginning of our journey, which allowed us more insight into the process than we had conceived to be possible.

As stated at the outset of the chapter, we decided that if we could train a group of interpreters—brokers—and at the same time provide them with marketable skills, we could serve at least two purposes. One purpose was to help the trainees explore a set of possible occupations for further work in the health field. The other purpose was to train and recruit several to work with us in the mental health setting.

The training program was developed in cooperation with the local community college and a county government agency established to deal with refugee issues. The latter agency administered federal funds from the Office of Refugee Resettlement, which facilitated job training, English language learning, and entrepreneurial endeavors. Our proposal for the program stressed having trained personnel from the refugee community in the most highly used medical facilities—people who understood their own community and its health needs but who also understood the local health system and basic medical terminology, processes, and procedures, and who could communicate with the doctors and nurses with a fair level of confidence. In turn, they would develop a set of terms useful in communicating with their own community members about health problems and related issues. One problem was that the refugee clients did not know what "mental health" was and, as they came to understand why they were referred to it, they resented the implication that doctors thought they were "crazy." We also considered it necessary for the health trainees to understand the mental health system and be acquainted with the terms used in that system of care. I have already discussed the difficulty in coming to an agreement about *social* and *culture*. Other definitions we agreed on included, but were not limited to, the following terms: *dysfunctional, hallucination, behavior, diagnosis, psychology, symptoms, stress* (García, 1984-1985).

The training program was to be embedded in the community college's already operating nursing assistant training program. The plan was that the trainees would take the regular nursing assistant program curriculum, English-as-a-second-language classes calibrated to the medical and health environment, and a training seminar in mental health. The mental health trainer would also be responsible for placing the students in on-the-job training internships.

The Paraprofessional Training

The announcement that we were looking for students to train as mental health nursing assistants was made through the County Refugee Program Agency. The response was better than what had been expected. We had close to 40 applicants and we could only select 10 for training. We interviewed all of the applicants. We were looking for students who had English-as-a-second-language training at least through the third year. As interviewers, we were also aware that there were other more implicit characteristics that we were seeking. We tended to choose those students who could be understood most clearly. That is, we were looking for students who spoke English well without an accent. We noticed that we tended to like those students most who were younger and dressed close to our unconscious notions of "American." Before we actually contacted the candidates about our selection, we revised our original list. We chose a few more older students, and we tried to balance the roster to include other Southeast Asian ethnic groups present in our community, that is, Mien and lowland Lao.

We began our training program with a curriculum developed for Vietnamese refugees (Cohen, 1979). An instrument that came with the training package was administered to measure the Hmong trainee's knowledge base regarding Western concepts of mental health and psychological dysfunction. The test indicated that there was no knowledge base whatsoever. We quickly realized that the curriculum, though thorough, was not intended for use by non-pre-Westernized refugees. The Vietnamese refugees, the great majority of them, had been exposed to Western society and culture prior to the refugee experience, whereas the refugees from the Laotian highlands had not. We then decided to use the training curriculum solely as a guide. We decided to take an experimental approach mixing some basic psychology and anthropology. I started with a curriculum reflecting presuppositions regarding Western mental health with concepts such as child rearing, parenting, personality, and psychopathology, but to little or no avail.

Out of frustration, I then turned to an approach based on Robert Edgerton's (1976) cross-cultural typology of deviance, which included a summary of traditional social science explanations of deviance as well as eight deviance categories for which cross-cultural data were used for illustrative purposes. Edgerton documented six explanatory categories: social strain, subcultural conflict, psychological defense or commitment, biological defect, human nature, and accounts, or insiders' explanation.

The explanatory category that the Hmong students seemed most interested in was "subcultural" conflict. Focusing on this explanatory category proved to be the means by which the conceptual gap between the Hmong and American worldviews regarding mental health and psychological dysfunction could be bridged.

Subcultural Conflict

The second explanatory framework of "deviance" is referred to as "subcultural conflict." The best example of this was called up from my being a member of a minority group. I recalled my experience as a child and adolescent living with my parents, one of whom was an immigrant and the other, a first-generation American of "immigrant" parentage. The immigrant was my mother, who preferred to speak Spanish, listen to Mexican music, attend Spanish-language movies, and watch Spanish-language television programming. My preference was the opposite, preferring English-language music, movies, and television as well as speaking English. One day while at a social service office, my mother asked a Mexican American to interpret for her. The person was unable to interpret because she claimed not to speak Spanish. My mother was so angry that she implemented a rule in our home that only Spanish was allowed in our house and English only outside. But the conflict continued to exist because of television (compare Romano-V., 1969; Saragoza, 1989). In time, I grew tired of having to interpret English-language movies so that my mother and grandmother could understand.

The Hmong trainees really enjoyed the story. All identified with the conflict in that they related several incidents in which their children were opposed to many things Hmong. They didn't like the *neng* (the shamans) to come over because they made too much noise; they disliked "sticky" rice and other Hmong food; they refused to listen to Hmong music unless it was upbeat and contemporary; they would refuse to see Hmong or Lao language movies; they were embarrassed about Hmong medicinal beliefs and especially the "rituals." They preferred to speak English, eat hot dogs and hamburgers, hang out with American kids or Americanized Hmong peers, and listen to Michael Jackson, to the exclusion of everything having to do with the old culture. In this acculturation process, the young reject their parents, inter-generational conflicts are created, and solutions are hard to come by. As my students reflected on my story and drew parallels to what they were going through, they became sad. On the other hand, there was some hope. There was relief that there was a solution. They felt understood for the first time. Someone could understand what they were going through. That their problems were being accurately described provided them with a label and a cure. It has been said that to put a label on an affliction provides some relief (compare Kleinman, 1974; Shaef, 1987). In this case, the relief was visually apparent.

I empathized with the Hmong nursing assistant students. I understood their pain. I also reexperienced my own adolescent behavior and relived shame for having put my parents, especially my mother, through the same experience 25 years earlier. I did not understand what my parents were going through as displaced members of society (Romano-V., 1969; Turner, 1979), just as refu-gee youth also did not understand that they were rejecting their parents who made the ultimate sacrifice in fleeing to a strange land so that they might live without violence. I disclosed my feelings to the students. I remember not liking to take "tacos" or "burritos" to school because everyone else took "sandwiches." I explained to the students that their children's behavior was not intentional. I explained, "Your children are only responding to pressure to conform." The pressure comes from the school system and the peer group. The only thing school administrators and teachers know is how to Americanize foreign-born children. The pressure also comes from their American counterparts. Thus their children, the Hmong-Mien-Lao children, are only responding to the pressure to be American. The refugee parents discussed the story in their own language in the classroom. There was a sense of relief. It was thick. The students were very appreciative of the story because it offered an explanation for their children's behavior. Now they understood what kind of force was operating on their children.

These training sessions were very helpful to me as the instructor and to the students. A relationship had been established. Elements of trust began to develop as they related parallel stories about what they were currently enduring in trying to understand America, what was happening with their children, and themselves, as parents, as Hmong refugees. I often left the classroom full of memories. In thinking about the plight of the refugee, I reflected back on what had taken place in my life and began to better understand what had happened. It wasn't until then that I really fully realized that Southeast Asians were the newest Americans. The varied reflections informed a different strategy.

The Minority Member as a Cultural Broker

This was a perfect opportunity to discuss the case of the Hispanics in America, their dilemma, and the options. I discussed my own experience growing up as a minority student, my conflict with parental values, and my pilgrimage to my mother's homeland when I was 18 years of age, eating cactus, riding horses, and carrying a weapon tucked underneath by belt, like my mother's deceased brother and her father before him. I had a personal growth experience as I talked about this period of my life.

It was at this point that I made a realization regarding my role as a cultural broker, that each one of the students could also do the same. I also realized that the students were all striving to become "American." This provoked in me feelings of envy. How could they become "American," fully accepted, if I had not achieved that status, even after years of education and experiences. Further, even after colonialization and decades of immigration, Mexicans have not been fully accepted by the host culture compared with the European immigrant groups (Elst, 1978; McLemore, 1980/1983; Romano-V., 1969).

The answers were found in several areas. One was that, even though they strived for assimilation, what guaranteed that once they arrived there would also be acceptance by the host society (see Sue & Sue, 1990)? The realization that there was no guarantee brought into focus that at the end of the assimilation road there was still racism to deal with. This was demonstrated to the students in various ways throughout the training program, not only with illustrations from the Mexican American experience but also experientially, as we continued to share what was going on with them and as I shared with them what was going on with me. Also, it was very helpful to reflect on explanatory frameworks, such as the implicit American caste system based on race, religion, and national origin. Opportunities did not necessarily become any more available, even if one were educated, English speaking, and articulate. I decided to take another approach, which was based on my training as an anthropologist.

I began with the question of American attitudes toward the refugees. Many had already experienced racism, disapproval, and the superiority expressed by mainstream Americans toward them in familiar situations such as supermarkets, shopping centers, schools, and even such places as recreational parks for fishing and hunting. The basic notion was that American society is not homogeneous and that every subcultural group would have a different view of the world. There is a main "referent" group, however, called WASP, which is an abstraction but refers to several identifying characteristics based on socioeconomic status, language, education, and religion as well as cultural history (Spindler, Spindler, Trueba, & Williams, 1990).

It was emphasized that the only "native" is the indigenous American Indian; everyone else is either an immigrant or descendants of immigrants (see McLemore, 1980/1983). It was mentioned that American society is stratified in many ways, but usually the last immigrant group to arrive is subject to animosity, discrimination, and less than favorable attitudes (unless WASP in origin). Moreover, the most recent immigrant group usually competed with the previous new immigrant group for jobs and other opportunities and was the source of much conflict.

The students were attentive as I pointed out the importance of maintaining their heritage. Many class sessions were spent providing them with a synopsis of New World history, migration and immigration patterns, and basically pointing out to them the tremendous diversity of immigrant nationalities making up "America." I asked them who were the real Americans. Some responded with "the American Indians" because they were first. I provided them with various theories of their origin including the Bering Strait and Kon-tiki theories, both of which pointed to the inevitable conclusion that Native Americans were of probable Asian origin and also immigrants (see Thompson, 1989). The Southeast Asian students in my class appeared overwhelmed by the information as well as relieved. On the one hand, they understood that all Americans were immigrants at one point in their ethnic history, and, on the other, they expressed the relief that they were not the only group that has burdened the resources of the host culture. Every ethnic group receives help from the hosts, then every ethnic group helps the next group down the line a generation or two later. Certainly, that was my feeling as I employed cultural concepts to provide cultural therapy to Hmong refugees.

It was pointed out to them that America is not only a nation of immigrants but also a continent, and hemisphere, of immigrants and that they were the most recent arrivals to the United States. It was pointed out that they would not be the last. The conflict in Central America was pointed out as the most likely place of origin for the next wave of recent immigrants and that they would probably also be refugees.

This last strategy was used as a result of a discussion with Marjorie Helm, Community Outreach Services Coordinator at Merced County Department of Mental Health, where it was concluded that we needed to recapitulate the "ethnic experience" in America for the Hmong students as many minority groups had experienced it in the 1960s. It appears, in retrospect, that the "ethnic experience" was important because minority ethnics rediscovered something positive in their racial and cultural heritage, and it helped them to rediscover self-determination. This experience helped them to build self-respect and self-confidence, and motivated them to achieve American standards of success without sacrificing their own identity (see the Racial Cultural Identity Development model in Sue & Sue, 1990). In discussions with support staff, it was suggested that denial of ethnic identity contributes to the weakening of the "ego" (see Devereux, 1978).

Making a Cross-Cultural Connection

From that point, I began to conceptualize a model that appeared to make more sense in introducing, inculcating, and immersing the students in the possibility of the idea of mental health and, by extension, mental illness. I cracked the communication barrier by reading to the students a legend that I found in a book by Bliatout (1982). The legend was the Hmong Creation myth. It was an interesting legend because it not only explained the origin of the world but also explained the presence of illness and evil and the creation of agents for cure, namely, *neng*, shamans. I read the legend in English, as in the book, while our translators interpreted the legend back to Hmong (Lao and Mien) from English. The class appeared quite captivated and focused. Some of the students said that they had heard the legend before, but different versions. Two of the students were Mien.

When asked if they believed the legend, they all said they did, especially the part regarding the power of the neng. This was quite a different response for a question put to them at the first training seminar when we asked them about their religious faith. They all responded that they were Christians. All of the students subsequently said they believed in the power of the neng and mentioned that they often appeal to them for help when they or someone in their family are sick. One of the female students said that her children don't like the neng because they make too much noise. This was an important point because the question of their children's ethnic identity was raised—whether they were concerned about their children maintaining their cultural and linguistic heritage. One student said that she did not want to teach her children their heritage because they were now Americans and she did not want to make it difficult for them to assimilate. When I asked them how they would feel if one of their grandchildren was born with blue eyes, the class was silent.

As I read the legend, I could sense a change in the affect in the group of Southeast Asian students as a whole. Some laughed, some started talking to each other in their own language, and there were some who appeared embarrassed that an outsider would know something about their inner spiritual processes. After reading the legend, it seemed like there was more trust between myself, as a Westerner, and the Hmong students, as Easterners. They experienced my acceptance of their worldview. It was at that time that all of the students admitted that some of the time they still believed in certain ideas and practiced certain behaviors that were not reflected in their previous responses that they were Christians. In the process of this revelation and inquiry, they were able to trust me as a person who would not and did not intend to ridicule them as human beings—something that they really feared.

After this particular training session, the nursing assistant students were comfortable talking about their beliefs and behavior in their cultural health system. I was able to rely on my Chicano-Mexican background and knowledge of Mexican folk healing traditions. From that point, I made more cross-cultural comparisons with Mexican immigrant rural beliefs regarding health concepts and healing behaviors. This was especially helpful when it was discovered in the process of discussion that both the Mexican rural immigrants and the Southeast Asian refugees based some of their health beliefs on the hot/cold and wet/dry system of balances for classifying both physical and spiritual maladies.

This experience was interesting because it led the Southeast Asian students into a reexamination of their background, a new-found acknowledgment of a past they did not know they had, and provided an opportunity for them to appreciate what they had, instead of discarding it without question. They rediscovered their "enduring self." The reading of the Hmong legend was a start in this direction. It led to a reexamination of their own past, their language, their beliefs, and their future and placed them in a positive light. It helped to reframe who they were and allowed them to be creative in their adaptation experience. The main message to the students was that it was OK to be Hmong, to believe in "ghosts," and to use neng to cure them of their spiritual grief.

The Training Program Ramifications

It is needless to state that the Refugee Mental Health Training Program was a successful endeavor, and most importantly, for the students. Of the 10 students, 8 of them became gainfully employed. The other two continued their education. One student went on to California State University, Fresno, pursuing a degree in engineering. Another student pursued social science studies. Those who became immediately gainfully employed found jobs as nursing assistants in hospital and community clinic settings. One student became a surgeon's assistant. Two continued their work in mental health. Several others worked and found time to continue their education at the local community college. The project itself received recognition from the California State Association of Local Mental Health Directors as one of the top three mental health promotion projects in the state of California in 1985.

In addition, many other interventions were developed as a result of the nursing assistant training program. Joe Torres and Pa Yang organized and developed a Hmong Woman's Support Group. Last year, in 1992, the group was still going strong. A day treatment program for Southeast Asian schizophrenics was also developed and modeled after the Spanish-language one. Later, as I gained a reputation as an ethnic mental health programs innovator, I helped other refugee communities in the San Joaquin Valley develop their own programs. A Southeast Asian Mental Health Treatment Team developed in Fresno County with consultation from Joe Torres and myself. In Tulare County, in collaboration with Lao Family Communication, Inc., we were able to develop bicultural effectiveness Americanization workshops, Parent-School Liaison Committees, and several grief groups for Hmong, Mien, and Lao elderly (see Levine & Padilla, 1980; Szapocznik, Santisteban, Kurtines, Perez-Vidal, & Hervis, 1983; Vega & Murphy, 1990).

Psychocultural Adaptation and
the Enduring Self: A Discussion

George and Louise Spindler's notions of psychocultural adaptation and their recent elaboration of "the enduring, situated, and endangered self" become powerful concepts when the anthropological practitioner and counselor works with refugees, immigrants, and other newcomers. Instead of passively observing, describing, and documenting painful processes, the practitioner can intervene proactively in culturally sensitive and appropriate ways. The Spindlers' adaptation notions helped make the Hmong mental health promotion project a success. When combined with their ideas, my American minority status offered a maverick perspective on the Hmong adjustment process that was helpful to the refugees. What we wound up with was a new light on the options available to immigrant minorities in the new land, not through hindsight but in the present as foresight.

The psychocultural adaptation model offered clear and concise information regarding the processes involved in adaptation to American society. Without the Spindlers' previous thinking as guidance, a grasp of the fundamentals of constructive and consonant adaptation would have been elusive. Psychocultural adaptation helped us map and understand the processes the Hmong were going through in their attempt to "fit" into the requirements of American culture. Some of the observations possible from the vantage point of the psychocultural adaptation model were salient, such as the fact that the younger refugees would have an easier time meeting the requirements of American culture than the older refugees. Some of the older refugees would not learn to speak English fluently. Most, if not all, would not be able to go to school beyond learning the fundamentals of the English language and thus would not be able be gainfully employed and provide the basics for their families. They retreated into a native orientation and survived psychologically. In this sort of survival, the "enduring self" dominates. Although it may not be financially viable, there is an inner peaceful resolution (see Spindler & Spindler, 1992).

There would still result a divergence of identities between the older Hmong and the younger Hmong. The model helped predict that those younger Hmong and other Southeast Asian youth who rejected their ethnicity would have a harder time psychologically as they encountered the stresses of racial cultural identity development within the American context (see Sue & Sue, 1990; compare with Cappelletty, 1986). The path of complete rejection of the enduring self leads to a false promise. The "situated self" is quite pleased with itself. Therein lurks the danger. The "situated self" becomes psychologically coterminous with the "conformity" stage of racial, cultural identity development. With the self-hatred and own-group rejection, coupled with the unchecked all-embracing uncritical appreciation of the dominant group referent class, Southeast Asian youngsters lose their identities.

This is one of the concerns that the older Hmong have about the younger Hmong, even now, 8 years after I left the Merced

County Mental Health Department. Now I see some of the same issues emerging at the university level, where many Hmong students attend and have to choose between one way of knowing the world (the old) and a new way, more American, yet not distinctly so (see Spindler et al., 1990). Even now there is emerging conflict in values that promises no easy solutions. For example, one young Hmong woman who is attending the local state university told me that her family is arranging for her marriage to a young man that she doesn't know. She has not told them about her boyfriend. They plan to get married eventually. It is producing quite a conflict in her and she doesn't have any solutions. Her family needs the dowry that will be produced by arranging her marriage. Yet, she does not want to marry the person her parents have chosen. This has not yet arisen as a problem within the family, but it is sure to. She does not know what to do. As a marriage and family counselor, all I can do is help her sort through her options and also help her become aware of the potential consequences for those options that she chooses. For example, making a decision on the basis of an American solution can isolate her from her traditional social support systems including her family of origin.

Psychocultural adaptation refers to those psychological processes most intimately linked with cultural change that are set in motion by "the confrontation of divergent cultural systems" (G. Spindler, 1962, p. 326). Usually, immigrant groups are not aware of the ways in which adaptation to a host culture can be achieved. In helping the Hmong nursing students become aware of the adaptation styles available to them, the implicit suggestion was for them to take the best of both worlds and integrate them into a new third system as desirable. This suggestion was based not only on our experiences as Chicanos, as offspring of immigrants and migrants, but also on a knowledge base of anthropology as well as in the knowledge base of marriage, family, and child counseling.

The point in providing these students with these ideas was that, given our experiences, the ability to have recourse to two or more cultural systems was inevitably better than having recourse to only one, not only for the whole cultural group but also for each and every individual, not only for the Hmong but for all immigrants and minority groups, and, yes, for all Americans, white and black.

Note

1. This term for this core condition was actually coined by Michael LeVine, a counseling student at CSUF, during one session of my seminar, Multicultural Aspects of Counseling (fall 1991).

References

Bliatout, B. T. (1982). *Hmong Sudden Unexpected Nocturnal Death Syndrome: A cultural study.* (Available from Sparkle Publishing Enterprises, Inc., P.O. Box 06569, Portland, OR 97206)

Bliatout, B. T. (1984, May 4). *Asian and Western concepts of mental health: The Hmong/Lao.* Paper presented at the Southeast Asian Health Conference, Northwest Church, Fresno, CA.

Cappelletty, G. G. (1986). *Psychological stress in the Hmong community.* Unpublished doctoral dissertation, California School of Professional Psychology, Fresno.

Cappelletty, G. G., Kenkel, M., & García, J. C. (n.d.). *The measurement of psychological distress within the Hmong refugee community.* Unpublished paper. (Available from California School of Professional Psychology, 1350 M Street, Fresno, CA 93727)

Cohen, J. D. (1979). *Indochinese Mental Health Training Project.* (Available from 2209 Van Ness Avenue, San Francisco, CA 94109)

Devereux, G. (1978). The works of George Devereux. In George D. Spindler (Ed.), *The making of psychological anthropology.* Berkeley: University of California Press.

Edgerton, R. B. (1976). *Deviance: A cross-cultural perspective.* Menlo Park, CA: Cummings.

Elst, D. H. van der. (1978, March 24). *Immigrants, ethnics, and minorities.* A paper delivered at the annual meeting of the Southwestern Anthropological Association.

García, J. C. (1984-1985). *Hmong ethnographic notes* [Personal files].

The Hmong: A struggle in the sun. (1984). *The Fresno Bee* (reprints from the McClathcey Newspapers, Fresno, CA).

Kleinman, A. M. (1974). Medicine's symbolic reality. *Inquiry, 16,* 203-213.

Lee, E. (1988). Cultural factors in working with Southeast Asian refugee adolescents. *Journal of Adolescents, 11,* 167-179.

Levine, E. S., & Padilla, A. M. (1980). *Crossing cultures in therapy: Pluralistic counseling for the Hispanic.* Monterey, CA: Brooks/Cole.

Martin, D. G. (1989). *Counseling and therapy skills.* Prospect Heights, IL: Waveland. (Original work published 1983)

McLemore, D. (1983). *Race and ethnic relations in America* (2nd ed.). Boston: Allyn & Brown. (Original work published 1980)

Owan, T. C. (Ed.). (1985). *Southeast Asian mental health: Treatment, prevention, services, training, and research* (NIMH, PHS, ADAMHA, & Office of Refugee Resettlement). Washington, DC: U.S. Department of Health and Human Services.

Quesada, J. (1987). *Wounded healer: The "social" in the health worker/ interpreter-refugee patient dyad.* Unpublished paper, University of California, San Francisco, Medical Anthropology Program.

Romano-V., O. I. (1969). The historical and intellectual presence of the Mexican American. *El Grito: A Journal of Contemporary Mexican American Thought, 2*(2), 32-46 (Berkeley: Quinto Sol).

Saragoza, A. M. (1989). *Mexican immigrant children in American schools: A brief.* San Francisco: Zellerback Family Fund, New Faces of Liberty Project, San Francisco Study Center.

Shaef, A. W. (1987). *When society becomes an addict.* San Francisco: Harper & Row.

Sluzki, C. E. (1979). Migration and family conflict. *Family Process, 16*(4), 379-390.

Special Services for Groups. (1983). *Bridging cultures: Southeast Asian refugees in America* (project funded by the National Institute of Mental Health, Grant No. 5 T 31 MH13084-08 SWE). Los Angeles: Asian American Community Mental Health Center, Asian/Pacific Social Work Curriculum Development Project.

Spindler, G. (1962). Psychocultural adaptation. In E. Norbeck (Ed.), *The study of personality: An interdisciplinary appraisal.* New York: Holt, Rinehart & Winston.

Spindler, G., & Spindler, L. (1957). American Indian personality types and their sociocultural roots. *The Annals of the American Academy of Political and Social Science, 311,* 147-157.

Spindler, G., & Spindler, L. (1991). Rorschaching in the shadow of Hallowell. In L. B. Boyer & R. M. Boyer (Eds.), *The psychoanalytic study of society: Vol. 16. Essays in honor of A. Irving Hallowell* (pp. 155-182). Hillsdale, NJ: Analytic Press.

Spindler, G., & Spindler, L. (1992). The enduring, situated, and endangered self in fieldwork: A personal account. In L. B. Boyer & R. Boyer (Eds.), *The psychoanalytic study of society: Vol. 17. Essays in honor of George and Louise Spindler* (pp. 23-28). Hillsdale, NJ: Analytic Press.

Spindler, G., & Spindler, L. (with Trueba, H., & Williams, M. D.). (1990). *The American cultural dialogue and its transmission.* Bristol, PA: Falmer.

Sue, D., & Sue, D. (1990). *Counseling the culturally different: Theory and practice* (2nd ed.). New York: Wiley-Interscience.

Szapocznik, J., Santisteban, D., Kurtines, W., Perez-Vidal, A., & Hervis, O. (1983, November 11-12). *Bicultural effectiveness training: A treatment intervention for enhancing intercultural adjustment in Cuban American families.* Paper presented at the Ethnicity, Acculturation and Mental Health Among Hispanics Conference, Albuquerque, New Mexico.

Thompson, G. (1989). *Nu Sun.* Fresno, CA: Pioneer.

Trueba, H. T., Jacobs, L., & Kirton, E. (1990). *Culture conflict and adaptation: The case of Hmong children in American culture.* Bristol, PA: Falmer.

Turner, V. (1979). *Process, performance, and pilgrimage: A study in comparative symbology*. New Delhi, India: Concept Publishing.

Vega, W. A., & Murphy, J. W. (1990). *Culture and the restructuring of community mental health* (Contributions in Psychology, No. 16). New York: Greenwood.

Peggy Wilson

8

Working on Cultural Issues With Students

A Counseling Psychologist's Perspective

PEGGY WILSON

Peggy Wilson is a member of the Pas Indian Band in northern Manitoba, Canada. She is a mother, counselor, and teacher. Her classroom experience began in a one-room school, where she taught Grades 1 through 8. Later, she was a classroom teacher in an isolated Indian and Metis community that had no access to mainstream amenities other than by bush plane, which arrived bimonthly, or by bombardier during the winter months. Since that time, she has been a high school teacher and administrator, a curriculum consultant, a cultural awareness trainer, a clinical psychologist, and a university professor. She received her doctorate from the University of California, Santa Barbara, and her clinical psychology license from the province of Manitoba. Since completing her doctoral work, she has been Visiting Professor at the University of Alaska in Fairbanks and Associate Professor of Counselor Education at California State University in Sacramento. Currently, she is on leave from Sacramento and is Associate Professor at the Saskatchewan Indian Federated College in Regina, Canada. She and her husband often work together conducting cross-cultural awareness workshops and seminars. Wherever their travels take them, they always return to spend their summers at their permanent home on the Pas Indian Reserve, where she operates a private clinical practice in psychology.

At present, the term *cultural therapy,* first used by George and Louise Spindler (1989), has a different meaning for each of us. Until a definition is generally agreed upon, one that clearly states what the process called *cultural therapy* is, then each person who uses the term must define it. In what follows, I present my understanding of cultural therapy and illustrate its meaning by giving several examples of how the process works.

I am a psychologist and a counselor, so I view the term through those lenses. I use the term *cultural therapy* to describe the process whereby individuals come to understand their culture—that is, their roots, connections, traditions, and values. Arriving at this understanding is a very personal quest. It is almost like taking a long journey during which one takes time to appreciate all the landmarks along the way. And at the end—if there ever is a final destination—the place is not important, but it is the stops and starts, the adventures, the hazards, and the enjoyment experienced along the way that make the trip memorable. Throughout life, individuals keep recalling, going back each time they encounter a new situation that makes them remember, and strengthening that which is already there. Getting to an understanding of each individual's own culture is that personal journey. The solid connection between all the events is what the Spindlers call the enduring self—the sense of continuity that people have with their past (Spindler & Spindler, 1989). And although this enduring self is somewhat idealized, it allows humans to make connections. The more people understand this enduring part of themselves, the more satisfied they are that they have a solid base to work from.

Cultural therapy, then, is a process in which individuals are involved and of which they are conscious. Counselors can help others find their own way. Counseling is a process of helping individuals understand their own journeys, their own cultures, and the biases that those cultures provide. What makes us do the things we do? What makes people choose to do things in a specific way? What are our values, our attitudes? Once we can begin to understand the cultural biases that we have, we can better understand how these biases affect the people around us.

But understanding the enduring part of self is not, by itself, enough to be functioning, healthy human beings; we must also interact with others. In the words of Hsu (1985), "The meaning of being human is found in interpersonal relationships, since no human exists alone" (p. 27). So we must also understand how we affect and are affected by others.

When the people we interact with come from another culture, we need to know that our cultural biases can cause suffering. For those persons who are involved in cross-cultural counseling or cross-cultural teaching, the process of finding identity in cultural terms is of prime importance. The purpose of cultural therapy is to alleviate the suffering caused when one's cultural biases are implicitly or explicitly forced upon another. By engaging in the therapy process, educators and counselors discover those aspects of self that are shaped by cultural forces. Although cultural therapy does not offer methods for alleviating mental disorder, the term *disorder* can be used in describing the nature of some inter-ethnic relationships.

Much of my work centers on training graduate student counselors and teachers. I am concerned when students don't know about their culture. I often hear Euro-American students complain that they don't have a culture. This indicates to me that these students don't know that they are cultural agents, that they transmit a culture that they aren't aware of in every movement, in every action that they take, in every word that they speak. They don't know how they affect their students in each encounter and personal connection that they either do or do not make (Spindler, Spindler, Trueba, & Williams, 1990). To make them conscious of this influence, I encourage them to learn as many counseling theories and teaching styles as possible and to apply them in multicultural settings. I am beginning to realize that, although this training is invaluable for working with others, its greatest value lies in my students' acquired ability to analyze themselves. It is their understanding and interpretation of their own experiences, their own cultures, and their own biases that assist them in seeing others more clearly. Cultural therapy is one way of getting to this cultural understanding. The degree to which students choose to accept, reject, maintain, enhance, or ignore their culture becomes a personal adaptation and these adaptations often make a visible difference in their ability to facilitate cross-cultural learning or healing in the children they encounter. When students see something familiar to them happening to the children they work with, they use this common experience as a place to begin to make connections. These common experiences connect, in some way, to the enduring selves of the counselors.

Using three case studies of situations that occurred within the past year in Sacramento, California, I will explore the notion of the enduring self, pointing out situational adaptations made by the counselors, the teachers, and the youngsters with whom they worked.[1] The children in these cases, like children everywhere, arrived in school carrying emotional baggage ranging from war-induced fear to self-doubt created in family dysfunction. They also came to school with rich cultural traditions and with experiences that could not be ignored by the adults who worked with them. I believe that these cases show that teachers or counselors who are able to explore, understand, and accept their own backgrounds are better able to adapt to a diversity of situations. The cases illustrate the ability of each of the helpers to establish rapport with children who are experiencing ordeals similar to ones that they themselves have had to deal with. They are able to see clearly that their clients are faced with having to make similar choices in confronting confusing situations.

In each of the following cases, I first describe the student and explain briefly the situation that made counseling necessary. I then provide a self-description offered by each of the counselors or teachers, and, last, I interpret the working relationship between the two.

Case 1: Miguel, the Reluctant Learner

Miguel is a 10-year-old Mexican American boy. He is in the fifth grade at a large elementary school in a depressed socioeconomic area of Sacramento. His classmates are predominantly Asian; however, there are also other Mexican American as well as African

American and Euro-American children in his classroom. Miguel is always well groomed and dressed according to the latest trend in clothing.

Miguel moved from Oregon to this city during the past year. He came with his parents and two older brothers, one in the eighth grade and the other in the tenth. The family moved to California believing that they would be able to get work and reasonably priced housing. Neither was the case. They lived in and out of their car for a month until Miguel's mother found work. They were then able to move into rented housing.

Miguel's parents do not have a formal education, although his father is self-taught and performs seasonal construction work. Miguel's mother does not read or write in either Spanish or English. She works as a waitress and is at her job site from noon until midnight every day. When Miguel's father is not working, he drinks a lot and his drinking has led to the parents' separation. Miguel's father does not live with the family at present.

Miguel has always been a good student; however, lately, he has not been completing assignments. He is part of a writers' workshop project in his classroom. Parent-teacher conference day is rapidly approaching and Miguel's teacher is encouraging him to complete his writing project so that he can get a grade and so that she can make a good report to his mother.

Laura, who is Miguel's teacher, regularly holds discussion circles in her classroom. The children sit in a circle and either they or Laura suggest a topic for discussion. In one session that Laura particularly remembers, the class discussed the following question: "Have you ever seen someone doing something wrong, and, if so, what did you do about it?" She recalls that, at that time, Miguel came across as being very confident, matter-of-fact, and almost flippant. When it was his turn to talk he said, "A couple of days ago there was a drive-by shooting near my house. I heard it and I ran outside. My neighbor's car got shot at. I ran to their house to tell them and they phoned the police." Classmates asked, "Were you scared?" Miguel responded, "Naw, what's there to be scared about?"

Several months after this discussion, Laura was preparing for parent-teacher interviews. In her classroom, students are asked to grade themselves and then to compare their self-evaluations with Laura's evaluation of their work. Together, they discuss the differences and similarities and negotiate the final grade for the class. Students were to have their writing projects completed before the parent conferences so that grades could be assigned. All the other students in the class had completed their writing, but Miguel continued to stress that he had just one more sentence to write.

Finally, Laura said, "Miguel, this Friday I'm meeting with your Mom. I would like you to finish your work so you can get a grade. Right now the grade that you have doesn't really show what good work you can do." Again the reply was, "Ya, Ms. C., I'll have it done. I have just one more sentence to write." Laura called Miguel at home several nights that week and each time she got the same response. Then finally, on Thursday, she said, "Miguel, remember that I'm meeting with your Mom tomorrow morning. I hope that you are going to be here, too." Miguel's reply was "maybe."

Early on Friday morning, Laura called Miguel's house to remind his mother of their 7:30 a.m. appointment. At the appointed time, Miguel and his mother arrived. Miguel did not have his work done. When Laura reminded him that he could not get a grade unless his work was completed, his mother began to berate him. She reminded him that every night she called home from work to see if he had any homework and he always told her that he either had none or was finished. As she scolded Miguel, Laura heard his mother repeatedly saying, "I just don't know what is wrong with you lately. You don't seem to care about anything." Laura had also noticed that Miguel's work had gradually deteriorated and that he was not the happy, carefree boy that he had once been. She realized that Miguel's inability to finish that one assignment was his way of asking for help. She also knew that he might not be aware that he was asking for help, but, nonetheless, she seized upon the opportunity to speak to both Miguel and his mother.

Miguel's Teacher

Laura, Miguel's teacher, had moved to the United States from the Philippines with her parents, her three older brothers, and one younger sister when she was 12 years old. At that time, Laura spoke Ilocano, the language of her home province of Laonyon. Both of Laura's parents are college educated and had met and married when they were in college in Manila. Before her marriage, Laura's mother had been a Fulbright scholar in Colombia. Laura's mother had always been more academically oriented than her father, and Laura felt some resulting tension between her parents.

In the Philippines, Laura lived with her extended family. Her grandmother was more a part of her early childhood than her parents were, as her grandmother was always present when Laura's parents went to college or when they went to work. In addition, the family always employed an *Ate* (big sister) who did housework during the day in exchange for tuition to night school.

When Laura was a child, her school classes began at 7:30 in the morning and continued through 5:30 every day. Children studied 12 separate subjects and carried their 12 notebooks and 12 textbooks with them on individual luggage carriers as they proceeded from class to class. Every evening, Laura spent 2 hours practicing piano and ballet.

When Laura speaks of her childhood now, she recalls puberty and reaching menses as the most traumatic time of her life. She believes that there is something about that event and the effect that it has had on the rest of her life that helps her to intuit, empathize, and connect with students who are having problems. Laura was 8 years old when her menstrual cycle began. At that time, her mother was attending college in Japan and was to be absent for the year. For 1 entire year, Laura carried the secret of her menstruation and believed that she could tell no one. She knew only that something was wrong with her and that she must take care of herself.

Laura also recalls that during that time her father would come home after work and drink beer (as was customary in her home province) for the rest of the evening. Grandmother accompanied her father by drinking *choctum,* a homemade brew. Together, the two spent their evenings in varying stages of intoxication, while *Ate* attended her night classes.

Laura developed a complex plan for taking care of her hygiene needs while protecting her secret. She had always been an excellent student, but during this year of fear and worry her grades gradually dropped. It was not until a year later when her mother returned from Japan that she was able to relieve herself of her secret and its accompanying fears. Then, the next year, in Grade 4, Laura began to regain her confidence and once again became a model student.

Shortly thereafter, Laura became the self-appointed leader of a gang of 22 little girls who acted almost as a vigilante group, protecting their younger siblings and watching out for injustices being done to those they considered to be less fortunate than themselves. Because of this affiliation, Laura was often accused by her teachers of instigating trouble and of being a negative influence on her peers. Although she was often called to task by the school officials, and was in fact instructed to disband her group, she knew that there was no wrong in what she was doing. Yet she had acquired the reputation of troublemaker and gang leader. She always knew, however, that her mother supported her activities and believed in her potential and her worth.

When Laura's mother was awarded a scholarship to study in the United States, Laura was pleased. Although the rest of the family was angry and disappointed with the prospect of the move, Laura saw a move to America as a way of getting away from a negative reputation. She viewed it as a way to steer her educational life in a fresh new direction.

Once in the United States, she became a top student in her classes. With the assistance of the only minority teacher in her school, Laura was placed in the gifted and talented educational stream. She continued on to the university. Her desire to seek justice attracted her to the Multicultural Teacher Education Center at California State University in Sacramento, where she obtained a teaching credential. She is now enrolled in a master's program in educational administration and takes classes toward that degree in the evenings. This is Laura's first year of teaching as a fully credentialed teacher.

Working With Miguel

Laura was sensitive to Miguel's needs and she knew that he needed help. Taking a piece of paper from her desk, she drew a large circle. She divided the paper into four parts. As she labeled the parts "mental," "physical," "emotional," and "spiritual," she carefully explained each. She told Miguel that every one of us is made up of these four parts. Then she said, "You know, Miguel, if something is wrong in one of these parts, it affects all the others. If you are sick, you can't think clearly. If you don't believe that something or someone is watching out for you and looking after you, you can't concentrate on school work either. Or if you are scared or worried about something, that makes it so you just can't settle down to doing work."

Laura went on to explain, "Your Mom has all these four parts, too, and so do I." Again she asked, "Are you hurting anywhere? Because if you are, that may make you feel sad. And when you're sad, you might feel that nobody cares. Then it's really hard to do your work." Miguel then said, "But if I tell, they'll be mad at me, and I promised not to tell." After much encouragement, Miguel finally told them that he had seen his big brothers beating a little African American boy. With more encouragement from Laura, Miguel finally talked about how scared he was at nights when he had to be alone. Miguel's mother thought that her two older sons had always been at home with Miguel after school. Unfortunately, this was not the case. Miguel was usually home alone in a crime-ridden neighborhood. More discussion resulted in Miguel talking about the drive-by shooting that had happened 2 months previously. Miguel firmly believed that, because the people he saw in the car were black, and because they were driving in his neighborhood, on his street, they must have been looking for his brothers.

Miguel believed that they were out to get revenge on his brothers for having harmed that little boy. He said that he locked the doors and sat by the window each night, watching, just in case they should come back.

What a relief it must have been for Miguel to finally talk about his fears. Miguel's mother also talked about her marriage's breakup and about how that had affected her ability to take care of her family. Laura had managed, by drawing upon her own experiences, and by taking time to show that she really cared about her student, to draw him out and to help him understand his own behavior. In addition, she helped Miguel's mother, who, as a result, became closer to her son.

It was not by accident that this situation worked out so well. On the surface, it would appear that Laura and Miguel are very different. Laura is Filipino; Miguel is Mexican American. Laura and her family are well educated; Miguel's family is not. Laura's parents had always held good jobs and were viewed as respectable, contributing community members. Miguel and his family struggled in a low-income situation and had even been homeless for a time. Yet Laura was able to see and feel Miguel's pain because, on a basic level, their enduring selves were much alike. Although Miguel was very young, he cared very much about justice. This same sense had driven Laura through much of her life. Both Laura and Miguel had suffered damage to their enduring selves. Despite this damage, Laura had acquired the instrumental competency that helped her both recognize and deal with their differences.

I was recently invited to dinner with Laura, her fiancé, her parents, and her sister at Laura's parents' home. It was during this visit that I began to clearly understand Laura and to see the basis for her self-assurance and her successful encounters with students from many different cultures.

Together, the family had prepared a wonderful traditional Filipino meal. Before, during, and after the meal, they spoke with pride of the customs and the traditions of the Philippines. They spoke of the need for excellence in whatever they attempted. They also spoke of their work with minority students and of how they supported and encouraged each other in their work. Finally, and with no hesitation, they entertained my husband and me at the piano with music and song. This was a family well grounded in and proud of their culture yet able to integrate it with aspects of American culture. In doing so, they had the best of both worlds. Laura, although only 25, has the self-assurance of a person who has been encouraged and respected for her own contributions. Her enduring self is well established and, because of this, she is able to readily make situational adaptations. Culturally, she is able to fully understand, appreciate, and respect her Filipino language, customs, and traditions. She can also accept and appreciate the customs and traditions of others who are very different than she is. Her life experiences, both positive and negative, enhance her interactions with others, because she has accepted these experiences as influences in her life that add to her instrumental competence. Laura has become a bicultural teacher whose efficacy is evidenced in her work with her students. She has gained competencies through her own biculturation, through the recognition of her own biases, and through sensitizing experiences that are acultural.

Although I do believe that a certain amount of cultural adaptation must take place before people from differing cultures can work effectively together, I also think that there are times when effective work can be done when this adaptation has not occurred or when the level of adaptation is not outwardly evident. The following case illustrates successful work between cultures. In this case, the counselor had not developed much of an understanding of her own culture. There were aspects of her background, however, that allowed her to recognize similarities in her life and the life of the child that she worked with.

Case 2: The Story of Benjamin

Benjamin is a 6-year-old African American child who was referred to the counseling center by his classroom teacher. Benjamin pokes and pinches his classmates, hits them, and calls them names. His teacher feels that these actions are calculated and planned because, in most instances, they occur when her back is turned. Benjamin's behavior has alienated him from other children of his age.

Benjamin does not seem able to concentrate on one activity in school for any significant period of time. He is constantly up and down. He resents any other child getting attention and he goes out of his way to destroy work done by other children. He does not complete tasks and seems entirely unable to focus. Benjamin's intelligence scores are average to high average.

Benjamin lives with his single mother in a one-bedroom apartment located in a lower-middle-class neighborhood. His mother has a high school education and works as a clerk in a bookstore. She makes sure that Benjamin is well dressed, has proper nutrition, and is, in general, well cared for. She is also very protective of her son. Benjamin's father lives in another state and has only minimal contact with Benjamin. Benjamin refers to him as "bad dad" and says that his father always lies to him and never fulfills his promises.

Twice previously during the past year, Benjamin had been referred to the counseling center. His first counselor was a 25-year-old African American man who was a graduate student in counseling. Jim tried repeatedly to work with Benjamin but was unable to make any connection. Benjamin would not talk to him and resented going to the counseling center. The next counselor who worked with Benjamin was a Euro-American woman, 30 years old. She was trained in behavior modification theories and was sure that she would be able to get through to Benjamin and effect changes in his behavior. Benjamin would not respond to positive reinforcement, nor would he carry on any conversation with her. His behavior in the classroom, on the playground, and at home only worsened. After a 6-month period of increasingly negative behavior, Benjamin was once again referred to the counseling center. This time his counselor was Elizabeth, a student-trainee working on a graduate degree in counseling.

Elizabeth is a 40-year-old Euro-American. She is married and is the mother of three teenage children. Elizabeth was raised in Iowa and is the youngest in a family of three. She has two brothers, the younger of them 5 years older than she is. Elizabeth was not able to converse easily about her culture. In fact, she seemed not to know that she had a culture. Somewhat hesitantly, however, she did speak about childhood experiences. Her voice is quiet and to adults she appears timid and somewhat lacking in confidence. Her unassuming manner and her quiet respectful ways were a determining factor in the success of her work with Benjamin.

How Elizabeth Connected With Benjamin

Elizabeth explained that her first goal and strategy in working with Benjamin was to establish a trusting relationship with him. To get acquainted, they spent most of their initial sessions just walking outside without either of them saying anything. They both felt comfortable in the silences. Elizabeth now recalls that she really made no attempt to deal with Benjamin's difficulties in the classroom. Instead, she was more concerned that he have a friend— someone he could trust and someone who would not constantly scold him for his behavior. I think it may have been at this point that the enduring selves of Elizabeth and Benjamin connected. Elizabeth had always needed friends—people that she could confide in. She had seldom been able to find this kind of friendship.

During one counseling session, Elizabeth had Benjamin work with play dough. It seemed that manipulating the play dough allowed him to vent some of his anger and frustration. When he made a representation of himself using the dough, it was without hands, arms, or eyes. She saw this as his expression of powerlessness. At other times, she allowed him to play in the sand. Each time he played, he would bury whatever play objects he had. The more time Elizabeth spent with Benjamin, the more she began to sense that he had been sexually abused. As she worked with Benjamin, she began to focus on her own childhood and on the shame of the rape that she had carried throughout her life.

As a youngster of 10, Elizabeth had been raped by her brother and his gang of friends. She had never dealt with the trauma nor had she ever mentioned it to anyone. Her own experience allowed her to intuit and empathize with her young client. Her enduring self had been severely damaged, but this did not stop her from sensing that Benjamin may have had a similar experience. In fact, the experience seemed to sensitize her. It was her sense of caring for this youngster that brought her to seek counseling for herself. She worried that she would project her experiences onto the child and that she would not be able to work with him in an objective way.

Elizabeth continued to work with Benjamin. She learned that he had been sodomized at the age of 3 by his mother's boyfriend and that Benjamin "thought about it all the time." Although the case had been reported, there had been insufficient evidence to convict the perpetrator. At that time, Benjamin's mother did not have enough money to afford counseling for her son. It was not until he started school and became a problem child that the school sought counseling for him. All this time, Benjamin and his mother had lived in fear of her former boyfriend's return. Benjamin's mother became so overprotective that she would not let him socialize with anyone outside of school. He had not learned how to play with other children and he was afraid to interact with adults.

Elizabeth worked closely with Benjamin for a year. She did not use any one mode of counseling. Instead, she allowed her own creativity and her ability to hear her client guide the counseling sessions. Benjamin first began to talk to her, then to play in the confines of the counseling center. Gradually Elizabeth brought other children into the sessions until Benjamin felt comfortable playing and talking in a respectful way with them. He has learned some important coping skills to help himself deal with the abuse, and he has learned that he can ask for help. Most important, Benjamin has found that some adults can be trusted.

As I guided Elizabeth through this case, there were times when I felt that Benjamin was Elizabeth's therapist. Nonetheless, he flourished under her guidance. Although both of them had suffered damage to their enduring selves, the experience, over a period of time, became a bonding agent in their relationship. He became a changed child and she became more confident in her ability to make situational adaptations. My hope is that Elizabeth will learn about her cultural background. Her first extensive practicum worked successfully. Maybe this was an accident and maybe it was not.

Elizabeth has the potential to work with many different people and, although she already knows that she can work well with those who have been abused, she does not know whether this will be the case with clients who have other needs. As she lives in California, chances are that many of her clients will come from cultures other than her own. Learning how she transmits her own culture as she works can only enhance her skills. It is this cultural knowledge and adaptation that I wish to explore in the next case, one in which an African American graduate counseling student finds herself working to understand the racist actions of her white client.

Case 3: White Power

Harley was referred to counseling by his teacher because of outward displays of racism. According to his teacher, Harley had written KKK on the chalkboard and on his notebooks during their first class meeting. After he established his territory that first day, he continued to attempt to demonstrate his power and to intimidate those around him. Harley appeared to be a leader among his peers and his leadership was causing division in the classroom. He frequently admonished his group of followers, "We must keep the white race pure," and he was fond of declaring, "Rockers rule."

Harley is 16 years old. He had previously always attended an all-white school. He lives in a predominantly white neighborhood within a culturally mixed city. His father belongs to an exclusive white motorcycle club, which Harley plans to join as soon as he is of age. Harley is a middle child with an older sister and a younger sister. He listens to rock music and enjoys flaunting his interest in both rock music and motorcycles. He also expresses openly and loudly his belief in white power.

Althea, Harley's Counselor

Althea is a 45-year-old African American woman. She was born and raised in Oakland, California. Her father, who was African American, was born and raised in Mississippi. Her mother, born in the state of Texas and raised in Oakland, identified herself as Caucasian. Althea's maternal grandmother was half-white and half-Ethiopian and her maternal grandfather was half-Choctaw and half-white. Althea's Native American heritage was never mentioned. It was only as an adult that she learned about it.

According to Althea, her mother frequently talked about being black as a curse from God. She referred to her children as Negroes and taught them that Negroes in general were dumb and ugly. Nappy hair was terrible. Thick lips and broad noses, she taught, were very much a part of the curse from God, as were big behinds and small ears. Her mother said that the smart Negroes tried to act like white people and the dumb ones didn't have the sense to know the difference.

Althea remembers that it always seemed as if her mother did not like either white people or black people. She always said that white people were not fair. They were selfish people who only thought of themselves. They treated their dogs better than they treated Negroes.

Althea's father had a different perspective. Although he had a fear of white people, he did not hate them. He simply did not trust them. He taught his children that white people might sometimes treat them differently and sometimes unfairly, but that was because they did not know better. He taught his children that people were people first and that no one was good or bad because of where they came from or because of what color they were. He did believe that basically white people were greedy, selfish, and dangerous because of what they had been taught. Althea's father taught her to stand proudly but quietly. He said that white people were in charge and that, because her family was not white, she must learn to cope. He taught his children that they must never trust white people totally but that they should never be outwardly hostile.

Althea was frequently the only African American student in her classes during elementary and high school. As a small child, she had only her parents, grandparents, and teachers for examples. She recalled having watched a little girl in kindergarten as she played on the monkey bars. How she wished that she could play with her. The blond, pigtailed little girl was named Nancy. Nancy was not allowed to have "colored" friends. Althea remembers that she was not angry about this fact, but she does remember feeling hurt.

When she was in junior high school, Althea attended an all-white church. The people in the church were not mean to her—they ignored her. She says, "It was as if I was invisible. I knew the reason I was ignored was because I was colored, so I tried to act as if it was OK. I actually wished that I could be white." Althea remembers that she used to sit in church and think, "When I die and go to heaven, God will remove his curse, and I will be white."

After experiencing many incidents of both subtle and blatant racism, Althea went through a period of rage. She was angry with the world. She had watched white people treat her father as if he were worthless after giving a lifetime of dedicated service as a train porter. She had attended a high school where she was excluded from many activities because she was black. Her family had experienced police harassment over and over again as the police attempted to scare the family so that they would move out of their all-white community. She had witnessed and experienced mistreatment in grocery stores, department stores, and public restaurants. She had visited Mississippi in the 1960s. The combination of all these experiences made her angry.

At the age of 18, Althea decided to attend an all-African American university in Alabama. She began to realize that many black students did not like themselves, and she watched and took part in a transformation. She saw students become color conscious, hair conscious, money conscious, and conscious of their physical features. Still, there was no cultural pride—no sense of positive cultural affiliation. Only the hierarchy had changed hands.

So Althea began, independently, to explore the positive aspects of her heritage, to look critically at her life and at the teachings of her parents. She has taken time to look at her life from a metaperspective. She accepts some, but certainly not all, of the things that her parents taught, some of the teachings of the all-black college, and some of the lessons taught to her in mainstream schools. She has studied her African heritage, is in the process of learning about Choctaw culture and traditions, and is carefully sifting through her findings.

Althea has been a classroom teacher for many years. She has a master's degree in educational administration and is currently working on a master's degree in both school counseling and in marriage and family counseling. While she is attending the university, she is also the interim director of an alternative high school program.

Althea is working on her own therapy and is learning to understand herself and her parents. She believes now that her mother strongly disliked white people out of fear. Her mother also disliked African Americans because she had been discriminated against in a racist society for her dark skin. Society taught her how to feel about people who were not white. She knew no other way to try and save her children from the hurts that she had suffered but to teach them to give up their African culture and to become what would be acceptable in white society. The small part of her that was Native American was to be denied because white society did not even consider Native Americans to be human. Because of her dark coloring, she could not claim her white heritage. Although her teachings were contradictory, they were her way of attempting to save her children from hurt.

Althea believes that her father never trusted white people totally, yet he taught his children that they must never be hostile. He said that they must "stand proudly but quietly." In retrospect, Althea believes that her father had the "good nigger" kind of fear that was taught to slaves in earlier times. That was how he survived in an otherwise dangerous society.

Because of Althea's personal experiences with racism and with her newfound positive knowledge of her cultural background, she has developed a special interest in social responsibility and human diversity. She has the ability to empathize with the victims of the destructiveness of racism whether they are oppressors or oppressed. She can feel the pain of both the victim and the abuser because she believes that both are victims.

Working With Harley

Althea chose to work with Harley first as part of a group, then individually. When she entered the classroom, she introduced herself as a counseling intern. She told the students that she would be conducting class meetings and that she would also be asking to see some of the students individually. She explained that participation in class meetings and in individual sessions was completely voluntary; however, while students did not have to take part in the discussions, they were required to remain in the room during the sessions. She explained her rules of confidentiality and made sure that every student understood what that meant.

Althea believes that Harley is the victim of a racist society. He cannot be scolded or shamed into accepting differences among people. He could not be forced to suddenly change his mind about his feelings and beliefs in white power. She knew that he must connect somehow to someone who was different than himself, and that he would have to voluntarily accept cultural and ethnic differences. The process, she thought, would not happen overnight.

Harley, until recently, had been exposed to a predominantly white environment. His parents were probably what are popularly referred to as "rednecks," and Harley has had extensive exposure to people who believed in stereotyping, racial put-downs, and slander toward people who were different. Althea suspected that now that Harley's school was becoming racially and culturally mixed, his feelings of superiority, cultivated at home, were being aroused. His new English teacher was Hispanic, and Spanish was her primary language. Several Spanish-speaking students in the classroom had conversed with the teacher in Spanish, and Harley could not understand them. This caused Harley to become agitated. After all, this was an English class and he was used to being in control of this group of students. He felt his power waning. To add further to his loss of power, a group of new African American students brought their rap music to school. Generally a person who listens to rap does not also listen to rock, so Harley may have seen the rap music at school as a display of defiance of his power and beliefs. Althea guessed that Harley's security in feeling superior was being challenged and threatened. He was busy defending and protecting himself.

When Althea entered the classroom, she was easily able to spot Harley and his group. She told the class that she wanted to get to know all of them better. She let them know that she was aware of the racial tension that was occurring in the school and that she thought that they might be able to help her with some questions of her own about that subject. She began by telling them a bit about herself.

"I am proud to be an African American," she began. "My mother is half white and the other half is divided between African American and Native American." She went on to explain her background and to ask if any of the students came from a mixed heritage. The students gradually responded to her queries.

"Do something for me," she requested. "Look at me and guess what kind of music you think I like." "Soul music," someone said. "Jazz," shouted another. "Rap, it's got to be rap." "How about the blues?" "Oh, I know, it's probably church music." She allowed the guesses to slow down before she admitted that her favorite music was country and western. Some of the students laughed. Others just showed their surprise. She explained to them that she could enjoy all music for a time, including rock, but that country and western was what she liked best.

Next she asked them to tell her their names. When she got to Harley, she said, with excitement, "I used to own a Harley." Talking to the class with most of her attention directed to Harley, she explained that she grew up with two brothers who were really interested in motorcycles. She told them also that she had lived very near 82nd Avenue, where one of the leaders of a well-known motorcycle club used to live.

When Althea discusses her initial encounter with Harley, she says that she could tell from Harley's responses and expressions that they had made a connection. This was what she had hoped would happen, but she had not expected it to be so rapid. An open line of communication was being established between them. At the end of that first class, she made her way over to Harley and was able to talk to him further. He spoke with pride about his bike and she was genuinely interested. She told him that she would like to see his bike and that she would like to talk to him some more. She also asked him if he would be willing to help her with a group counseling session that she hoped to set up with five or six of the young men in the class. When he responded positively, she knew that she would be able to talk with him not only in the group but individually as well. The connection was made and there was potential for friendship between Harley and someone from a very different cultural and ethnic background.

On an individual basis, Althea worked at building a relationship with Harley. They spent time talking about their families—what they liked about them and what they disliked. They agreed that they could still love and respect their parents even when they did not agree with something that they said or did. They talked about school and teachers and, of course, they talked about bikes. Harley became protective of Althea, instructing her on the correct way to ride a bike and on what to look out for. Only when a firmly established relationship had been built did Althea begin to speak about Harley's feelings on white supremacy and the KKK.

Harley finally confided that he was scared of the black students. He said that many times they had called him "white boy" or "rocker" and "stuff like that." According to Althea, she tried hard to listen to Harley without having a judgmental attitude toward what he was saying. When they were able to connect on a personal level, it was not hard to believe him and to understand his fear. Without pushing or preaching, Althea was able to explain that as we get older we are sometimes able to understand things differently and that it is all right to take time to think things through. He might, she told him, even change his mind about some of his firmly held ideas.

In these ways, Harley and Althea began to talk openly of their confusion about some racial issues. They both understand that one person's actions do not speak for the entire group. Harley still wants people to know that he is proud to be white and that he still likes rock music. Nonetheless, he has made a commitment not to hurt people when he is scared. Althea has taught him some appropriate behaviors that he can use instead of his previous acting out, and she helped to introduce him to an African American youngster his own age who shares his interest in motorcycles.

Althea and Harley continue to meet twice a week. He helps her with the weekly group counseling class. Rather than being suspended from school, Harley is becoming a role model to other white youngsters who would not otherwise see positive behavior directed toward minority classmates.

In each of these three case studies, the Spindlers' notion of cultural therapy is one way to interpret the outcome. Both counselors and the teacher presented here found ways to intervene that helped their students to resolve conflicts between their enduring and their situated selves. Laura was able to understand Miguel because she was reminded of her own childhood and how she had struggled in silence, thinking that there was something wrong with her. Likewise, Elizabeth was able to recognize the loneliness and shame that she often felt and was able to help a client with similar feelings. Althea spotted a conflict she, too, had been involved in. By relating her own search for a resolution to her client's situation, she was able to work positively with someone from a very different background than her own. She had consciously decided to acknowledge her biculturality and to live with it. All three recognized that it was not a personality quirk that was creating problems in their clients but that the social context of the school or community had created the problem. Thus they dealt with their own situated selves and with their clients' situated selves so as to make a connection. They then relied on their enduring selves to help their clients make situational adaptations, ones that perhaps will have an effect on their enduring selves. Cultural therapy has happened for both the counselors and their clients.

Laura and Althea have made significant cultural adaptations. Both accepted aspects from more than one culture and are using these aspects to enrich their primary cultures. Neither was able to do this until she fully understood and accepted her primary culture. In the process of learning about themselves, they have both established a positive self-image and have acquired powerful skills that they can use with their students. Their work with students is not coincidental. It is purposeful. Their enduring selves are well established.

Elizabeth, on the other hand, was able to draw upon her own experiences but was not secure in her knowledge or skills. Her enduring self has been damaged. Until she learns more about herself, she cannot feel a sense of explicit purpose or direction in her work. She often works in the situation without making conscious connections to her enduring self. Unconscious events sometimes occur that allow her to contact and use her past.

My fear is that all three will become marginalized as they become successful in their work. As Laura works successfully with students that other teachers are not able to reach, these teachers may become resentful. Although she is humble and respectful about her successes, others see her as being too subjective, too emotional. "Her students have too much fun, they can't be learning," her colleagues allegedly have said. Increasingly she is finding that she cannot positively interact with the other teachers at her school because their conversations often center on their dislike for their students. Staff-room conversations often take the form of blaming the students for their negative behaviors. So Laura stays in her classroom during class breaks.

Elizabeth and Althea are still students themselves. They must find ways to cope in a society that does not accept their successes or they must accept being marginalized. For Laura and Althea, that is already part of their acculturation experience. For Elizabeth, acceptance of this marginalization may be very difficult.

These cases illustrate the increasingly apparent fact that teachers and counselors must understand their own backgrounds, their cultural ties, their traditions, and the significance of their experiences to see their culturally diverse students through caring and unbiased eyes. The more sensitizing experiences the helper has had, the more likely it will be that meaningful emotional connections will be made with students. It seems that these sensitizing experiences form a large part of the enduring self and make situational adaptations possible.

During counseling training, students are repeatedly reminded that they must come to terms with their own problems before they can work with clients. Teacher education students do not often receive this caution. And while counseling students learn that an understanding of their own culture is part of this learning, education students very often are not even exposed to the tools for dealing with their own emotional problems.

An increasing amount of literature is appearing on the process of multicultural counseling. In most cases, this literature deals with training the mainstream, usually white counselor or teacher to work with minority clients (Pederson, Draguns, Lonner, & Trimble, 1989; Sue, 1981). The literature seldom focuses on self-learning and seldom focuses on the minority counselor or teacher working with students from cultures other than her own. As the makeup of the population changes, it is becoming increasing important to study and learn how minority counselors and teachers can best work with their clients, whether they are people of color or Euro-Americans. I suggest that the experiences that they bring to the learning situation, combined with their own sense of caring, empathy, and genuineness, are probably the most vital tools that they can possess. Used with sensitivity, these practical tools will work across all cultures and allow cultural therapy to take place.

Note

1. To protect the identity of the teacher, counselors, and students involved in the case studies mentioned, all names are pseudonyms. I do wish to acknowledge and thank the three people involved for the fine work that they continue to do and for allowing me to write about it.

References

Hsu, F. (1985). The self in cross-cultural perspective. In A. Marsella, G. DeVos, & F. Hsu (Eds.), *Culture and self: Asian and Western perspectives* (pp. 24-25). New York: Tavistock.

Pederson, P., Draguns, J., Lonner, W., & Trimble, J. (Eds.). (1989). *Counseling across cultures* (3rd ed.). Honolulu: University of Hawaii Press.

Spindler, G., & Spindler, L. (1989). Instrumental competence, self-efficacy, linguistic minorities and cultural therapy: A preliminary attempt at integration. *Anthropology and Education Quarterly, 20*(1), 36-50.

Spindler, G., & Spindler, L. (with Trueba, H., & Williams, M. D.). (1990). *The American cultural dialogue and its transmission*. Bristol, PA: Falmer.

Sue, D. (1981). *Counseling the culturally different: Theory and practice*. New York: John Wiley.

Shelley Goldman and **Ray McDermott**

Seth Chaiklin

9

Crossing Borders Electronically

Mentoring Students via E-Mail

SHELLEY GOLDMAN
SETH CHAIKLIN
RAY McDERMOTT

Shelley Goldman and **Ray McDermott** are grade school teachers turned anthropologists. They care most intensely about understanding and confronting the easy acceptance and reproduction of inequalities in American culture. They live with their children in a university dormitory, experiencing life firsthand at the opportunity end of the educational system. At present, Shelley is Senior Research Scientist at the Institute for Research on Learning, where she heads the Middle-School Mathematics Applications Project supported by the National Science Foundation. Ray is Professor of Education and Anthropology at Stanford University, where he works on problems in the history, social function, and cultural context of reading, writing, math, and money exchange.

Seth Chaiklin is on the faculty at the Institute of Psychology, University of Aarhus, Denmark, where he teaches pedagogical psychology and codirects a program with Mariane Hedegaard that prepares students to work as consultants in educational institutions. Two current research projects are "Culture in School and Society" (with Mariane Hedegaard), which is investigating the schooling of children of Turkish immigrants to Denmark, and "Understanding Physics," which is applying principles of developmental teaching in a physics teaching experiment at a Danish upper-secondary school.

AUTHOR'S NOTE: For helpful comments on earlier drafts, we thank Bernadine Barr, Ann Mathison, Karen Powell, and George and Louise Spindler.

247

When Frederick Law Olmsted designed Morningside Park in Manhattan, he could not have known it would be a twentieth-century site for the racial struggles he observed during his famous travels through the antebellum South (Olmsted, 1856). For 12 long blocks, the park separates the predominantly African American community of Harlem from the mostly white Columbia University campus and its residential complex, the Cathedral of St. John the Divine, and various other imposing institutions.[1] Olmsted's park is an embarrassingly literal example of social stratification, for, in addition to the few hundred feet of grass, trees, and athletic courts that divide Harlem on the east and Columbia on the west, there is a 20- to 50-foot rock wall that allows Columbia to overlook Harlem. The two communities are connected every few blocks by long rock staircases running up the sides of the walls to what is appropriately called Morningside Heights.

By fact and fiction, it is not an easy border to cross. For facts, there are high crime rates and two private police forces that patrol the sidewalks on the Columbia side of the border. For fiction, there is the folklore that bad things happen to any resident of the Heights who uses the park, a rumor mill that gives rise to and feeds off defensive behavior patterns, such as the periodic unsuccessful efforts among the upper echelons of the area to lock the gates at the top of the park after dark.

The three of us lived and/or worked on the Heights for a decade. Although we were border-crossers who worked with children on the Harlem side, we were often in the position of discovering still other ways we inadvertently helped to make the border. For example, like everyone on the Heights, when we needed to go to midtown by public transportation, we walked four long blocks west to catch the bus; years went by before we noticed that only 200 feet from our door, 40 feet down the stairs and 160 feet across the park, was a bus that went to the same place in much less time. We had read that Protestants and Catholics did the same in Belfast (Boal, 1965), and whites and African Americans in nearby Philadelphia (Ley, 1974), but in both cases people seemed to know what they were doing. We did not know the pattern could develop simply because the information channels about local bus routes were so well tuned to the details of social stratification. The rock walls of the Heights made stratification visible and literal, and information about the buses made the same stratification covert and subtle. The border was ubiquitous.

This chapter is about a moment of crossing the border, a case of opening the gate for person-to-person contact and the passage of information. It is the story of a mentoring relationship between an adult (Seth Chaiklin) and two 10-year-old, sixth-grade girls in a school near the park. More important, it is about how crossing borders and enabling unlikely relationships to develop could actually help inner-city kids break from the gate. The channel for the mentoring relationship was minimal, namely, the telephone wires that allow computers to exchange electronic mail (E-mail) messages, and the data for our analysis are correspondingly minimal, an exchange of 42 messages across 6 months (and brief exchanges in the ensuing years). Most of the messages are less than a page long, and together they take up only 35 single-spaced pages.

Each of us has been amazed at how much of concern to school-children is taken up in the letters. No one letter is remarkable. No one reveals secrets. No taboos are broken, or even raised. But cumulatively, they present a record of what awake, reflective children might ask adults if, as a matter of course, they happened to be walking through the same world together, sorting the conditions of their lives in and out of school, and working on the details of that "collective illusion" called culture.[2]

The description of a culture at work is notoriously difficult. Because everyone is connected to everyone else in multiple and diverse ways, the behavior of people in a culture, we are often reminded, requires "thick description" (Geertz, 1973). We offer instead a thin description of people in contact with each other only briefly and along a single channel. These limitations are a good frame for an important observation: Despite the apparent strength of the borders that separate the members of the Harlem and the Upper Westside communities, and despite the narrow range of the electronic channels that connect these particular children and an adult, there is a wealth of mutually accessible culture and educational wonder in their communications.

We use this observation to make two simple educational points and two complex theoretical arguments. We cannot offer firm conclusions, and we use the E-mail exchanges only to shape our considerations. The first educational point is that mentoring relationships between children and an adult in their wider community offers possibilities for organizing learning and growth across the social borders that are usually left impenetrable. We note that, in most successful educational systems, such relationships occur as a matter of course. Our second point is that, whatever the logistic, legal, or bureaucratic reasons for mentoring not being a significant part of American education, mentoring by electronic mail bypasses most of the problems, and, as sterile as it sounds, E-mail might be a great way for children and adults to have safe and interesting conversations with each other.

The theoretical points develop even less obviously from the data but are nonetheless crucial. First, despite constant claims that children on opposite sides of social and cultural borders are different than each other in ways that are consequential for their learning potential, these E-mail exchanges suggest that it is quite easy to communicate across some of the deeper social barriers found in our cities. The children in this case are not only from across the tracks, both are children of immigrants, from Jamaica (only weeks before) and Malaysia (10 years before). Certainly we cannot deny our experiences that tell us that communicating across linguistic and cultural differences can be difficult, but this does not mean we should stretch our experiences into an account of school failure.

The success of these E-mail exchanges suggests instead that problems with people on different sides of the border have to do with the forces that organize the borders and not with differences in the communicative styles and values of the cultural groups on the different sides (Drummond, 1980; Frake, 1980; McDermott & Gospodinoff, 1979; Ruskin & Varenne, 1983). Much of what stands as a characterization of people from different groups may have the same relation to reality as the knowledge of alternate bus routes on the Heights; it may be based on ignorance, but that ignorance is finely tuned with the structure of the borders and is consequential for their maintenance. In seemingly bypassing the borders that divide the worlds of a Harlem school and the Bank Street College of Education, E-mail exchanges allowed the participants to use the knowledge and concerns made available by their mutual participation in American culture.

It is important to note what we are not claiming. We are not using this example of an electronic mentoring relationship to suggest that E-mail gives the students something they were lacking in the way of good teachers or significant adult or familial relationships. We are not saying that kids or their families were so deprived that their lives were altered by a little time on a computer network. Quite the contrary, we believe strongly that inner-city children are rarely deprived of learning potential, although they are often lacking institutional connections that middle-class children have. If inner-city students have fewer connections than students in other segments of society, electronic networks may have some interesting possibilities for creating access to connections. At the very least, crossing borders electronically can show us the humanity and intelligence on both sides.

The second theoretical point speaks to mentoring as a particular version of cultural therapy, an intriguing idea, long ago suggested by George Spindler under the name of "anthropotherapy" and more fully developed in recent papers by George and Louise Spindler (1989, Chapter 1 in this volume) from which this volume has developed. Although it may be the case that E-mail bypasses some of the communicative barriers that keep children and adults from different communities apart, it is also the case that E-mail makes use of, and in fact requires, tremendous cultural input to be successful. Because these exchanges occurred serendipitously as an aside to a wider project involving whole classrooms of children in communication with each other (and with other children around the world), the interactional foundation for E-mail was in this case well developed. More important, what was not well developed, programmatically, interactionally, or culturally, is exactly what much of these E-mail exchanges are about, namely, the self-conscious inquiry into the relations that make the lives of the children and the adult mutually intelligible. The children want to know what constitutes their culture and how to adopt a pathway to its rewards. Creating pathways would be easier for children if they could periodically share with someone their discovery of and reactions to the arbitrary cultural and institutional practices in which they are participants. The children want to figure out where they stand for themselves, and, for a start, they want to know it through the eyes of a mentor. They want to know what it means to be a student, an adult with a job, a researcher, or an adolescent who likes to talk to adults. The adult in this case is fortunately not one of their teachers charged institutionally with the job of sorting and documenting them into piles of successful and unsuccessful students. Nor does the adult know the answers. Together the three correspondents wrestle, from their different vantage points, with the specifics of what makes them, in varying ways, part of the same culture, namely, their birthplaces, their families, their lives at school, and their relationships with other kids and other adults. The articulation of possible pathways through a culture can be of tremendous value to children.

In an excellent book on pathways to maturity in modern Japan, David Plath (1980) has given us a formulation of the world in which long-term relationships can be maintained. The same formulation can be used to describe how even less intimate relationships, even those across electric wires connecting faceless others, can make a difference:

> Culture, character, and consociates weave a complicated fabric of biography. The process is not only lifelong; it is longer than life. Consociates begin to shape our personal course even before we are born, and may continue to renegotiate the meaning of our life long after we are dead. To this extent, a person is a collective product. We all must "author" our own biographies, using the idioms of our heritage, but our biographies must be "authorized" by those who live them with us. (p. 9)

Growth and development are a collective enterprise for Plath, and guidance, feedback, and authorization are essential to anyone's acquisition of culture. This is easiest to picture in the small societies of our imagination, societies in which everyone is in face-to-face contact and signposts to the one good life are everywhere and unambiguous. A century of ethnographies from small-scale societies reveals that our imaginations have failed us, that, in fact, no matter how small the society, growing up is always difficult, more a case of placing the right bets than knowing the right path. Culture is always an ambivalent and contradictory guide and is perhaps better understood as a list of uncertain hopes and promises than a sure model to the future.

Now imagine the difficulty of growing up in a society driven to reproduce complex class, ethnic, and racial divisions. Now imagine growing up in Harlem, or having just recently arrived in Harlem from Jamaica and Malaysia. Where is guidance to come from? From what idiom is one to author a life path? And with whose authorization? There are many ways to go, and we all need to feel our way around in search of a place to stand, in search of a center, and that in a world that will not stand still. Again, Plath (1980) states the case with startling clarity:

> The processes of human maturation . . . seem to be legislated by a parliament of prodigals: there can be immense pain and waste; tragedy and future-shock can overcome anybody; growth must always be seen in the context of a discouraging potential for regress. Nevertheless, given time enough and health we do appear to have the potential to continue growing as persons indefinitely. (p. 6)

Culture is a "parliament of prodigals," with members always on the verge of being out the door they would prefer to go in, or vice versa. We all need a cultural therapy, and the more a cultural therapy speaks to the arbitrary cultural divisions that have us feeling left out, dropped out, and pushed out, the more the therapy has a chance of giving us access to the crowd and to reorganizing the crowd to a better end. Triangulation, multiple points of view, and comments from metalevels are essential to maturation in any culture but perhaps most of all in a class-divided, capitalist nation in which members can be forced to pay so dearly for living on the wrong side of an arbitrary cultural divide.

A cultural therapy is helpful to the extent it informs everyone, all the prodigals, those seemingly giving the therapy and those seemingly receiving it, of the arbitrary categories that keep us locked in relationships that could be transformed for the better. This chapter cannot deliver an account of what a full-blown therapy might involve, but by showing how easily difficult borders can be crossed electronically, it suggests that the people of the Heights and the people of the valley are more than enough like each other to share in the same rewards of the cultural system; the difference between them is in the structure of the opportunities available to them. Such a realization is the beginning point of a politically sophisticated cultural therapy.

The chapter proceeds as follows: First, we give an account of the school and the telecommunication project of which the E-mail messages are a happy by-product; second, we summarize the content, style, and relational fabric of the messages; and, third, we conclude with the implications of the messages for our educational and theoretical points.

The School and the Earth Lab Project

Carver School serves neighborhood students in Grades 4-6. Most of the students who attend Carver live in housing projects directly adjacent to the school yard, although a few students come from tenement-type residences on nearby blocks. Approximately 85% of the students are African American, 14% are Hispanic, and 1% are Asian or white.

Education at Carver is constrained daily by conditions that exist in many inner-city schools: Poor economic conditions and lack of resources are immediately obvious; academic failure and alienation are strongly institutionalized and felt; the school seems to have few connections with its community; major social problems, crime, and drugs as well as poverty harass everyone coming and going around the school; and the folklore about what happens to children passing through the park echoes the stories told on the Heights. Each of these conditions shapes the educational experiences available in the school. Perhaps the most invidious constraint on learning is a sense of every person's isolation from everyone else. Over the course of an entire year, it is possible for any student at Carver to know and work with as few as five adults, almost all of whom interact with students only in large groups. With classes of 30-35 children, there are few opportunities for individual attention. Only "special" and "exceptional" children in compensatory programs receive one-on-one time with an adult. Students are also isolated from each other. For most of their day, students sit at desks engaged in activities and tasks they do independently. Almost all of their assignments are completed and evaluated on an individual basis (Newman & Goldman, 1988). Students sometimes work and talk together, but only when forced by circumstance, for example: two students to each computer or book, because there are not enough to go around, or special activities like field trips for which grades are not given. Students and teachers interact freely with their peers only when it "does not count," that is, before school in the morning, at recess and lunch, and in the computer room—all scenes that carry no grades or other institutional consequences.

Carver School has a number of hardworking teachers who are trying to improve what the children are offered. Since 1984 they have directed much of their attention to integrating technology with the curriculum in the school. Despite much rhetoric about how computers are the savior of American education, there is considerable evidence that computers in most inner-city schools simply sit and gather dust or get used in ways that leave classroom operations and outcomes unchanged (Cuban, 1986; Mehan, 1989; Piller, 1992). This is no surprise to critics who anticipated that patterns in social relations could easily overwhelm a new technology and that technology pales before politics as a source of social change (Aronowitz & Giroux, 1985; Bowers, 1988). There is no bypassing human relations in teaching and learning. *Communication* and *learning* are two terms for the same phenomenon (e.g., Bateson, 1972; Vygotsky, 1986). If the introduction of computers into the classroom is going to change learning practices, then there has to be a corresponding change in the possibilities and forms of communication between teacher, children, and possibly others.

The teachers at Carver School brought telecommunication in as part of a research project called Earth Lab (Goldman & Newman, 1992; Newman & Goldman, 1987, 1988). Unlike most efforts to introduce interesting technology into classrooms, Earth Lab was designed to produce materials well tuned to the activities of the children who used them. In addition, Earth Lab researchers worked closely with the teachers to help orchestrate a classroom that could make intelligent pedagogical use of the computer and the multiple connections that could be made to increase students' communication with others in their classrooms as well as with the world beyond the school (for the theoretical conception of mind and pedagogy underlying Earth Lab, see Newman, Griffin, & Cole, 1989). For example, earth science education on weather and climate was focused on actually collecting weather data daily and communicating about the data with students from across the globe. Inside the classroom, children were asked to collaborate with each other, face-to-face and on-line, by creating and sharing data files, analyzing them, and writing reports together. The goal of Earth Lab was to increase communication possibilities for the students. Every step in the research process and every move in the classroom was analyzed for its consequences for communication among the participants.

The technology that supported the mentoring relations under analysis started with an enhanced electronic post office. First, in everyday terms, imagine a room with a set of locked mailboxes. In this room, you can put a letter into any mailbox, and you can read any messages in your own mailbox (but not the others because they are locked). With appropriate software, one can create an analogous situation on a computer. Users of the system can compose and deliver messages to all other persons on the same system but only read messages delivered to them. Users can read and write their messages independently, because the computer saves the messages. It is not necessary for a sender and recipient to be using the computer at the same time.

In this particular case, the technical arrangement that supported the communication was a combination of a local area network (LAN) and a bulletin board system (BBS). A LAN has two or more computers, usually in the same building, directly connected to each other via some kind of cabling and appropriate software, and a machine for sharing files and/or programs. A LAN often has an electronic mail service that allows its users to communicate with each other.

A BBS can provide a variety of services, for example: Persons can read and write private messages to each other as described above; a person can write public messages that many people can read; or a person can communicate in real time with other persons who are connected to the BBS at the same time. The actual possibilities depend on the particular BBS software being used.

The special feature of a BBS system is that it can be accessed remotely. That is, the people who use the BBS are physically located at some distance from the computer that runs the BBS. There are different technical methods by which one can gain access to a particular BBS, but typically one accesses a BBS over a public telephone line, using a hardware device (modem) that converts signals from the computer into a form that can be passed over the phone line and received by the BBS computer at the other end. The practical consequence of this arrangement is that people in different physical locations can communicate together through this common meeting point—the BBS.

A BBS program can be supported on a microcomputer, even a small machine like those usually found in school classrooms. BBSs have been prevalent among home users of computers, but in recent years schools, businesses, and private and public organizations have initiated BBSs. Beyond the idea of a BBS, there are also a variety of networks, associated with universities, large corporations, and governments, enabling the transmission of electronic mail messages to thousands of computers around the world. Commercial services sell access to a central computer that can be accessed worldwide via a packet-switching network. Services often have memberships that number in the tens of thousands. The resources and possibilities of computer-based communication continue to expand and develop. In short, the use of a BBS for communication between mentors and children is not particularly unusual or exotic.

The children and the mentor communicated over a system that involved both a LAN and a BBS. In Earth Lab classrooms, the students wrote messages on a LAN in their school.[3] The teacher would take these messages on the LAN and upload them via modem to a BBS at Bank Street College. The mentor could receive and reply to the messages on the BBS. The teacher would download the mentor's replies from the BBS and send them to the students on the LAN.

In 1986 a teacher in an Earth Lab classroom told two of his students about a researcher at Bank Street, Seth Chaiklin, who was doing work with junior high school students on garbage disposal policy in New York City. The students thought the idea was interesting, and each one wrote Seth a letter (December 8, 1986) on the LAN in their classroom. The next day, their teacher added an introductory note and uploaded their letters to the BBS at Bank Street College. Seth could also access the BBS, where he could read and reply to the letters. Here are copies of the note card and the two student letters.[4]

From: paul
To: seth
Subject: Student letters
Date: Tue Dec 9 12:44: 06 1986
Seth,

Here are two letters from my students. Respond to Carver School. The masthead is generated by the mail system in Earth Lab.
paul

To: BSE in class: class 1
From: Natalie in class
Subject: letter
Date: 12/08/86

Dear Seth,

Hi! My name is Natalie I am a student at Carver School in Manhattan. I am ten years old. I was told by mister Roades to write this letter. I am very interested in what you and your students are doing and would be very happy to probably be informed about your projects or basically anything., I would also be very pleased to receive a letter or letters from students and you yourself.

Why are you searching in garbage? is it to see how much food people throw away, Per Day, Per month, per year or just something else).

Cordially Yours,

Natalie

From: Rena in class
Subject: A Friendly Hello
Date 12/08/86

Dear Seth,

Hello, as you see above, my name is Rena. I am in Carver School, class 6-213. mister Rhodes told me you are working with some High School students on a garbage project. I think that is very interesting and I would very much like to hear from you or the students you are working with about your project or anything else.

Is searching in garbage cans part of your research on garbage? Do you know how many garbage new Yorkers produce every week? I would every much like to know, if you can, please tell me.

That's all from me now.

Yours Truely,

Rena

Less than 2 hours later, Seth had written an answer to both children, and they set off on an exploration of the worlds in which they live. There could have been other ways for Seth to become a mentor to the children. He was, for example, working face-to-face on the garbage project with children from another school. But in this case, E-mail was an easy and efficient way to start together for conversational points unknown. Little effort was required. The border seemed less marked, and there were few personal or social structural risks. There were things to be learned, conversations to be had, and a channel for having them. That was apparently enough.

The Messages

Topics

In their first messages, Natalie and Rena open with the garbage problem, but they move quickly to other topics. In his first letter to Natalie, Seth invites her to talk about anything she pleases:

[Seth, December 9, 1986]
I'll tell you what. I will tell you a little about the garbage project, and then I will ask you some questions, and then you can write back to me about any of these things . . . [explains garbage project]. Maybe you could tell me what your favorite things to do are. Do you like to listen to music? Who are your favorite musicians? Do you like animals?

Rena receives a similar invitation. Garbage remains a concern, and it appears in 13 of the next 38 messages (17 in all). The students move quickly through Seth's suggested topics: from Natalie the next day, a minimalist response, "I like animals very much," and from Rena 2 days later, "You asked me what my hobbies are, well I have a ton of them! I love to read, skate, swim, write stories, play volleyball, play kickball, watch TV, work with the computer etc. I better stop naming them."

That is the end of animals and hobbies, but 22 other topics get taken up and developed across messages over the next 6 months. Seven of the topics and most of the messages have to do with school: Teachers get 12 messages; junior high school admissions, speech contests, and using computers in class all get 8 messages each; exams, graduation and honors, and the science fair get 6 each.

After garbage, the most addressed topic is technology—the medium the three of them are using to do their communicating (14 messages):

[Natalie, March 11, 1987]

In your latest letter you told me that you are using the Logowriter. I like using the Logowriter very much! Its fun and really gives you some challenge in getting your direction correct. We mostly use the Logowriter in Computer Club because when we come to the computer room during school we almost always have something to do.

Although the establishment of the electronic mail process was initially made possible by the girls participating in the field-testing of Earth Lab, the network was in its infancy and not always working perfectly, and it often constrained users to its idiosyncrasies. The system-level demands on users made their way into the communications. The letters almost by necessity mentioned the technology, its use in the school, and ways of handling technical problems and mistakes, such as erasing or losing files and deleting letters. There was some recognition that the electronic medium left some features of communication unattended, such as face-to-face contact.

The weather comes up in 11 messages, not as a conversational filler but because Earth Lab curriculum had the students gathering data and writing reports on the weather as an analytic topic.

[Natalie, January 30, 1987]

Before I sent you the Thank You letter we got an assignment to put down on paper all the questions we didn't know the answer to about Hurricanes as a group. Then we were assigned to find the answers by using various books and encyclopedia's. After all that hard work we had to send our questions and answers to the other groups, who in turn sent us their's.

Then we had to take our questions and answers and compare them with their's. After we were finished we wrote back through the mail electronic function and quarreled over the questions and answers.

Out of it all our teacher told us that we have to write a report on the topic. But she also said if we can get more information by any source that's okay. So if during your studies you come across any information on Hurricanes please let me know. But don't go out of your way.

Geographic locations, birthplaces and home cultures, and holi-days all get a heavy share of the discussion (nine, eight, and eight messages, respectively). The discussion of where in space and time people are in relation to each other seems almost necessary to most conversations around the world (see the exemplary de-scriptions of place talk by Basso, 1990; Frake, 1992). E-mail net-works provide an occasional exception, because they can cater to strangers who do not want to get together and who will work hard to omit their own demographic particulars. The students and their mentor, on the other hand, seem to take every opportunity to identify shared locations. These friendly messages across social borders seem to cry out for a mutual tuning of space and time coordinates.

[Natalie, December 10, 1986]
    I only came to New York a few weeks ago so would you mind telling exactly where Joan of Arc High School is?

[Seth, December 10, 1986]
    I was born in Brooklyn, but you wouldn't know that if you saw me and didn't know anything about me. About 4-6 months after I was born, my parents moved to New Haven, so about all I know about Brooklyn is which subway lines go there.

[Rena, December 17, 1986]
    I mentioned that I have a friend in Malaysia. You may have never heard of this place. My parents were born there. But I was born in New York City.

[Natalie, May 28, 1987]
    Do you know how to get here? If you are going to come by subway take the I.N.D. "K" train to 125th Street then walk one block west to reach Morningside and then walk two blocks on Morningside Avenue when you reach 123rd Street you have to walk down a few feet and then you come to a building with the Star Spangled Banner in front. It is a brick building and is brown.[5]

The directions were part of a message about meeting Seth. Meeting each other face-to-face in the last week of the school year, after 6 months of correspondence, gets some high-charged attention across six messages.

[Natalie, April 8, 1987]
What do you look like?
Are you going to come by any chance come to our school before we leave for 7th Grade?

[Rena, May 27, 1987]
I heard that you are going to come to my school with your garbage project. I can't wait! Natalie and I have been dying to find out what you look like.

[Rena, June 1, 1987]
Thanks for your letter. I just read it a few minutes ago. Do you know that I am very cheerful right now? Well, you letter made me even more cheerful and happy. Life is wonderful, isn't it? I am glad you will be coming this afternoon.

There are exchanges on surprising topics. There is a lively discussion on "working with kids" that takes up space in seven messages (which we examine in a later section), and six messages contain concern for a paper that Seth is writing about learning algebra:

[Rena, February 20, 1987]
About what you said about writing a report on how children learn algebra, I think I can tell you some things about it since I have learned it a little in the program which I go to called Prep for Prep. (If you would call it algebra)
What my math teacher first did (I think), was to teach us to solve one step equations, after that, we learned how to solve two steps equations, then, we learned to graph coordinates, then, we learned how to do/solve, equations with to variables.

Seth follows with more questions, in the long run reports finishing his rough draft, and announces that he has started work on a physics paper. He gets no response.

The range of topics and the willingness of the participants to stay with them over many exchanges is interesting. There is nothing extraordinary about any one of the letters. The excitement is in the way they build on each other and display the rhythm of the year as they rush to junior high selection, the science fair, graduation, and honors. Unless their respective new schools just happen to be set up with access to E-mail networks and bulletin boards, it is likely that their relationship will end.

[Rena, June 19, 1987]

This is probably the last time I am going to be able to write to you. On Monday, I will be graduating. I am going to miss this school.

Well, I don't really have anything to say except that I wrote to say good bye.

Bye.

Their new schools, it turns out, were not equipped with E-mail capacities. The following September, Seth managed to get the students access to terminals at Teachers College, but the relationships slowed down and petered out of existence. Five years later, Natalie returns to her old elementary school and tries to send a message to Seth, who has moved to Europe. The message arrives, through an intermediate E-mail stop:

[Natalie, June 24, 1992]

Dear Seth,

I don't know if you remember me. I used to write to you along with Rena. About a year ago I lost contact with Rena when she moved. I've tried writing to her at her old address but there has been no answer.

Next year I will be a senior in high school. I go to the Spence School now. After I graduated from Carver School I went to De La Salle Academy where I remained for seventh and eighth grade.

After De La Salle I went to Spence. I am now embroiled in the whole college admissions process—SAT prep, visits to colleges, reading several college brochures. So far I really like Brown but haven't had a chance to visit but my friends who have tell me its wonderful. Well, what else is new? My parents separated and now I live with my mother. It was for the best. I was really relieved. I heard that you got married—Congratulations!!! Well, I look forward to hearing from you.

Natalie

P.S. I was typing pretty fast so I don't know how good the punctuation or spelling is in the letter.

The short extracts we quote in this chapter cannot do justice to the complexity of the relationships developed over the wires. Nonetheless, we can focus on two patterns—affiliation work and questions about sharing their culture—that can help us to make our educational and theoretical points.

Affiliation Work

It is an old and sometimes useful distinction that every message has two dimensions: a content dimension that delivers what is being said and a relationship dimension that delivers information on the relations between the persons in the communication (Bateson, 1972). In face-to-face communication, the latter is often handled either without words or tied to words in ways that make them difficult to transcribe. When using E-mail, transcription is the only source of communication. There are no gestures, no tones of voice, no different kinds of strategic uses of silence and delay. Relations must be tended with the same words that carry the content. The messages that Seth and the children send to each other are filled with relational or affiliation work that answers the questions of who we are and what we are doing communicating with each other. As time goes by, they become more self-conscious about what could be barriers to their affiliation, and their messages become increasingly didactic about the differing aspects of our culture that drive them in their current positions. They become cultural therapists for each other.

Affiliation work appeared across the messages and can be seen, however minimally, in every letter. We use the term *affiliation* to include the work they put into defining relationships, setting boundaries, citing commonalities of experience and interest, and establishing connectedness.

Sometimes affiliation was obvious, as in introductions, displays of support, and advice seeking and giving. These activities possibly helped to foster the close ties and trust that were referred to and called upon in subsequent communications. One example is the exchange of biographical information and personal opinions, which can be seen early in their beginning communications when they request information about their backgrounds, hobbies, likes, and dislikes. These pen-pal letter gambits are typical in school settings and appear widely in school-based telecommunications (Levin, Rogers, Waugh, & Smith, 1989). Seth initiated the pen-pal genre in his response to the first letters he received from the girls, and this established an initial context for communicating. The pen-pal writing faded after only four turns of communication, and more intensive affiliative interactions began emerging, for example, asking for and receiving advice and the exchange of opinions about various issues (Riel, 1990; Riel & Levin, 1992).

Other forms of affiliation are less obvious. For example, the degree of formality and informality in the letters was negotiated, and in their negotiations we can see the participants not only being attentive to each other but displaying that attention for the others to see. Affiliation becomes evident when each topic, query, or musing receives a response from the other side. When the girls request information for school project work on hurricanes, Seth responds with information. He reads some of the proverbs the girls wrote as part of a network exchange activity, and when Seth sends the girls a computer-generated image of Garfield, the mass-culture cartoon cat, they proudly share their treasures with others in their class. The network relationship culminates and is displayed publicly near the end of the year.

[Natalie, April 28, 1987]

Dear Seth,

Mrs. Moore said she would love to have you and your students come and show us your project. Mrs. Moore has also asked me to ask you to send some dates of when you and your students can come. . . .

In my last letter I forgot to include that I met a friend of yours who also teaches at Bankstreet. His name is Mr. Kook (Cook?) Micheal Kook. We (Rena nd I) werew talking to him and he was answering our questions that we came up with. It was great talking to him. . . .

Conversational topics, terrain, and timing were negotiated. When the girls initiate the E-mail correspondence, they both start with what they perceive as Seth's interest—the garbage disposal problem. He responds by opening the agenda in his first responses to Rena:

[Seth, December 9, 1986]

Thank you very much for your nice letter. I would be happy to write to you about my work with garbage, or if you want, we could write about all sorts of things. . . .

Meanwhile, maybe you could tell me what your favorite things to do are. Do you like to listen to music? Who are your favorite musicians? Do you like animals?

I hope I hear from you again when you get a chance.

And after explaining the garbage project to Rena:

If you want to keep writing, we could write some more about garbage. (I know quite a bit about it.) Or, if you wanted, you could write to me about other things. For instance, do you have any hobbies? Do you play any sports? Are you interested in music? I hope to hear from you sometime.

This query about the girl's interests sets the stage for a more personal kind of communication—one that is not limited to school-appropriate topics. This is reinforced by the tone of Seth's response, which is warm, friendly, and curious. The students also show off their attentiveness to Seth by modeling his written and interactional style. In the early letters, the three correspondents adopt a formal letter writing style complete with greetings, body of letter with separate paragraphs for each of the discourse threads (Black, Levin, Mehan, & Quinn, 1983), salutations, and closings. This formal format prevails and becomes juxtaposed with the informal, friendly tones that are expressed through the use of punctuation, capital letters, ways of representing prosody and metacomments.

[Seth, December 9, 1986]
   Hmmmm. That seems like a LOT of garbage to me.

[Rena, December 11, 1986]
   Ooops! I am late for library work. Well this is all from me for now.

[Seth, December 16, 1986]
   Dear Natalie,
   I know that I answer your letters TOO QUICKLY. But that is just the way I do it. Don't worry. I am not insulted if you do not answer right away. . . .

[Natalie, January 5, 1987]
   . . . I still want to wish you a belated "MERRY CHRISTMAS AND A PROSPEROUS NEW YEAR."

In answering a query about whether the garbage at the dump smelled, Seth responds with humor:

[Seth, December 19, 1986]
   Dear Rena,
   To tell you the truth, the tons of garbage did not stink. However, I was looking at it from behind a glass window. . . .

[Rena, January 5, 1987]

[Last line of letter] Well, I better go now, I have to write up my book list. . . . UGH!

Sincerely

Rena

P.S.—I am sorry that this letter is jumbled up together. But I am just too excited. Though I don't know why?

P.P.S.—I loved the library at Bank Street

Near the end of an extremely long letter to Natalie, Seth responds to Natalie's questions by discussing teachers, grownups, a "theory of psychology," and whether or not he is married. The letter has a relaxed tone, even in the face of "thinking out loud" on some serious topics. Being able to deliver and handle the humor is part of the pleasure of this affiliation work.

[Seth, May 4, 1987]

. . . So it is possible that you are becoming mature faster than your friends, so they seem more like children to you. I do not think this idea explains all the reasons, but it might be part of it. Anyway, you should continue to talk to the people that you want to. (Hmmmm . . . this reminds me of a silly joke that my friends used to tell me when I was in college. "You can pick your friends, but you can't pick your friends' noses." Yuck.)

I don't mind you asking me if I am married. In fact, I am not married, and I do not have any children. I guess you don't always have to be married to have children, do you?

Well, I hope things go well for you. Sorry to write such a long answer. I guess my fingers are just relaxed today (hee hee).

As always,

Seth

[Rena, May 20, 1987]

Dear Seth,

A note of warning, PLEASE DON'T BE EATING OR DRINK-ING WHEN YOU READ THIS LETTER ESPECIALLY IN THE SECOND PARAGRAPH . . .

About the garbage that is floating around the ocean, what do you think of it? I think that the garbage should be taken and burned. That way we can probably use it by recycling it. Sometimes, though, the thought that the soda cans I drink from could come from the garbage was togather with dodo. Or even worse they could be from the things we flush down the toilet really gets me sick. Isn't it disgusting?

Do you happen to know what they do to cans that can be recycle? I mean, do they wash them first? . . .

Seth, in his turn, seemed to take on the job of reorienting the students to the E-mail conversations after vacations and extended periods of no contact. These are people making room for each other. This became so true that occasionally one of the students would write a letter with no particular topics and invite Seth to respond with a topic:

[Natalie, January 5, 1987]

I don't have anymore questions at the moment so it's your turn to ask me some. And if there is anything you are curious about please ask.

[Natalie, March 3, 1987]

I'm in a hurry but there's just one question I'd like to ask because I can't remember. Do I owe you a letter or do you owe me one?

Some messages were about affiliation and nothing else. In letters just prior to Seth's visit to the class, affiliation looms large. Once the time and date for Seth's visit are confirmed, Natalie writes with directions to the school. She is excited about the visit and looking forward to sharing the news with Rena, who is out of school in observance of Ramadan. As she closes her communication, she expresses her excitement in a "slip" of sorts by which she manages to tell Seth twice how much she wants to meet him:

[Natalie, May 27, 1987]

. . . Hope I see you soon. Tell your students we look forward to meeting you too [authors' note: *you*, not *them*].
Your Bankstreet Writer, Natalie.

Rena also does affiliation when she writes to Seth on the day of his visit:

[Rena, June 1, 1987]

Dear Seth,

Thank you for your letter. I just read it a few minutes ago. Do you know that I am very cheerful right now? Well, your letter made me even more cheerful and happy. Life is wonderful, isn't it?

I am glad you will be coming this afternoon. As I said before, Natalie and I are dying to meet you. At what time will you be coming?

About keeping in touch after I graduate, I think that would be great! . . .

It's nice to get grandfatherly advices; I don't have a grand-father . . .

I think I'd better stop now; if not, there might be nothing for us to talk about later, if we get to talk!

The messages are thick with affiliation work. With many topics to cover and a pleasant relational space for communication, the conversations touch on issues of importance to the lives of each involved. The correspondents co-construct a space for the mutual exploration of their individual and shared lives.

Questions About Sharing Culture

In her first response to Seth, Rena raises questions about Seth's work with kids:

[Rena, December 12, 1986]

Do you like working with kids. Since you are working with some Jr. High students, I guess you must like working with kids. I know I do. But then again, I am a kid.

Seth follows with a question on why, just because she is a kid, she likes working with kids. She replies with what she calls a "pretty ridiculous and ununderstandable" reason:

[Rena, December 17, 1986]
     You see, since I am a kid, I just have to like working with kids or else I won't be able to work with myself. Do you understand? I hope so.

Seth adds that Rena makes sense and wonders if kids make much better sense with each other than they do when adults are around:

[Seth, December 19, 1986]
     Your reasons for liking to work with kids makes perfect sense to me. It just seems to me that when kids are by themselves, without adults around, then they act very grownup, and then when the adults get around, then the kids think to themselves, well adults are here so I guess that I should act like a kid. I think that is too bad. Do you ever see that happen from your perspective as a kid? I would be really interested to know.

Rena offers an agreement that kids "by themselves . . . try to act like adults" and an important point of clarification: "but we don't necessarily stop because adults are around." Seth bows to her point and offers an account of why he asked. This sounds like the beginning of a good conversation. Children and adults should ask each other for candid opinions, and of course they should negotiate their accounts for a reciprocity of perspective. This can be the groundwork for mutual guidance at some later point. Almost 4 months later, Natalie raises the same issue in a more personal way:

[Natalie, April 28, 1987]
     There is a question I have been trying to find an answer to and I thought you probably would be able to answer it. When I talk to grown-ups I feel so comfortable and learn so alot, but when I talk

to kids my age I feel sort of uncomfortable and so I find I talk to grown-up more. Can you solve this?

Natalie uses E-mail to organize a question that may be difficult to ask those around her. Imagine an anthropological version of her query:

> We seem to have system here in which there are persons called adults and persons called kids, and they seem to have separate arenas of activity, separate roles, and access to quite different rewards in the world. I, Natalie, seem to be having a hard time squaring the cultural definition of these things, on the one hand, and my experience, on the other. Can you get this organized for me?

We cannot expect our children to ask this sort of question, but Natalie gets close. Nor can we expect adults to answer them very easily:

[Seth, May 4, 1987]
> I am afraid I cannot answer your question because I have the same problem!!! That is, when I talk to grown-ups my age, I often feel uncomfortable, but everyone once in a while I meet a person who is very mature, who knows alot, and then I really like talking to them. But I don't meet them very often. So I decided I had to become like these people to, instead of waiting to find people who would be like grownups to me the same way they are for you. Does that make sense?

Ethnographers cannot expect natives to tell them all that they need to know about their culture, and children cannot rely on adults to tell them exactly what cannot be known. But ethnographers and children are alike in profiting in the attempts of others to figure out how the world works, and the more they participate with others in asking difficult questions, the better their grasp of the shared situation. Seth does not remain inarticulate about the relations between children and adults. He becomes professional, cites findings from contemporary psychology, and goes on to explain

how the same person can be different in different settings and how
girls mature faster than boys. He seems to think aloud on paper
about the difficult question she has given him. They are not sure
they are having the culturally correct experiences as children, and
he seems pretty sure that he does not fit the adult mold perfectly.
Together they seem to wonder if anyone has it right.

The students are equally direct in putting other issues up for
Seth's scrutiny and advice. Consider the following exchange on
the class valedictorian and questions about what Seth does at
professional meetings:

[Rena, May 20, 1987]

Sometime next month, on June 22, the sixth grade is going to
graduate. The teacher (I think,) are going to choose a student to
be the grade valedictorian. Mrs. Moore, our (Natalie and I) teacher
said that they will choose the top student who can speak best in
the grade and willing to make a speech. I know that I'm pretty
good student and speech maker, but I am not sure if they will
choose me. I really want to be class valedictorian. In fact I think I'll
kick myself if I don't get choosen. Do you know of any tricks that
would make them choose me? If you do, could you please tell me.

When advice was given, it was well received:

[Rena, June 1, 1987]

And thanks for the grandfatherly advise about getting selected
class valedictorian. It's nice to get grandfatherly advise; I don't
have a grandfather. My Mom's Dad died when she was only four,
and I'm not close with my Dad's, I'm not even close to him!

The students also ask direct questions about the adult world. On
April 19, Seth tells Natalie that he is going to Washington to a
professional meeting of the American Educational Research Association. She replies and asks the difficult question: "So at that
meeting of teachers you were telling me about in your last letter.
Is the purpose of this to find new and better methods of teaching?"
Seth offers facts about kinds of persons and kinds of projects but

leaves untold the possibility that the emperor has no clothes, that in fact no one knows exactly how to generate better methods of teaching. Instead, Seth suggests that Natalie perhaps should go to AERA to get everyone straight about how children are to be taught. Two years later, the children from Earth Lab deliver a demonstration lesson and the results of their work to a packed house at AERA. Cultures cannot always handle direct questions, but sometimes they can grow and expand from the kind of questions Natalie is willing to direct at the world.

How do children ever know that they are doing the right thing, having the right experience, and moving in the right direction? This is a particularly difficult question in a society that is well organized to have many schoolchildren fail. While we have never seen a child publicly applauded for failing in school, it is nonetheless the case that failing is one of the two most obvious ways of going through school in America. How then can children figure out where they are fitting in, where they are going, or where they will wind up? What are their questions and to whom can they be put? Is there a neutral voice somewhere? Can they expect anyone to give "grandfatherly" advice? Similarly, are there contexts in which adults can capture the concerns and voices of children in ways that are not tied to the institutional agenda that has given the children their problems in the first place? Seth did not expect sixth graders to ask about his professional meetings or the details of his paper on algebra. He did not expect them to ask about how he interacts with other adults, and he did not expect to find that they feel better with adults in the same ways he feels better with children.

Culture as an Object of Therapy

There are tremendous limitations to the claims that can be made for the mentoring by E-mail exchanges we have presented, particularly when we refer to them as cultural therapy. By most accounts, therapy is supposed to go deep down inside a real and enduring self, where every object and event is filled with significance.[6]

In contrast, we have only reported that two children and an adult have asked some simple questions of each other. The news is that, given where they live, this is news. The questions are not only asked but answered, and in ways that enable everyone to notice that Seth and the two children are far more like each other than local customs and local borders might allow.

While it is certainly the case that culture both cuts deeply into every person and fully organizes our lives by arbitrary and in some sense false conventions, it is also the case that culture has a flimsy side, a surface set of tricks that keep us from asking interesting questions about ourselves. A cultural therapy could be about the mutual release of people from the behavioral details that keep them from questioning their own life paths.

Our E-mail cultural therapists can profitably address such details, because they are locked into the same culture, but from different places in the system. Such a therapy does not alter the selves involved, but it does give them a sense that other selves are struggling with the same issues. It does not alter the borders separating those who have from those who do not, but neither does it allow everyone to think that borders separate different kinds of persons as much as they separate persons with different points of access to the wider system. Cultural therapy could force us in the long run to go deep into our enduring selves, but it can also raise questions about how we came to think that we had such real selves independent of the workings of the world. The sociologist John Meyer (1986) has recently claimed that the modern person "is both obliged to and institutionally supported to construct a valued subjective self somewhat immune from reality, experience, and action. . . . The modern individual is licensed to construct a strong myth of the self immunized (with much legitimacy and professional support) from the organized social reality" (pp. 200, 216). This is a difficult illusion to maintain. Suppose we could find out from each other that all of us started to worry about our subjective "real" selves independent of the world around us in much the same ways at about the same time in history. Suppose we could find out from each other the many ways we together construct a world in which we seem so distant from each other. In

the case of inner-city schoolchildren, we can imagine how empowering this kind of discovery might be.

Culture gives us limited and limiting answers to the difficult
questions about who we are, and these need to be confronted.
Culture also gives us ways of staying away from questions about
who we are, and these must be confronted also, particularly when
they are in the crass service of lining people up by class and race.
A cultural therapy, by bringing people to a mutual consideration
of the cultural categories that have acquired them, of the cultural
categories that live the lives of the people rather than the other
way around, might be a good way to initiate a confrontation with
the local categories that constrain our relations with each other.
With that version of cultural therapy under way, we would have
begun the hard work of reorganizing the access people have to
resources and, for they are much the same thing, the access persons have to themselves.

Two Educational and Two Theoretical Points

*(1) One-to-one mentoring is a good educational idea, and it is
unfortunate we do not use it more.* It is difficult to imagine a child
who does not need to share experiences with a nearby adult who
is nothing more than on the child's side. A surprising number of
our children now go without thick connections to the people
around them, and mental health professionals, particularly the kind
who keep records, have not filled the gap (Cicourel & Kitsuse, 1963;
Erickson & Shultz, 1982). Traditional communities have been loaded
with such people: grandparents, aunts and uncles, neighbors, and
pastors have all had their turns. Successful programs for people
in trouble consistently invent a mentor's role. Around the world,
members of Alcoholics Anonymous have their sponsors (Bateson,
1972). In urban Tokyo, local businessmen are assigned to local
teenage toughs to guide them in the right direction (Wagatsuma &
DeVos, 1983). And in Guatemalan villages, individuals wandering off
the cultural map are assigned a squadron of concerned persons to
reorganize their lives in what Paul (1963) has called "milieu therapy."

We cannot point to any corresponding fix-up powers in Seth's communication with the students. It is not clear that the students needed any fixing. Much like the rest of us, they needed institutional connections and some guidance now and then. No doubt they had numerous sources, but in their communications with Seth they got another angle, another voice, from the other side of the border. Children do not usually have the opportunity to observe and discuss the daily activities of an adult. The interactions that we have described show that the children were able to learn about aspects of adult life, to share thoughts about problems they were facing, and get perspective from a person who has had more experience. Both adults and children benefit from the interaction. The children benefit from being exposed to Seth's social institutions and the activities that go on in them. The adult benefits from learning to respect and appreciate the considerable maturity that a 10-year-old child has already developed. They got enough to stay with the effort; in January, Rena apologizes for her letter being "jumbled up together. But I am just too excited. Though I don't know why?" It is always worthwhile to have someone to turn to for no particular reason.

(2) E-mail may be a particularly useful medium for a mentoring relationship. Once the system is set up, it is efficient, it takes little time, and it is safe. Who is this man talking to these children? Just what is his interest? These contemporary suspicions will not go away. E-mail requires no face-to-face contact, and the messages are accessible to those maintaining the network. Seth was months into his exchanges with Rena and Natalie when Shelley Goldman started to read them and treat them as data, and other students and Bank Street faculty also followed the exchange and entered the conversations periodically.

Computers alone are not sufficient to change the fundamental problems of education. They only provide a tool that can be adapted and developed in pursuit of educational goals. Even in the short history of computers in schools, we see the institutionalized problems of schools short-circuiting the educational applications of computing. The computer, in its practical application, is neither a neutral goal nor necessarily a great equalizer (Bowers, 1988).

We are concerned about the development of a bifurcated society of computer users and computer nonusers, and we do not want the haves and the have-nots of computers to become the next border that is difficult to cross. We are aware that many of the children in inner-city schools do not come from homes where computer-based opportunities are available. We are aware that most inner-city schools currently have in place the technology base that can support telecommunication. The use of telecommunication in the school context could possibly provide students experience with a socially significant communication network.

A distinctive feature of these telecommunicated interactions is the playing down of power relationships between the mentor and the children. This is one of the few interactions that we know of in which an adult and child can come together as relative social equals. The children have no reason to expect that the adult mentor is going to report the conversations to the teacher or their parents. The adult mentor has no obvious control over the material conditions of their lives. The lack of face-to-face interaction may help to support this coequal relation. Physical size, strength, age and institutional setting differences are neither immediately apparent nor intimidating.

(3) The American educational landscape is filled with varying kinds of people often in communities marked off from each other by well-defined borders. It is a mistake to assume that the various ethnic, racial, and class borders that separate different communities define the learning capacities of the children. The mentoring E-mail exchanges can alert us to how the borders we tend to assume are impermeable—to bus passengers and school competencies, for example—are in fact easy to cross. Given where they live and go to school, it is easy to imagine how Rena, Natalie, and others from Carver School could be denied access to middle-class institutions in America, and easy to imagine, with only our brief view of their lives, how they could be given a chance. Either way, they can be wonderful and capable people. Which way they go depends on what kind of access they are given. Their E-mail exchanges may have helped, for it takes little to make a difference to an individual life. To make the difference for their whole school, or the whole of the Harlem community, takes

much more of an effort, not the least of which will be a new understanding and a reconfiguration of ways in which the knowledge of
the people on the Heights gets privileged and the knowledge of the
people in the Harlem valley gets disparaged. We need no more
theories about what is not known on the wrong side of the border.
We need to cross borders, invent ways for people to establish relationships that confront the stereotypes, and produce and maintain change
in the opportunities available to children; if we do that enough, we
may not need any theories of school failure (Horton, 1991).[7]

(4) A great deal of what is called success in America is not the simple
product of the training people bring to bear on certain problems. Often,
success depends more on strategic moves made in specific contexts on the basis of information only momentarily available to a
few. Whereas Americans used to think in terms of a Protestant
ethic that encouraged and rewarded hard work, increasingly the
socially mobile must think in terms of being in the right place at
the right time (Jackall, 1985). School success is an institutional
success, not to be confused easily with the distribution of actual
knowledge and never to be confused with anyone's potential. The
well-to-do of this country can be quite ordinary people, as dull as
stone even, but they have had to be in the right place at the right
time. In the middle-class school, quite ordinary children, if they
simply follow their noses and do a minimum of work, can do quite
well; by the contours of the same game, children on the other side
of the border can get locked out from the information, contacts,
and connections they need to proceed up the ladder. Everyone could
use a little advice, a little guidance, and not everyone has been getting
their share. There is the promise that more contact can help us to
explore the arbitrary ways in which we have constructed what
counts as useful information. Behind every schoolchild there is
likely to be a system of injustice that organizes our differential
access to the rewards of the system. Cultural therapy over E-mail
is one small way to get kids access.

Notes

1. The neighborhood includes the Bank Street College of Education, where Goldman and Chaiklin worked while collecting the

materials for this chapter. The college is only four blocks from the south end of the park and about a half mile from the school at the north end of the park.

2. On culture as "collective illusion," see Murphy and Murphy (1986); for the short form, "collusion," see McDermott and Tylbor (1983).

3. There were over 600 messages sent on the Earth Lab network from December through June (see Goldman & Newman, 1992), and from this total we separated 41 letters passed between Seth and the two girls over a 6-month period of time. There were a few additional letters that were lost because they were written before we installed a program to collect them automatically or they were not saved properly on the system.

4. The letters reproduced here retain the original grammar and spelling. The full corpus of letters can be obtained by writing to Shelley Goldman at the Institute for Research on Learning.

5. People on the upper side of the Heights would rarely use this route. It starts with the wrong train out of midtown, wrong in the sense that it winds up on the wrong side of the border, and would have a person walking through, as the natives like to say, a "bad neighborhood."

6. On the computer as a target of significance, see the enticing paper by Broughton (1989).

7. We do not suggest the mass marketing of E-mail mentor programs as a cure to the social problems of schooling. Once E-mail relations become institutionalized as a programmatic part of the school, we fear they could lose their effects.

References

Aronowitz, S., & Giroux, H. (1985). *Education under siege.* South Hadley, MA: Bergin and Garvey.

Basso, K. (1990). *Western Apache language and culture: Essays in linguistic anthropology.* Tucson: University of Arizona Press.

Bateson, G. (1972). *Steps to an ecology of mind.* New York: Ballantine.

Black, S. D., Levin, J., Mehan, H., & Quinn, C. N. (1983). Real and non-real time interaction. *Discourse Processes, 6,* 59-75.

Boal, F. W. (1965). Territoriality and class: A study of residential areas in Belfast. *Irish Geography, 6,* 229-248.

Bowers, C. A. (1988). *Cultural dimensions of educational computing.* New York: Teachers College Press.

Broughton, J. (1989). Machine dreams: Computers in the fantasies of young adults. In R. Rieber (Ed.), *The individual, communication, and society.* New York: Cambridge University Press.

Cicourel, A., & Kitsuse, J. (1963). *Educational decision-makers.* Indianapolis: Bobbs-Merrill.

Cuban, L. (1986). *Teachers and machines: The classroom use of technology since 1920.* New York: Teachers College Press.

Drummond, L. (1980). The cultural continuum. *Man, 15,* 352-374.

Erickson, F., & Shultz, J. (1982). *Counselor as gatekeeper.* New York: Academic Press.

Frake, C. O. (1980). The genesis of kinds of people in the Sulu Sea. In A. Dil (Ed.), *Language and cultural description: Selected essays of C. O. Frake.* Stanford, CA: Stanford University Press.

Frake, C. O. (1992). A church too far near a bridge oddly placed. In K. Fukui & R. Ellen (Eds.), *Beyond nature and culture.* Oxford: Berg.

Geertz, C. (1973). *Interpretation of cultures.* New York: Basic Books.

Goldman, S., & Newman, D. (1992). Electronic interactions: How students and teachers organize schooling over the wires. *Interactive Learning Environments, 2,* 31-44.

Horton, M., with J. Kohl & H. Kohl. (1991). *The Long Haul.* New York: Anchor.

Jackall, R. (1985). *Moral mazes.* New York: Oxford University Press.

Levin, J., Rogers, A., Waugh, M., & Smith, K. (1989). Observations on educational electronic networks: The importance of appropriate activities for learning. *The Computing Teacher, 16*(8), 17-21.

Ley, D. (1974). *The black innercity as a frontier outpost: Images and behavior of a Philadelphia neighborhood.* Washington, DC: Association of American Geography.

McDermott, R., & Gospodinoff, K. (1979). Social contexts for ethnic borders and school failure. In A. Wolfgang (Ed.), *Nonverbal behavior.* New York: Academic Press.

McDermott, R., & Tylbor, H. (1983). On the necessity of collusion in conversation. *TEXT, 3,* 277-297.

Mehan, H. (1989). Microcomputers in classrooms: Educational technology or social practice? *Anthropology and Education Quarterly, 20,* 4-22.

Meyer, J. (1986). Self and lifecourse: Institutionalization and its effects. In G. Thomas, J. Meyer, F. Ramirez, & J. Boli, *Institutional structure: Constituting, state, society, and individual.* Newbury Park, CA: Sage.

Murphy, Y., & Murphy, R. (1986). *Women of the forest* (2nd ed.). New York: Columbia University Press.

Newman, D., & Goldman, S. (1987). Earth Lab: A local network for collaborative science classrooms. *Journal of Educational Technology Systems, 15,* 237-247.

Newman, D., & Goldman, S. (1988). Supporting school work groups with communications technology: The Earth Lab experiment. *Children's Environments Quarterly, 5,* 24-31.

Newman, D., Griffin, P., & Cole, M. (1989). *The construction zone.* New York: Cambridge University Press.

Olmsted, F. L. (1856). *A journey in the seaboard slave states, with remarks on their economy.* New York: Dix & Edwards.

Paul, B. (1963). Mental disorders and self-regulating processes in culture: A Guatemalan illustration. In, *Interactions between the social environment and psychological disorders.* New York: Milbank Memorial Fund.

Piller, C. (1992, September). Separate realities. *MACWORLD,* pp. 218-231.

Plath, D. (1980). *Long engagements.* Stanford, CA: Stanford University Press.

Riel, M. (1992). Making connections from urban schools. *Education and Urban Society, 24,* 477-488.

Riel, M., & Levin, J. (1990). Building electronic communities: Success and failure in computer networking. *Instructional Science, 19,* 145-169.

Ruskin, F., & Varenne, H. (1983). The production of ethnic discourse: American and Puerto Rican patterns. In B. Bain (Ed.), *Sociogenesis of language and human conduct.* New York: Plenum Press.

Spindler, G., & Spindler, L. (1989). Instrumental competence, self-efficacy, linguistic minorities, and cultural therapy: A preliminary attempt at integration. *Anthropology and Education Quarterly, 10*(1), 36-50.

Vygotsky, L. (1986). *Thought and language.* Cambridge: MIT Press.

Wagatsuma, H., & DeVos, G. (1983). *The heritage of endurance: Family patterns and delinquency formation in urban Japan.* Berkeley: University of California Press.

Frank H. Logan

10

Youths in an Intensive
At-Risk Program

A Critical Look at Cultural Therapy

FRANK H. LOGAN

Frank H. Logan recently received his Ph.D. from the Stanford University School of Education. About a year ago, at a school of education social, he was asked what he wanted to be when he grew up—a joking reference to his age (50+), student status, and varied past (he is a Vietnam vet and has been a high school teacher, a commercial fisherman working off the West Coast of the United States and Canada, and "homesteader" on a very remote island). He has spent the ensuing year trying to think of an answer to this question. From day to day, the answer varies from "Do I have to grow up?" to "Aren't grownups allowed to have fun?" But when pressed about the future, he expects it will be spent mostly off the ocean and back in civilization. "Overall, if the next decade is half, even 10% as fun and interesting as the previous decades, then I will be completely content." Meanwhile, the saga continues: After a one-year postdoc at the Center for Particle Astrophysics at the University of California, evaluating their self-examination of the culture of science ("one of the strangest native cultures yet to be examined by an anthropologist"), he has taken up an appointment as assistant professor of teacher education at the College of Saint Rose in Albany, New York.

Might there not be an anthropology in which the observer is seen as part of what he observes; in which his observing is taken into account as affecting what he observes? If it is by not asking such questions that stability is maintained, then by asking them might there not be some anthropology to do with change? If we stand back

from the part of ourselves that is part of what we see—between
these two parts of ourselves might there not be freedom for change?

Nicholas Mosley (*Hopeful Monsters*, 1990, pp. 293-294)

In this chapter, it is my intention to illustrate some of the concepts of "cultural therapy" through my experiences studying a
youth at risk program. To help me in this inquiry, I will especially
rely upon the experiences of two of the youths in the program.
William and Lawrence were best friends in junior high, until they
entered high school. William had been one of the people who
helped teach Lawrence about the United States when he moved
here from Nicaragua because his grandmother feared he would be
conscripted by the Sandanistas or the Contras.

Lawrence: Yeah, when I came here, we went to [the same junior high] and
we used to hang out there. It was queer 'cause me and William was
close. We were real close. As soon as we moved into high school ah,
the movie *Colors* came out. Have you seen that movie?

F: No I haven't. Should I?

Lawrence: You *should* see it. Yeah. And it's pretty wicked that way it came
out because you know it got a whole bunch of people in gangs again.
You know, William's black. He took his Crips' side. You know, I'm
Spanish so I took my friends' side. And so we just started battering
each other. You know, we just used to fight all the time. And then, at
the [Ten-Day Summer Program], I was just arguing, and William got
up and said, "You remember, Lawrence? We were friends, man. We
were the closest friends. What happened? As soon as that movie, that
gang movie came out, you took your side." He goes, "We almost
killed each other. I wanted to kill you. You wanted to kill me" and
things like that. He said, "It wasn't worth it. I don't think a friendship . . ." I told him that after that . . . you know I thanked him
after . . . you know because he made me realize, it's not between a
rag[1] that's going to ruin a friendship.

The summer program Lawrence referred to impelled the participants to undergo a thorough self-examination, a reinterpretation

of their lives. One of the by-products of this was their "opening up," which provided a rich contextual body of material about their experiences and the meaning they assigned to them. This material opened my eyes in much the same way that it opened the eyes of the participants, and in doing so it demonstrated the value of what George and Louise Spindler call "cultural therapy" in the first chapter of this book.

Based upon my study of the youth at risk program, I see cultural therapy as having two main thrusts. The first is the same as that proposed by the Spindlers: to facilitate situating the youths in the mainstream culture by showing them how cultural factors in their own biographies and their schooling have interfered with successful adaptation. This includes showing them how the counter-culture's values are perversions of their enduring traditional values.

The second role is more strictly therapeutic: to provide a means for the youths to get things off of their chests, to provide catharsis for the built-up pressures that have resulted from internalizing adverse experiences—to somehow redeem the enduring self and its role of providing self-esteem. Both of these functions were visible in the program I observed.

The Program

The program featured two components: a 10-day summer program and a 1-year follow-up or consolidation. The participants consisted of 55 youths who volunteered to "turn their lives around" and many support people including approximately 150 adult volunteers who worked with the youths during the intensive 10-day summer program, 20 professional consultants who supervised the summer program, and 75 adult volunteers who worked with the youths during the year following the summer program. Of this latter group of adults, approximately 65 were mentors to the youths and approximately 25 served as organizers and facilitators for mandatory monthly meetings. Some adults filled multiple roles. The youths were volunteers who signed contracts to observe the rules of the program after being identified by school counselors and social workers.

The summer program was strong medicine, but, observing the youths during the early days, it was clear that strong medicine was called for. The youths had signed an agreement to leave their gang paraphernalia behind, but the boys still moved around together in their gangs, and when the adults pressed them get rid of their colors, they used hand signals to take the place of the colors. During the first days, they were surly and there was tension in the air. One of the facilitators told me, "It may look like we're losing it, like we're going to lose it, but we know what we're doing. We have to bring things to a head before they can be resolved."

A look at one of the early interactions will help in visualizing the program's methods. The instructor, Arnold, began the session by asking: "Tell me something you're resigned to." This was followed by an outpouring of information of the kind that makes your hair stand on end.

Mike: Cheating myself, because I don't get better grades. My aunt said I should get my GED. I feel bad. My sister does well in school. But now I've accepted the situation. I barely get by. I hate it. I get in moods. In the back of my head, I'm thinking what a fucker I am. I get in arguments with my parents.

Robert: Trying to live up to others' expectations. I was adopted by my parents, and I never got good grades. They were always dogging me. I wonder if she actually cares. I'm living others' lives, not my own. It's also difficult to have my dad out of the house.

Kenneth: I'm in a cycle of getting kicked out of the house and going off to juvenile. This has been going on for 2-3 years. I get sent to a psychiatric hospital and locked up. I get in physical fights with my stepdad, and Mom calls the police. He used to hit me, and I'd go around with all the bruises. Finally I got fed up and hit him back. My mom says she hates me, and tells my sister to hate me. I thought hitting him back would stop him, but it didn't.

Luke (jumbled): When I was 3 years old, my mom was still young, 17. My dad held a knife to my throat at the door to make my mom do something. [Luke's mother is addicted to drugs. This led to his little brother getting locked up for possession of cocaine.] Mom wanted drug money. She forced him to carry drugs. Pinned him down.

Anthony (crying): Mom fucked me up too. When I was little, I was like a little brain child. (anger) My mom never said shit. She's never seen one of my report cards. At least Mike and Robert have parents who care enough to get on your case. I've never gotten a hug from that bitch. I haven't had a hug from anyone since my grandmother died. Then my dad raped my sister—I was supposed to go with her to help at the store, but I was too tired, so my younger brother went with her. My mom said it was my fault my sister got raped. I almost shot my dad, I swear to God, I had the gun out of the drawer at his store. This is the first time I've ever told anyone this.

Abe (who was crying even before he began): I never had anybody to love me, I never had toys or nothin' when I was little. I've never told anyone. (falls back into his chair) I got abused sexually. It went on and on. I was 8 years old, and I thought it was normal. I didn't know there was anything wrong with it. It was a friend of my family's. It went on for 5 years . . . then later I discovered it wasn't normal . . . (pause while Abe pulls himself together) . . . I started doing drugs to hide myself. I wanted to kill myself. People would hold a gun to my head for a joke and I would say, "Go on motherfucker, shoot me, I'll pull the trigger myself!" I'd get black moods and I'd just go out and shoot somebody. I've hurt people, killed people. I'm not good for nothin'. I got stabbed, I wish I'd been shot, to take away my pain.

Patricia: I was sexually molested for 8 years, just like Abe. I thought it was normal too. It was my four cousins and I never told. By the time I realized it was wrong, when I was 14, I felt it was too late. I've never told anyone. I'm very insecure, I don't have any self-respect. My parents don't know. I don't get any love from my dad. I'm afraid to tell them.

Elizabeth: I was coming across a field at school and I felt something, I thought it was a shadow. There was a security man but he was too far away to hear me. I got raped. I stopped going to school. I can't get close to anyone. I can't report it because my mother thinks that if I'm not a virgin, no man will want me. The man knows where I live, he was on PCP when he raped me. Later he broke into my house and tried to rape another girl. She got away and he was placed in jail. He writes me messages from jail. "I'm going to get you" and things. The worst of it is that I can't talk to my mother any more. To her, my virginity is all I have to offer a man.

Denise: I was molested twice and raped once. I was living with my grandmother at the time, and it was my older cousin. I was 6 or 8. Then, when I was 11, my mother's friend raped me. When I got raped, I thought it was my fault. My parents know. I didn't go to court. I didn't want to go through all that stuff.

Robert: I want to tell Abe that he isn't the only one. My stepdad molested me in the living room. Later he told my mom, who was asleep. My mom blames me.

Passages like this have changed me and changed the way I look at inner-city youths and cultural therapy. It is common to see youths like these as being irresponsible, but from their words it now seems to me that they are hyperresponsible. They are victims of horrible experiences, but they accept responsibility for those experiences and allow them to define who they are. They are nonvirgins, cheaters, fuckers—the kind of people for whom things don't work out right. Before they had a chance to develop belief in themselves, irresistible outside agencies overwhelmed them. Abe thought sex with adults was normal; now he hates himself for allowing something unspeakable to be done to him without protest. Elizabeth lost the only thing she had to offer a man, so what future does she have left? Patricia doesn't have any self-respect; she, too, thought the unspeakable was normal. Luke and Anthony were not able to protect their siblings from their parents and they blame themselves!

It is common to blame school failure for self-esteem problems. Self-esteem deficits are attributed to failure to acquire instrumental competencies and to the low expectations of teachers and others. But these are weak forces compared with being put into hopeless situations and learning to lose. This process begins before the child enters school—in some instances, before birth.

Self-efficacy perceptions are not entirely self-determined. They are an interpretation of experience. Experience is open to alternate interpretations, but these are often beyond the control of the child, and it is easy to see that appalling experiences have the power to take control of children's lives away from them. At the same time, the fact that some children are able to survive the worst surroundings suggests that different interpretations are possible, even if not totally within the individual's control, and that we can address such problems through addressing the interpretations people give to their experiences.

The Spindlers correctly note that failure to become situated in the mainstream culture leads to "reaffirmation, withdrawal, constructive marginality, biculturalism, and assimilation" (Spindler & Spindler, 1989a, p. 8), but missing from the picture is how these reactions manifest themselves upon the next generation through physical abuse, sexual abuse, and emotional abuse—all of which are by-products of the failure to become situated—manifestations of the endangered self.

Getting the individual to consider alternative interpretations is a part of the process the Spindlers had in mind when they said, "Perhaps both teachers and students have to become ethnographers, studying each other and themselves" (Chapter 1 of this volume).

The program I observed set about the process in a logical way. A look at another of the early interactions will help in visualizing this process.

The instructor, Arnold, began the session by asking: "Where is the probable future?"

This was a confusing question and nobody rushed to answer. Arnold drew two circles on one of the blackboards. One, he labeled "the past," and the other, he labeled "the present," and then he asked: "Where does the present come from?" Several of the youths answered: "The past."

Arnold said, "OK. And where does the future come from?"

"From the present!" answered several youths, in chorus.

"OK. So where is the probable future?" Again, the youths were puzzled by the question, so Arnold said: "The present comes from the past, and the future comes from the present, so where is the probable future?"

Mark ventured, "In the past?"

Arnold answered, "In the past!" He drew an arrow from the past to the future. "You're saying that the past shapes what you do now. Is there really a future if your life is shaped by your past?"

Mark grappled with the question, without saying anything clear enough to summarize. Arnold said, "Your future is a conversation. If your present is colored by your past, then you're living your future in your past. If you're living your future in your past, then your future is totally predictable. That's your probable future."

This was unclear, and Arnold went over the same progression again, and again: "It's like a railroad track. It starts here, and it goes here (pointing to the two circles on the blackboard)—you can't get off the track."

Denise objected. The microphone was taken to her and she was asked to stand. "My parents used to drink and do crack. . . . Now they are both ministers and have their own mission in the neighborhood."

Arnold was delighted with this: "Yes! There is always the possibility of a different future. A possible future. It's like a railroad track, but there are branches. You have a choice of destinations."

Arnold called out a student's name: "Mike, you heard that you were not going to graduate, so you quit trying. You hear it all over, you're Hispanic, Mexican, Eastside. You ain't got no chance." He called out another student's name, "Abe, you have no chance. No support. No avenues or examples. You have to go with what you know and you don't know shit."

We have now seen examples of course work designed to fulfill the two functions that cultural therapy must perform if it is to be effective. Immediately above, the instruction was designed to open the participants up to new interpretations of their lives. Earlier, the session in which the participants were encouraged to get things off their chests allowed them to purge the emotions they had stored up that interfered with seeing themselves as redeemable. Both these functions have to do with the enduring self, which can redeem the situated self, but only if it is relatively intact. But in the cases we have seen, which I believe are typical, the enduring selves were not intact, and before they could play a role in redemption, they had to be salvaged.

The program's use of both these elements appeared to be effective. I have already mentioned how my passive participation opened *me* to new interpretations. For the active participants, the effects were often electric. One of the most dramatic openings came during a night session midway through the summer program. It began earlier when Abe said he was going to get out of the gang and Lawrence jumped up in exasperation or disgust and said, "Abe, you talk brave about getting out of the gang! Here in the course room is one thing, but it's not going to be like that back in the neighborhood. They're going to read you out!"

A short shouting match ensued between Abe and Lawrence about whether Abe would have enough backbone to get out or not. (As a matter of interest, Abe told me in a pre-course interview that it would be impossible to get out of the gang *because* he would have to be read out—a ritual similar to running the gauntlet—sometimes fatal.)

Then William jumped up: "I can't believe this is you, Lawrence! You weren't like this as a kid. I hung around with you all the time and you weren't like that. Lawrence, you've changed. What happened? The gangs are just what Arnold is saying. I wish I'd never joined. How many of you guys wish you never joined? [lots of hands and a roar of assent] Come on, Lawrence, don't you wish you'd never joined?"

The climax to this drama came the next evening when Lawrence said, "Ah, eh, after yesterday we were talking it over late last night. I learned . . . I guess a lot of people know me better than I know myself. So I'm . . . I'll have to give it up."

Arnold asked, "You'll quit the gang?"

Lawrence answered, "Yeah."

It is important to understand that part of the process that allows cultural therapy to explore the elements of a person's culture that interfere with cultural transformation is the construction of a cultural climate that supports the process. The Spindlers suggest that schooling is a "calculated intervention" in people's lives, but we should note that schooling also consists of uncalculated interventions. Often the uncalculated aspects of a school's culture negate the calculated ones. Part of cultural therapy consists of bringing the uncalculated interventions under control. This is done through consciously designing the school's culture, whether a public school or an intervention program. The program for youth at risk provides an excellent example of this.

Cultural Therapy and the Program's Culture

Much of the program's effectiveness came from its success in designing its own culture.

William: It was, it was, it was, it was, see, for all the gangsters it was cool. . . . We was in heaven 'cause we could kick it. Lay back, you know, go to sleep. Like you couldn't sleep out here—here in the park—you couldn't sleep out here.

F: 'Cause why?

W: Somebody come over and stab your ass or something . . .

F: It was their first time to rest?

W: Yeah. They could act like kids. They could act like kids. "ahhh" (playful kid noise).

Abe put it in terms similar to William's: "Being here is like being in a fantasy world. I have to go through four neighborhoods when I'm at home, and I have to run. It's hard to go to adults for help, because they're my enemy."

It will be useful for those who are considering cultural therapy to take a look at how the program built this special culture, what William called a fantasy world, to enhance its effectiveness.

A key element was the program's intensive effort to pour adult support on the youths, which began with the enthusiastic entrance of screaming and yelling adult volunteers into the course room on the first day. Adult support was lavish every day during the physical exercises, in the mess hall, in the course room, and at night in the dormitory. If the youths had concluded that adults were the enemy, here was refutation. Even with the youths in adolescent rebellion against their parents and in generational rebellion against school authorities, these efforts of the adult volunteers to reach out had an effect. By the end of the Ten-Day

Summer Program, relationships had been formed between many of the youths and the facilitators, who lived in their dorms, attended class with them, and ran all the physical training with them. The work of the adults to support the youths was one of the things that made the Ten-Day Program a safe place to "kick it" in William's words and also helped make the monthly meetings into "a clearing," in the program's words. As the participants became comfortable in the group, even if becoming comfortable was only a matter of becoming familiar, the process led to a degree of acculturation that brought the program's intellectual and emotional content along with it.

Forging the individuals into a society was facilitated by a group of strictly physical provisions during the summer program consisting of the way the course room was set up. The youths and adult facilitators were compressed into a tight group, much like the way fans are compressed during a basketball game. Everybody was touching the persons next to them. In the heat of summer, nobody could move without bumping somebody. Privacy barriers at first rebelled against the closeness. Boredom and body odors made this personal violation all the more offensive. What makes a society is common psychological forces combined with a common experience, and soon the common experience of heat and discomfort of the course room and the high emotional content of the meetings began to form the participants into a society, and the acceptance of the touch and smell of neighbors became a form of social support as privacy barriers came down. Thus a primarily physical marriage in the course room became a strong force in facilitating a marriage of minds, and there began to be a group response to the instruction with the end result that a culture was formed, one whose precepts had been skillfully managed by the program's facilitators.

I must point out that the program's ability to use these tactics depended upon the youths' fulfilling the contracts they had signed. To use such measures in a school setting would require some similar means of ensuring compliance.

This acculturation of the youth was increasingly apparent during the winter meetings. Youths I interviewed were able to verbalize the lessons and testified convincingly that they believed them and had internalized them. Many were highly resistant to the group meetings in the beginning, with some acting out while others were a sullen presence in the back of the room. But by the end of the program, most had become comfortable with the group. They engaged in the group's hugging culture. They were cheerful and respectful in their interactions with the adults.

I hope the point is clear, then, that there needs to be more to cultural therapy than a mutual analysis of the participants' culture: There also needs to be culture that will condone the process and accept the participants as new members. In his classic analysis *The Rites of Passage*, van Gennep showed how the first step in traditional rites of passage is to kill the culture being left (van Gennep, 1960). Clearly, this is something that cannot be done from within the old culture—it is something the old culture would not tolerate.

The program's culture building centered on a group of key cultural values: commitment, responsibility, support, communication, relationship. Acting from these values translates them into instrumental competencies. Accepting and learning to act from these ideals would situate an individual in the culture he or she defines.

The value "commitment" was integrated with a view of "the self" and the value put upon "responsibility." If you accept that the self is redeemable, then the next step is to be responsible to a commitment for change. Through this logic, responsibility became one of the chief cultural values of the program.

The Culture of Responsibility

One key cultural "distinction" was the program's maxim that you should not blame others for what happens to you but should take responsibility for yourself. It is both a practical imperative and an ethical rule. Practically, you cannot be the captain of your destiny if you do not take responsibility for it. You cannot both take responsibility and blame others for how it turns out.

The logic of this ethical rule was problematic for several of my coworkers in the evaluation of the program. Telling the youth to forgive their parents for egregious abuses (for example) shocked them, and they worried that this would prevent the youth from dealing effectively with the psychological effects of the abuse. I think the opposite turned out to be true. Airing these problems and encouraging the youths to forgive their parents had a therapeutic effect. By the end of the year, one youth told me he took the major step of confronting his father and that this finally laid the issue to rest.

A girl told us in the course room that her father was abusing her physically. When she took this issue home and confronted her father, it led to her mentor and several public agencies becoming involved. This was a difficult situation. In the end, everybody decided that the father was not guilty of abuse but was trying to give appropriate discipline. But in the process, everybody learned how father and daughter were engaged in reciprocal emotional abuse. Bringing the issue out into the open made it possible to begin to resolve the problem, and by the end of the year progress had been made.

A history of abuse exists for each of us, but what are we to make of it? Does it not all trace back to the same kind of mistakes and failures that we are, ourselves, all prone to? And if this is so, then how should we hate or blame someone for acting as we might have under the same circumstances?

The program's answer is forgiveness. Forgiveness does not mean approval, it just means understanding it and putting it behind you. It means being able to put yourself in the other's position. It means compassion, empathy, love. Most youths do not put themselves in their parents' place—in fact, for most, the parents' place is completely incomprehensible. They see only the behavior, not its causes. The program began the process of demystifying the parents and showing how they had been affected by their surroundings in the same way as the youths. In this way, they developed variations on the Christian themes of turning the other cheek, forgiveness, and loving your enemy, with a secular rationale—one that explains that self-determination is impossible without forgiveness. It should also be noted that this process was one of the ways the program delved into the culture of the participants in a way that was personal but not ego threatening—which of course is what we mean to do with cultural therapy.

I hope it is clear that "responsibility" is both a cultural instrument that led to a cultural situation and also, once introduced to the youths, a means of continuing the process of reinterpreting their lives. Thus the lessons of responsibility and forgiveness both helped the youths become situated into a culture that draws power from being responsible and used that power to put back together the fragmented enduring self, so it could be a source of self-esteem.

The Culture of Support and Communication

Because self-image is important in the acceptance of criticism, this culture of responsibility demands a stable, positive self-image. Therefore it is logical that the second major cultural more of the program was its support and communication ethic, which had the practical purpose of improving self-image. The idea was that communicating and giving and accepting support are instrumentalities that give power to those who use them. During the year, these concepts increasingly came to define the culture of the program. But like responsibility, support and communication were also methodological tools used in the course's day-to-day operation. The program's Socratic teaching methods relied upon the youths' willingness to communicate. Successful Socratic teaching created a bond between the course's intellectual distinctions, the youths' lives, and their emotional and normative being. This led the youths to stop blaming themselves for their past experiences and to begin to see themselves as lovable.

Communication facilitated the development of relationships between the youths and their mentors, and these relationships reinforced the youths' seeing themselves as lovable. Communication allowed the youths to get things off their chests. Communication gave the youths the support of knowing that their problems, mistakes, and sins were not unique. Hearing and understanding, and saying and being understood, led the youths to feel the support that was available. And it felt good! It felt good once the youths dropped the barriers that had made it impossible to feel it.

Communication and support were modeled in the same way responsibility was. One of the chief purposes of the daily physical activities was to create a milieu where support could be modeled and where the youth could see how helpful it really was. It was a context where it was more socially acceptable among their peers to give and accept support than in less physical situations.

Is This Really Cultural Therapy?

I think the treatments of this program clearly are an instantiation of cultural therapy. The machismo ethic is a strong cultural force in the Hispanic and black communities. He who is macho is never wrong, never to blame, never needs help, never allows criticism. Might and strength make everything right. We tend to ascribe machismo primarily to Hispanic culture, but it is a more universal trait that is amplified among those who react to the threats to their personal and cultural efficacy beliefs engendered by low social status. *Machismo* is the Hispanic term but there are alternatives from other cultures, such as *face, pride,* and *hubris.* Machismo was discussed in the course room and several of the adult volunteers gave examples from their lives where machismo had had bad effects.

In addition to ethnic cultures, machismo is associated with adolescent society. Among adolescents, it is not far-fetched to say that the macho way of devaluing responsibility, support, and communication is cultural, even though we are now edging into the psychological realm. If it is proper to talk about an adolescent culture as distinguished from adult culture, then this way of looking at responsibility is cultural. One consequence of the adolescent self-identification process is being hypercritical to advice and criticism. "I want to do it my own way," is the adolescent's rallying cry, even if it means making mistakes and getting hurt. This is probably because a developing identity is insecure.

When a strong sense of personal identity exists, advice and criticism are nonthreatening, even welcome. Some people, on the contrary, are perennial adolescents and a common reason for this kind of arrested development is the failure to build a strong sense of identity and/or self-identification with a negative image.

Opening up. As mentioned earlier, one of the chief benefits of cultural therapy is opening up and getting things off your chest. Some of the preceding excerpts offered examples of how it went. The youth who blamed himself for letting his father rape his sister, for example, told me later that the chief benefit of the program, for him, was getting things off his chest. This opening up is doubly therapeutic because it acts both as an end and as a means. The value of being open (openness as an end) was evident from the relationship between students' self-improvement and their willingness to accept criticism and to offer contributions to classroom discussions. As a means, the opening up provides data for the self-reevaluation process discussed immediately above. A side benefit is the information it provides others about the lives of the participants in such a program. This is not circumstantial. For such a therapy to work, I think "both teacher and students have to become ethnographers, studying each other and themselves," to repeat the quote from the Spindlers (Chapter 1, this volume).

Earlier, I presented two conversations between William and Lawrence. These two conversations focused my attention on Lawrence and William, so I followed them through the program. As a result of their opening up, I got an excellent tutorial on California gang organization, history, and culture.

Lawrence came to the United States at age 10. By age 18, he had a solid understanding of the local gang culture, the rites of the gangs, and their historical roots. I conducted my interview of him while we were walking through a local mall so he could show me some of his gang's hangouts and explain their activities.

L: See those guys there? That's the way I used to dress. Baggy pants—take charge pants. It's the regular way, 'cause there's no guy that gangs around and they're going to be wearing tight pants and stuff like that. You always have to wear very loose, 'cause you don't know what you'se going to expect from the gang fight. So you have to be wearing loose clothes so you can fight better, you can kick better, or whatever comes up. So you always have to be wearing loose clothes. And that's how you know how a gangster looks.[2]

Explaining the motivation for these gang fights, Lawrence said: "It is crazy. It was [used to be] for your land, where you live. That was what you used to fight for. After a while it went from where you live, to a rag."

F: A rag is?

L: A rag is a, you know, the color they claim. Red, blue, maroon.

Beatrice (Lawrence's mentor): Bandannas rolled up a particular way.

F: During the Ten-Day they asked what the purpose of the gang was, and the answer was "to protect the neighborhood." Does the neighborhood need protecting?

L: Part of it was to protect the neighborhood. Part of it. 'Cause sometimes other gangs used to come and get your cars and stuff like that. Part of it was to protect where you're from. What you're coming from, what you're going to do in the future. You *think* you're down for your shit. What you believe in. That the rag you carry in your pocket, *that's* what you're down for. But see, now that I'm just kicking back, I'm laying low, not in gangs. I finally understand that a rag . . . A rag right here can cost you what? 49 cents?

Beatrice (Lawrence's mentor): 98 cents.

L: OK, 99 cents, a dollar at the most. You carry that rag around in your pocket. You get shot. How much is your life worth? 99 cents! For carrying a rag, when that rag was meant to what, to carry to blow your nose, to clean your sweat. It goes on and on and on. (Lawrence points to a group of boys) See?

F: Are they blues?

L: Yeah. You can only tell by the blue bandannas they have on. And it's just like that. If we used to see them like that, we'd stop them, "Are you guys claiming or what?"[3]
"'Yeah, we're down for our shit.'"
"Well, we're down for ours, so let's step outside."

Boom, boom, boom, boom, the fight used to go on. They used to kick our asses, but we used to kick their asses. It was over.

This led to a discussion of the different gangs:

L: The *Sudeños*, which are the Hispanic blue raggers, come from Mexico to the United States. And the *Norteños*, which are the red raggers, they're born here. They are Chicano. They believe in the United States. They're Mexican Chicanos and the Sudeños come right here and try to take over their land.

F: OK, how does a Nicaraguan fit into this?

L: I came here and I wasn't born here,

F: So that makes you ah,

L: That makes me, like ah if I wanted to claim something, I would claim like blue. But my family, I have uncles, they believe in red![4] So I'm gonna believe in red.

F: Some guys grow out of the gangs. If times get tough, might they be called upon?

L: Yes.

F: And would you be in that position?

L: If my family was getting in trouble? Yes. [. . .]

F: I'm still not sure I got it right. The Bloods . . .

L: All right, now I'm going to tell you every little thing the gangs are supposed to know. There was three kinds of gangs. The "N" came out because the "N" is the fourteenth letter in the alphabet. So that's how the "N" came out and that's how the number came out. The "N" never used to stand for *Norte*. It stood for *Nuestra Familia*. Our Family. The "M" is the thirteenth letter in the alphabet so that's how they used the 13 and it never stand for Sul, it stands for Mexican Mafia. There was Nuestra Familia and the Mexican Mafia and the Border Brothers. The Border Brothers were the kind of Mexicans they used to come from the border and tried to claim the South. So there was three different gangs. And then in time the North, you know, the "N" came to stands for Norte, and the "M," it stood for Mexican Mafia, you know, the 13 came to stand for the South and then in time the Border Brothers disappeared.

. . . Ask any little gangster, you go like this (makes an "N" with his fingers), tell them, "What does the 'N' stand for?"

"And they say, 'Norte.' "

"What does it stand for?"

" 'I don't know. I'm a color because my parents were in it. My friends were in it.' "

That's the stupidest reason that they can give you.

F: Well, why were you in it?

L: I got in it 'cause my parents, my dad he used to treat me like shit, like I didn't exist. So I got in it because the gang was my family. They used to take care of me.

For Lawrence, joining the gang was a process of drifting, and he views the gangs as having lost their original meaning. This view was reinforced by what others said. Jacob, who had been recently released from prison for burglary, described becoming a gang member in a similar way:

J: I used to get good grades. Most the people in the program . . . not most, but some that I grew up with. I mean they went to the same school I went to, and stuff like that, and we just grown up and when we hit the teens, like 13, 14, it was time for to do something else. Just time to do something else.

William also appears to have just drifted into gang membership. The way he explained it, the group of boys he associated with as a child just naturally came to be associated with the Crips as adolescents, and when the movie *Colors* came out, they just naturally adopted blue as their color.

William also explained how membership in rival gangs estranged him from Lawrence: "We weren't really fighting, just verbally. We wasn't really fighting. You know, we wasn't really fighting. Naw. We, we almost had a couple fights, man. We almost had a couple. 'Cause of his friends, you know, his friends, you know, 'Ah, Lawrence, who's that? Talk to him.' All this and all that shit.

"I was like, 'You shut up.' I guess Lawrence, he had to step in with his friends. It's like, his friends say something to my friends. My friends say something back, and they'll look at me and Lawrence, you know."

William's previous description of how taunting leads to fighting is similar to Lawrence's picture of mall confrontations: " 'Are you guys claiming or what?'

" 'Yeah, we're down for our shit.'

" 'Well, we're down for ours, so let's step outside.'

"Boom, boom, boom, boom, the fight used to go on. They used to kick our asses, but we used to kick their asses."

These two pictures should be familiar to any one who has seen *Westside Story*. For that matter, this exchange from *Romeo and Juliet* (act 1, scene 1) should make it plain that this is a universal form of confrontation:

Abraham: Do you bite your thumb at us, sir?

Sampson: Is the law of our side if I say ay?

Gregory: No.

Sampson: No, sir, I do not bite my thumb at you, sir, but I bite my thumb, sir.

Challenging Popular Scenarios

The way these young men describe the adolescent passage into gangs challenges two popular scenarios that describe how minority youths fail. A "deficit" scenario follows the sequence: Youth fails school tasks, youth fails to learn mainstream culture, youth seeks alternative source of self-esteem, the gang becomes the only society that will have him. In the Spindlers' words, "Children acquire deficits in self-esteem when they fail to master essential instrumentalities" (Chapter 1, this volume).

The second scenario, the resistance theory scenario, views the youth as being tormented by having to choose between family and mainstream values. Out of loyalty to the family, the youth chooses family values and the gang. The Spindlers refer to this as "doing what persons coming into a new cultural situation must do if they wish on the one hand to 'get along' and learn and at the same time to keep their identities" (Chapter 1, this volume).[5] The problem is that getting along, and keeping their identity, are often incompatible with learning.

Neither the resistance scenario nor the self-esteem deficit scenario fits the stories told by my informants. To be sure, the techniques I used to gather information did not have the ability to probe early school factors, which are commonly discussed in the literature in this field, and which give poor and minority youths poor self-expectations, but there were several things that came out in my interview that changed the way I look at the matter.

First, we have the contention of William, Lawrence, and others that they were exemplary students up to high school—at least in their own estimation. If so, it was not failure to learn or adapt to mainstream culture that pushed them into the gangs. Rather, they formed natural associations with their peers and, without their making conscious decisions, these became gang affiliations. They did not choose gangs; in a sense, the gangs chose them. But by becoming gang members, they associated themselves with the expectations the public has of gang members. In other words, an identity choose them, which had been constructed socially out of the expectations of people from their set and from the outside, without their having made a conscious decision one way or the other.

Resistance theory views such youngsters as rejecting the mainstream, but such views ignore the positive attraction of instrumentalities that are adaptive in a marginal culture, such as dealing drugs, fighting, and talking ghettoese. This should be held firmly in mind when analyzing what some have seen as resistance. Positive reinforcement is a much more practical cause than the abstract negative motive of cultural loyalty that is usually attributed as a cause of resistance and "antisocial" behavior. In fact, the gangsters' behavior is as antisocial to their neighbors as to the mainstream, which also argues against the idea that resistance comes from loyalty to family. We must not confuse dark, reactive, self-destructive behavior with behaviors that are adaptive within the subculture of the youth. The gangster's loyalty is cultural loyalty only in terms of the specific culture of the gang. I view the gang as a culture with its own instrumentalities, and membership as a form of cultural situation. Many of the self-destructive elements of gang membership should be ascribed to conflicts between the enduring self and the situated self, because gang values do not successfully reflect the traditional values of the enduring family culture.

One of the critical factors that is thought to lead to resistance is the demand to substitute the enemy's ethos for the ethos of their family, but after talking to William, I questioned whether the ethos of his family, as defined by his mother and brother, was very different than the ethos of middle-class America, despite the thick ghettoese accent that is discernible in William's speech. William made a major point of contrasting the culture of his home with that of his friends:

> My family. As far as my family wise. Mom and that stuff . . . if you come to my house, you wouldn't think bad gangsters, you know, live up there. 'Cause we got trophies, you know, and family pictures sitting up. Like they call our house the Brady Bunch. They think that we're classics. . . . You go to my house. . . everything's clean. That's my mother. Everything's clean. 'Cause she lived her life already in that, she's done that. She already done all that. It's still in her, but she's got kids now. Most parents, most young parents, at the time, they don't think about that at the time. You can't be doing what you still doing.

As far as I could tell, William and his friends were motivated by the desire for the things that all Americans are taught through advertising to desire. Where William's associates differ are the means they are taught will fulfill their desires:

> A lot of my friends, they get into drugs 'cause they got to have things. They ain't got no diploma to get no job, so the best thing they got going for them like . . . it's good and it's bad. See, it's bad. All of it's bad. But it's good if you don't get caught. That's the good part about it. Like my cousin, he's my age. You know he's got a Benz, Cutlass, eight, nine cars. . . . Right across the street, right across the street from me . . . where you parked your car . . . That's the dope man's

house. You know, that's the big house. And he don't make it!? Right now! So he's got his men working for him right now, running around for him and everything. And they, they they just want to have things. That's it. You know, and most of it's just junk. Like, you know, like when you're young you want to have everything your friends have. Like we used to go, we still, you know, you see a brand new G.I. Joe toy on TV. You know, we ain't ever seen that. So when you're older, everything you didn't have, you'll want. Like if I'm just sitting here. I want that car to buy it. If I have to sell dope I'm going to, to buy that car, to get that car.

It is difficult for me to see resistance to white ways and values in William. It looks more like a struggle to achieve the whites' status through whatever channels are available. This was even more clear when I asked William about his uncle. I had arrived at William's home a few minutes early for an interview, and nobody was home, so I sat in my car to wait for him. Soon two men arrived in a pickup truck and began to work on the truck's brakes. After one of them finished working under the truck, apparently bleeding the brakes, the other started racing the truck down the street and then stopping with a screech of the brakes. Then he would repeat the sequence in reverse. Apparently, they were trying to adjust the brakes so they didn't pull off to one side. I had begun to wonder if William had stood me up, so I went over and asked the man who was standing by watching if he knew William. "Sure, he's my nephew," he said.

He was an older man with only a few teeth left, wearing dirty, old, ragged clothes; a man who had been severely battered by life, you could tell. The combination of a heavy Louisiana accent and missing teeth made it difficult to understand him, but it was immediately clear, despite a forbidding appearance, that he was not going to be dangerous to me. He was quite friendly and we stood talking for several minutes.

When William arrived, we took a drive and William showed me the neighborhood. I commented that it looked like a decent place to live. He snorted: "Huh? The police helicopter practically lives over my house at night, shining its searchlight through my window." And he went on to give the local crime report that doesn't make the papers. The woman raped over by the freeway, the drive-by shootings, rival gangs running down the streets, guns in hand. At one corner, he pointed out the local "acid man" serving cars that pulled up alongside for an instant and then sped off again.

I mentioned talking to his uncle and said that he seemed like too good a mechanic to be out of work. By this time, I had the tape recorder going, so I got everything William said when he responded: "That worthless old piece of junk? I ain't never going to be like that. He's a ruin. He got no pride in himself. He's dirty. No class. No, there's no way I'm going to turn out like that." Later in the interview, William said, "I want to have stuff, want to. . . . You know, unlike my uncle, I don't want to be doing that shit. Working on other people's cars, all dirty and ugly and shit. He's ugly, and that's, that's, ughh, I can't see myself like that."

Maybe William overreacted because of a suppressed fear that he could end up like that, but even if this was the case, clearly it was an end he feared, not respected. Resistance theory credits the young with more sympathy for their elders than I believe exists. I think that, if there is a reaction against white ways, it is more a case of sour grapes than loyalty to family.

This is an important point because one thing about sour grapes is that nobody ever chooses the sour ones when the sweet ones are available—in less metaphorical terms, a youth who has formed a reaction against "white ways" because they are unavailable to him will rarely turn down a nice car, jewelry, house, job, and the "white" way of talking that goes with them, once they are offered.

There are complex push-pull phenomena at work here. The pull of the counterculture lies both in its adaptiveness for its milieu and for the self-sustaining approval it gives those who have suffered ego damage from coming up against the prejudices and low expectations of the mainstream. The "push" relates to negative social expectations of the children of poverty. Terrible things happen in all segments of our society, but they are expected to happen to "certain kinds of people." When they are not expected and happen, as for mainstream children, they are seen as anomalies; but when they are expected and happen, they become self-fulfilling prophecies. Tell a clearly definable segment of the population they are incapable, and every failure confirms that view, and self-esteem suffers. Low self-esteem creates black moods and leads to destructive behavior and at the same time it leads the affected individuals to seek sources of self-approval, such as the gangs.

Self-efficacy is a term that shows up several times in the Spindlers' discussion of cultural therapy, one they suggest is similar to instrumental competence. Self-efficacy is just one of two types of expectations involved in this kind of situation: The second is the belief that an action will have a desired result. This is called an "outcome expectation." When we look at the development of instrumental competency, we must focus not only on the child's ability (and belief in her or his ability) to learn the competencies but also on the child's belief that the competencies will help gain the desired ends.[6]

Efficacy expectations are beliefs that one can or cannot perform a particular action. Outcome expectations are beliefs that the behavior will or will not have the desired effect. To illustrate, imagine that a teacher says, "You must do this homework so you can get a good job." Children may fail to do the homework because they do not believe they can succeed in doing it (self-efficacy) or they may fail because they do not believe that succeeding will lead to a good job (outcome). Such beliefs come from both the person's own expectations and others'. Such beliefs may be very well founded, or they may be poorly founded; in either case, they have a strong effect on action and success.

Self-efficacy has an extremely powerful influence on a person. If you do not think you can do something (like solving a math problem), every difficulty you encounter will confirm your belief; consequently, your goals, your persistence in reaching your goals, and your explanation of why you fail to reach your goals will all be affected (Bandura, 1986).

I hope the interaction of social learning, self-efficacy, and cultural situation of the self through acquisition of instrumentalities is now becoming clear. Reaffirmation, withdrawal, constructive marginality, biculturalism, and assimilation are not always the result of failure to acquire the instrumentalities of the mainstream culture in causative terms. Rather, children become situated in counutercultures in a way that is as natural as acculturation into the mainstream is for mainstream children, but this acculturation into the alternate culture too often forecloses the option to learn the instrumentalities upon which membership in the mainstream depends.

Looking back to the youths I introduced earlier, it is not adequate to say that they acquire "deficits in self-esteem when they fail to master essential instrumentalities," that "self-esteem is damaged not only by actual failure but by negative perceptions and low expectations of them by teachers and other students" (Chapter 1, this volume). They also picked up low expectations by accepting their history as their fate and by observing and living others' lives vicariously. They assimilated society's way of looking at them through their mothers' milk, in the way suggested here by Dewey (1916):

> Every individual has grown up, and always must grow up, in a social medium. His responses grow intelligent, or gain meaning, simply because he lives and acts in a medium of accepted meanings and values. Through social intercourse, through sharing in the activities embodying beliefs, he gradually acquires a mind of his own. The conception of mind as a purely isolated possession of the self is at the very antipodes of the truth. The self achieves mind in the degree in which knowledge of things is incarnate in the life about him; the self is not a separate mind building up knowledge anew on its own account. (p. 295)

But all these social media are open to individual interpretation. William is the perfect example of how perverse this experience can be. Take the relationship between William and his brother, the superathlete, superstudent, superexample.

W: Shit, I'm not him. I'm nothing like him. That's why, that's why I took a different route, so they could look at me for me. You know, that's him, he's doing what he's doing, and I was doing what I was doing. 'Cause, see, he was always trying to put me in the shadow every time. Every time we did something, like if I. . . . Like football. I was, I was real good. I got [an award] but they never said, "William got it," they said, "Sam's little brother got it." Even now, "You Sam's little brother?" I'd say, "No, I'm his brother."

F: Looking back on it, do you think you did the right thing?

W: I should of . . . Nawww. It was envy. It was envy. Like . . . See I started messing up in sixth grade. 'Cause up until sixth grade I had a B average. All Bs. Straight Bs. That's why I get in so much trouble now when I get . . . They don't even like me to get Cs, 'cause they know I can do better than that. I just don't devote my time to it. I like being in the streets.

My brother, he devoted his time to being the best one. That's what I want to do to, I just don't. I won't take the time to do all that, 'cause I feel, I feel, I feel I might miss something out on the street or something, so I won't do that. I want to be out on the street where everything is happening. That's the kind of life I like. I like to be in anything to take advantage.

So there is more than school deficits, low social expectations, and family loyalty involved in the way William moved into gangs and the gang scene and retreated from his former exemplary behavior in sports and school. There were also elements of reaction against high social expectations where envy and rivalry opposed the pressure on him to be like his brother and caused him to make a counterdemonstration to establish his own individual identity.

In living out his early life this way, William influenced the way his environment reacted to him, and this created strong pressures on his development—on his movement into gangs—and made it all the harder to reform. William was accepted as a gangster and was expected to act like one.

I wasn't planning on fighting all that crazy stuff, I didn't plan on that. That just happened, that just happened because of them, of them thinking of, thinking me being the same. Of them thinking William this, of them thinking, you know, "William, if we just say this to him, he'll fight us. You know, he'll fight us. Just go up to him and do this, he'll fight you for anything." You know, and I wasn't doing that, but, and they started pushing me. You know pushing me, push, push. I went to my house and all kind of crazy stuff you know.

The interview with William from which many of the above excerpts were taken took place after he had completed the youth at risk program, and I think his words show how cultural therapy clarified, for him, some of the fundamental values he inherited from his family. Implicit in all of the youths' testimony that you have seen is a sense of what's right and wrong about the youths' lives that did not come solely from the program or from the neighborhood gang culture. Thus, even though the youths had become situated in the counterculture, there remained an enduring self that advocated the values of the traditional/historical culture.

Self: Enduring, Situated, and Endangered

This endurance of the gangsters' original family values leads me to think that situation in a culture that violates the values of the enduring self threatens the enduring self. Abuses suffered as children appeared to have had ruinous effects on these youths' enduring selves—effects that followed them into every cultural frame they entered. In this light, the gang is yet another threat to family values; I suspect that the more the gang experiences deviate from the traditional values, and the longer the gang values become ingrained, the more the enduring self will be fragmented and stilled. I sensed in the youths' tortured portrayals of their lives a sense of loss, and I can't help wondering if there will be a time, down the road, when they can no longer make contact with their enduring selves, and when the sense of loss will become replaced by the loss: a void.

In the course room, it took very little effort to break down the ethos of the gangs. On one occasion, when the course leader took apart what the gangs stand for, nobody was willing to stand up and argue for the gangs' values. Many of their values were in the area of retribution and revenge. They justified bad things because they were payments back for bad things done to them by others. They were still having to reconcile their situation in the gang culture with their enduring family values, something that was difficult to do, something that created dissonances.

All this supports my conclusion that youths do not fail and join gangs from resisting, if resistance means being loyal to the families' historical/traditional culture. Actually, I see little difference between the enduring values of the different historical/traditional cultures. Furthermore, I conclude that the behaviors associated with being "at risk" are not simple reactions to failure to learn instrumental competencies. There is implicit in the Spindlers' description of "failure to become situated in the mainstream" a sense of rejection by the mainstream or, perhaps, a sense of retreat, but what we see in the cases of William, Jacob, and Lawrence is more like a positive attraction to the alternative culture of the neighborhood, which is, after all, the culture they grew up in.

What this means in terms of theory is that we must make a better accounting of the self in our conceptualization of the larger category, culture. The youth at risk program made this clear, for, while it focused on the cultural values of "responsibility," "support," and "communication," all of these values were arrayed around the program's concept of self. The key to the whole program was the belief and assertion that you can take control of your life. You can make yourself into whatever you want to be. You are not defined by your past. You believe you are defined by what has happened to you, but it is *your interpretation of what has happened to you* that defines you, and *that* can be changed. You cannot change what happened, but you can change how you see it. This concept of self is parallel, if not congruent with, the Spindlers' view of enduring and situated selves (G. Spindler, 1978; Spindler & Spindler, 1982, 1989a, 1989b, 1991, 1992).

The experiences of the youths I have described affirm the Spindlers' view and fill in a lot of the corners. The youths have clearly grown up in a climate of cultural conflict. Some have been unable to acquire the instrumental competencies of the mainstream culture, especially as translated into school curriculum, and some have compensated by joining gangs that provide alternative channels and competencies. The youths are short of self-esteem and what self-esteem they do have is built up around their alternative gang culture. But there are also many who appear to have chosen the gang, or have been chosen by the social expectations of their community, particularly their closest circle of peers—people for whom failure to learn school competencies appears to be an effect of the gang rather than vice versa.

An additional factor in the failure to acquire school competencies and in self-destructive behavior is the evil that has been done to the youth involved. The Spindlers (1989a) suggest that the enduring self could survive failure to acquire instrumental competencies and remain relatively intact. But this class of threats to the self affects the enduring self deeply. Episode after painful episode in the course room illustrated how destructive experiences had undermined the youths' self-concepts: Sexual abuse, emotional abuse, failure, low expectations—all became evidence justifying interpretations of low self-worth, leading to self-destructive and conflicted behavior.

In such a milieu, it is surprising they had been able to maintain any remnants of their enduring selves and enduring value systems, but they had. In conversation after conversation, it was clear that the situated selves and situational antisocial value systems that they had constructed were fragile constructions that the youths maintained only by ignoring the clamoring of their enduring selves. The situated value systems were shallow and the deeper enduring systems constantly plagued the youths with unpalatable messages. The youths could only pretend their situated competencies in the gang culture had a future, were justified by the way life was treating them, and demonstrated positive self-worth. But these pretenses were emotionally and psychologically unfulfilling. Their probable futures seemed no different than their parents' and neighbors': poor employment or unemployment, alcoholism, failed marriages, jail.

The youths were all volunteers, so we cannot conclude that the predominance of their enduring selves over their situated selves is a phenomenon common to the youths who did not volunteer. It is also possible that in time the situated values and competencies become fully internalized, that the situated values become better justified by excuses and hate.

Still, I believe it is impossible for this kind of justification scheme to be fully adaptive. I think the enduring self would always be trying to break through, creating the kind of conflicts Abe experienced, leading to black moods that compelled him to go out and shoot somebody for no reason at all.

The program's explicit purpose was to empower the youths to change, by identifying the misinterpretations around which they had situated themselves and giving them alternatives. In addition to the value put upon responsibility, support, relationship, and communication, the program identified two beneficial cultural instrumentalities whose failure to develop had prevented the youths from becoming culturally situated. They expected that this understanding would ultimately allow the youths to change. The two cultural instrumentalities were (a) the way to handle mistakes and (b) a method for handling emotions.

In the program's view, to handle your mistakes by making excuses and justifications gives your power to the excuse. To lock in your emotions gives the emotions power over you. Emotions, they suggest, should not be locked in but should be dissipated through communication. Communication, as they demonstrated in the course room, feels good, it lets the emotions out, and it allows you to accept support.

The program's alternative method for mistakes was to take responsibility for the mistakes and put them behind you. "That was then, this is now. I am not now who I was then."

The cultural therapy was inextricably interwoven with the issue of responsibility. I see the youths as having been very responsible. They held themselves responsible for everything that had happened to them: for breaking up their parents' marriages, for having been sexually abused, for not being loved, for failure. Self-blame is not a healthy kind of responsibility and the program gave them an alternative: "You are not your behavior." Responsibility means acknowledging your mistakes and putting them behind you—not tying them around your neck and carrying them around with you for all your life.

This view of self, which is quite similar to the Spindlers' concept of the enduring self, is just one of many efforts that have been made to explain the seeming paradox of a single self with multiple selves inside. Theories, such as behaviorism, that have tried to do this without keeping something like the enduring self have had difficulties as a result. We need a way to conceptualize the self-conscious mind Descartes perceived within the body (Descartes, 1955). In the course room, Arnold called this "your Sony Walkman," "you're already listening," "the little voice in the back of your head." Whatever it is, it speaks to each of us in many voices—one is commonly depicted as a figure with a halo and another as the figure with horns and spiked tail.

We should keep in mind that theories and concepts such as enduring self and situated self are metaphors that struggle to explain a more complex reality. Self-object psychologies are other attempts to explain multiple selves. According to Foulks and Schwartz (1982), "the self-object psychologies of Kohut (1971, 1972) and Kernberg (1975, 1980) provide a new conceptual scheme," in which humans are seen as mediating between a "good self" and a "bad self."

> In self-object psychology, a key determinant of the nature of self, and hence a key predictor of one's relationships with others, is the extent to which an individual has been able to integrate images of the good and bad self. In some individuals, these images are polarized into separate psychological entities representing a tendency toward "splitting of the self." (Foulks & Schwartz, 1982, p. 256)

With the youths I observed, the image of an enduring self, which mediated among or hid behind the different situated selves, seemed more apt than a view of polarized selves. In the self-object psychology view, I would expect the good self to be relatively unaffected by the consequences of the bad's machinations. But the selves who came out under Arnold's questioning in the course room appeared to be tormented selves—good selves fully aware of their evil deeds. How they faced up to those deeds varied situationally. In the course room, they were repentant. Among their homeboys, they were proud of their misdeeds. Among police, they were defensive and full of excuses and self-justifications.

The situated self is defined by a person's efforts to become situated in the mainstream culture and by being situated in alternative cultures. But the enduring self is always in the background both mediating the experience and being reinforced or compromised by it. This explains how one can supersede the situated self—how one can change oneself by changing the interpretation of past experience. To make such a change as an effort of will, there has to be someone in the driver's seat. The suggestion that you can somehow willfully put yourself above yourself to look at your interpretations of your experiences and to see how these interpretations have influenced the formulation of your self—and to see how they can be altered to create a different self—all this presupposes a separate self from the situated self.

Cultural Therapy as a Solution
to the Complexity of Social Turmoil

Social theories are often attempts to simplify social milieus that are too complex to understand without some sort of simplification. But such theories inevitably fail to capture all the relevant aspects of the situation. Moreover, as Dewey pointed out, today's theory and the actions it leads to have the ability to change tomorrow's reality. I have been trying to show just how complex and interdependent are the many causative factors involved with cultural transformation—a transformation that we all are undergoing as the present becomes the future, regardless of which culture we belong to.

The complexity of the human mind allows many things to be going on at the same time. Even more simple organisms are capable of acting out, simultaneously, interactions between self, behavior, and environment. The environment that influences the organism has in turn been affected simultaneously by the presentation the organism makes to it. The self observes its own behavior and its results, even as it changes its self-concept to stay in tune with what is happening.

Part of the complexity of social analysis arises when different levels of analysis are confused. Some social analyses give the impression that students resist schooling, resist acculturation into the mainstream. Based on my analysis, I think it is fairer to say that historical oppression led to the development of a counterculture that requires drastically different competencies than the mainstream culture. Students cannot simultaneously occupy both cultures but must either choose one or switch roles as they move back and forth from one to the other.

Many succeed in situating to both cultures, but for many students whose lives are chaotic and adversely affected by existential factors in their environment, of which we have seen some egregious examples, it is natural to conclude that they are the kind of damaged goods who are destined for life on the street, life in the "hood," life in the gang. Once they become reconciled to their status, it is difficult, often impossible, to learn a second culture academically, especially when the actual culture in which they are sited is so demanding.

It is important to recognize that the counterculture is not the historical/traditional culture and, while the counterculture has admirable qualities, it also has qualities that seriously threaten its members and their neighborhood—not to mention mainstream society.

One of the most central questions social scientists have is this: "What distinguishes the children who succeed in becoming situated in the mainstream from those who don't?" From this analysis, it seems quite likely that an essential part of the answer to that question is the effect of childhood events on the enduring self. As the Spindlers (1989a) point out, "Despite failure to develop instrumental competency in such a setting, an individual may preserve an enduring self or identity that is comparatively intact and positive" (pp. 7, 8). This is an issue, because, conversely, some children do not manage to "preserve an enduring self or identity," and therein lies the problem.

It was my observation that what put these youth at risk, above the risk that we all face in trying to live our lives, was that, for them, the enduring self was not adequate to sustain their self-esteem. The enduring self serves as a moral anchor, much like the land exerts its influence over the Apache through the connections with their oral tradition and place names in Keith H. Basso's "Stalking With Stories" (Basso, 1984). As the enduring self is endangered by its experiences, it loses the ability to guide, but not the ability of judging and self-condemnation.

I concluded that, for the children I observed, the crises of their lives were direct assaults upon the enduring self and that they tried to repair the damage to the enduring self through the types of adaptation the Spindlers referred to in the 1989a essay: reaffirmation, withdrawal, constructive marginality, biculturalism, and assimilation.

In this sense, I have come to see the enduring self as a phenomenon associated with something like Jung's collective consciousness or Rawls's (1987) overlapping consensus. Rather than seeing the enduring self as the "self that is sustained above and beyond the situated self," I now tend to see individuals as being situated in multiple cultural frames, perhaps in the manner of Goffman's (1974) frame analysis. So, if self-concept is assailed in one milieu, a person typically will find an alternative culture, such as the gang, the gym, or the local theater group, where self-esteem can be compensated.

But youth gangs only parody family values such as machismo and loyalty, and the parodied values of the new culture often oppose the values of the historical/traditional family culture in fundamental ways. Consequently, the attempt to bolster self-esteem is bound to be problematic, because either the enduring self has to be silenced for the situational self to be served or a system of rationalizations has to be developed. It makes sense to kill rival gang members or to plunder local liquor stores during riots only from the twisted perspective of the gang, not from the perspective of the family's traditional values.

Based on this interpretation, then, while I do not question that the minority cultures demand not to be white, or that most children succumb to this social pressure, I think it is inappropriate to call this "resistance." Calling it "resistance" ignores the most important levels of causation in favor of the mere impression of the end effect.

The utility of cultural therapy, as a concept of social improvement, is that its breadth accommodates these complexities. The idea of cultural therapy does not require a fixed image of the participant—in fact, it posits that the facilitator and the participant will interact reciprocally with their environment, in a manner that allows individual differences and that evolves over time.

I have described the act of opening up in terms of both process and effect, showing how the program opened people up and what came out. Opening up is therapeutic for the participant and instructive for the facilitator.

I am not fond of describing social problems in terms of power differentials, but without relying upon the neo-Marxist view of power relations, I can still see the benefit of putting both facilitator and participant on the same conceptual plane in this kind of interaction, because doing so offers a solution to the ethical problem of justifying the right to interfere with another person's life. When the facilitator does not take a superior position, but is a fellow student, the conflict of rights recedes.

A look back at the thoughts of Lawrence and William, which I presented earlier, shows that, in addition to having been opened up, the two of them were prodded into thinking constructively about their position vis-à-vis their many cultures. Their comments showed us that they had their traditional family values to hold up to these experiences as a standard—traditional values much like the mainstream's values. This was clear from Lawrence's statements: "It's not between a rag that's going to ruin a friendship." "It is crazy. It was [used to be] for your land, where you live. That was what you used to fight for. After a while it went from where you live, to a rag. It was red and blue." It was clear from William's "That's why, that's why I didn't graduate on time. I didn't get kicked out, I would have graduated. See, and all that, all that's because of gangs. 'Cause I wore my red shoes to school one day," and "I knew I was messing up. I was, I knew I was messing up but I couldn't—I could have got out of it, but I couldn't have. I could have got out of it, but I wasn't looking to get out of it."

The Spindlers suggest that cultural therapy works because it depersonalizes a person's problems by putting them into cultural terms. I think this is true, but paradoxically it also appears that in this case it worked by taking the person out of the usual social milieu, thus giving a chance for close personal reflection.

Theoretical explanations of the problems associated with poverty disagree about causes and solutions. Cultural therapy avoids these theoretical differences by dealing with culture and people on an individual basis, and this is one of its strengths. It is effective, so, regardless of the theoretical reasons given for its working, it is a valuable tool for addressing the problems associated with class and race in the United States today.

Notes

1. A rag is a colored bandanna that is worn to designate gang affiliation.

2. During the TV coverage of the L.A. riots, after the Rodney King verdict, I heard a policeman justify arresting a group of young blacks who were driving around in a pickup truck because their clothing was loose and oversized and because the truck wasn't registered to them.

3. *Claiming* means declaring allegiance to a gang.

4. Without irony, Lawrence uses the term *believe in* to denote allegiance to a color.

5. It is, of course, unfair to ascribe these views to the Spindlers out of context. I only do so to show how important having the whole context is.

6. These ideas about expectations came from Albert Bandura's social learning theory (1977).

References

Bandura, A. (1977). *Social learning theory.* Englewood Cliffs, NJ: Prentice-Hall.

Bandura, A. (1986). *Social foundations of thought and action.* Englewood Cliffs, NJ: Prentice-Hall.

Basso, K. H. (1984). Stalking with stories. In E. M. Bruner (Ed.), *Text, play and story: The construction and reconstruction of self and society.* Washington, DC: American Ethnological Society.

Descartes, R. (1955). Meditations on the first philosophy in which the existence of God and the distinction between mind and body are demonstrated. In R. M. Eaton (Eds.), *Descartes: Selections.* New York: Scribner.

Dewey, J. (1916). *Democracy and education.* New York: Macmillan.

Foulks, E. F., & Schwartz, F. (1982). Self and object. *Ethos, 10*(3), 254-278.

Goffman, I. (1974). *Frame analysis.* New York: Harper & Row.

Mosley, N. (1990). *Hopeful monsters.* Elmwood Park, IL: Dalkey Archive Press.

Rawls, J. (1987). The idea of an overlapping consensus. *Oxford Journal of Legal Studies, 7*(1), 1-25.

Spindler, G. (1978). Introduction. In G. Spindler (Ed.), *The making of psychological anthropology* (pp. 7-38). Berkeley: University of California Press.

Spindler, G., & Spindler, L. (1982). *Doing the ethnography of schooling: Educational anthropology in action.* New York: Holt, Rinehart & Winston.

Spindler, G., & Spindler, L. (1989a). Instrumental competence, self-efficacy, linguistic minorities, and cultural therapy: A preliminary attempt at interpretation. *Anthropology and Education Quarterly, 20*(1), 36-50.

Spindler, G., & Spindler, L. (1989b). *The self and instrumental model in the study of cultural change and urbanization.* Stanford, CA: Stanford University School of Education, CERAS.

Spindler, G., & Spindler, L. (1991). *The American cultural dialogue and its transmission.* Bristol, PA: Falmer.

Spindler, G., & Spindler, L. (1992). The enduring, situated, and endangered self in fieldwork: A personal account. In L. B. Boyer & R. Boyer (Eds.), *The psychoanalytic study of society: Vol. 17. Essays in honor of George and Louise Spindler* (pp. 23-28). Hillsdale, NJ: Analytic Press.

van Gennep, A. (1960). *The rites of passage.* Chicago: University of Chicago Press.

Conclusion

Reflecting on Applications of Cultural Therapy

GEORGE AND LOUISE SPINDLER

Did we accomplish what we set out to do? The colleagues who contributed chapters to this volume did successfully apply various aspects of the framework we provided in Chapter 1. In doing so, they enlarged, and in some cases challenged, those aspects.

The essential strength of these efforts is that they are empirically based. Projects requiring months of work and hundreds of hours of on-the-spot observation, interviewing, and participation were required to carry on these projects. The essential weakness of these efforts is that most were interpreted as cultural therapy in retrospect, ad hoc, ex post facto. There is an "ah hah!" quality to the interpretations that is both exciting and dangerous. "Look! What I did was cultural therapy!" The authors were aided and abetted in this by us, the editors—and, in a sense, their mentors—partly out of habit (most of them were at one time students of ours). We explicitly suggested, in some instances, that what they had been doing was cultural therapy—and it was.

The results speak for themselves. Every chapter shows us something important about a complex process we have labeled "cultural therapy." It was a good thing to do the first time around. We now have some parameters, some signposts, that designate a territory, and now it is time to design and execute programs that are intentionally and explicitly cultural therapy. Otherwise, we are in peril—that everything invoking a conversation about cultural diversity becomes cultural therapy. In a sense, it is, and perhaps we need to accept this inherent ambiguity and do the best we can to develop ground rules and procedures that will give us some control over the dynamics of the process.

Being academicians, we have to develop ways of distinguishing our special interests. As starters, we can say that cultural therapy is a process that enables actors in social scenes to be aware of the cultural basis for their perceptions and behaviors relating to other actors on the scene. The teacher—Roger Harker as prototype—learns to think about his or her perceptions, opinions, judgments, about students. She or he may think first, "That kid is resisting everything I am trying to teach him." Second, "What is my background that may make him seem this way?" And then third, "What are the reasons, given his background, or the culture of the school, or class, that may make him resistant (if he is)?"

Good teachers have always "thought thrice." At least now we have a name for it—"thrice-thinkers."

Cultural therapy requires self-other awareness in the above sense. It also requires explicit intentionality. Labeling is dangerous, as every professional educator must know. But it is also essential that we have a cognitive sense of what we are trying to do. If we are doing cultural therapy, we need to be clear that is what we are doing and what we hope to achieve by doing it.

What we are doing may not always be explicitly labeled "cultural therapy," however. There are dangers in this label. People object to receiving therapy when they don't think they are ill. And the most ill are often those who object the most vigorously. Further, everyone is "ill," culturally, in a complex society of great cultural diversity and inequity. We proceed through each day exercising our prejudices, our stereotypes, our preconceptions. We live by illusion and self-delusion, as humans do in all cultures. To rise above our own paranoia, we need help from someone outside the immediate situation we are in. The cultural therapist, if well trained, aware (a good "thrice-thinker"), can instigate, support, and, to some careful extent, guide the self-other examination process that results in self-other understanding and acquired skills in recognizing cultural diversity.

This leaves us with unresolved questions (we didn't promise you a rose garden!). One of the most perplexing is this one: "When does cultural therapy end and psychotherapy begin?" The answer is this: when *personal* problems dominate *cultural* problems. The two are not easily separated, but there is a boundary, however ambiguous it may be at times. Roger Harker serves again as an example. He had personal problems. He was hostile to his father and identified very strongly with his mother. He was, however, latently hostile to her domination but this hostility was deep in his unconscious and expressed only very obliquely in quite disguised form. He was curiously detached from his self-stated goals, apparently because he wasn't sure these goals were really *his*.

Did the complex personal relationship to his parents enter into his cultural therapy? Did George talk to him about them? Did he exhibit pathologies in relationship to male, or to female, children that demanded attention? The answer is no, no, and no! We dealt with his perceptions of and behavior toward children who represented greater cultural diversity than he, the unicultural teacher, could relate to effectively. There are psychological elements in this interaction, to be sure, but they were not the focus. We could improve his ability to recognize and relate to the culturally different (than himself) child. That was what we could do to make him professionally competent as a teacher, and eventually as an administrator. We did not resolve, or try to resolve, his complexes of identification and resistance. If he had exhibited significant behavioral manifestations of identity problems in his classroom, we would have had to bring in the psychiatrist, which we did in a few cases. The problems that cultural therapy can deal with most effectively do not require this deeply personal treatment.

A problem of quite a different order is represented by the tendency of those exploring cultural therapy as a remedial process for teachers and students in schools to be drawn more to ideas of *self* than any other. This is evident in several of the chapters. Good use is made of the concepts of enduring and situated selves but the other concepts—instrumental competence, adaptations to rapid and disjunctive culture change, and hidden cultural assumptions that affect perception, judgment, and behavior in classroom management—are underused. Why is this happening? We think that it is due to the pervasive bias in professional education toward psychological explanations. Psychology captured professional education years ago. Testing and measurement of everything in psychological terms is the sine qua non in scientific efforts in education. The curriculum must be psychologically based. Pedagogy is *psychopedagogy*. Cultural process and cultural diversity are passed over, avoided, or even rejected. Psychological concepts, methods of research, and procedures have done service for education at all levels. It is time now to consider cultural process at all levels.

We have for the past 40 years at Stanford, 7 years at the University of Wisconsin at Madison, and 5 years at the University of California at Santa Barbara, as have our colleagues at many other institutions in the United States, been presenting a cultural point of view, particularly in teacher education and in research methodology, stressing ethnography in advanced professional preparation, and we have published extensively. The effect on professional education has been minimal, though there have been effects. Until explicit, intentional cultural input, provided by qualified professionals, is a part of every teacher training and professional educational program in the United States, we will be fighting an uphill battle to do anything resembling cultural therapy in the schools.

This is the discouraging aspect of the situation. The positive aspect is that we have gotten started, and the recognition of cultural factors in "multicultural" education, and of the real situation in our culturally diverse schools and communities, is growing, as we try to cope with reality in America.

As a last comment in retrospect—we are surprised to find that nowhere in this volume is much attention paid to the influence of gender on perception and behavior in our schools. Gender is a basic form of diversity. In all of our work in schools in California, Wisconsin, and Germany, gender has proven to be a major factor in everything we studied. Whenever we paid careful attention to gender differences in perception and behavior, it proved to be more important than any other single form of influence including parental occupations, religion, degree of urbanization, and even age.

Perhaps gender is so pervasive an influence that we take it for granted except when it causes trouble. We all work with gender differences (and similarities) all day, every day. We "know" that females mature faster than males, that girls are generally less trouble in class than boys, that more African American females than males succeed in school and that many more apply for college entrance, that in modernization programs abroad as well as at home it is the young women, not the young men, who move most quickly and effectively into jobs and job training, that males are better at math and science, and so on. Of course, gender differences are social constructions—that is, gender is given meanings by humans in every human community—but there are some cross-cultural regularities. The "facts" are observable but the explanations of them are complex, and politically loaded. We have tried to untangle the knot in our own way for the cultures we have worked in (Spindler & Spindler, 1990).

Do females respond differently to cultural therapy than do males? Are they more sensitive to cultural diversity, expressed in social relations and communications, than are males? Do males retreat more often and with greater intensity to peer relationships as a source of security? Are males more likely to be resistant to learning as academically phrased? These and many more questions call for study—not in a search for inherent differences but in a search for the cultural politics of gender as they affect behavior in schools. There is a great body of literature on behaviors related or relatable to cultural therapy. Special attention can be paid to gender and reflectivity, communication, self-revelation, interpretation of past experience, empathy with others, and so on during the process of cultural therapy. These questions and problems are not treated in the nine chapters responding to the framework we set forth, and they are not issues in the statement of the framework itself.

There is much more to be said about the chapters in this book, and about cultural therapy, but this seems to be a good place to stop—with a challenge, some self-criticism, and some questions.

Reference

Spindler, G., & Spindler, L. (1990). Male and female in four changing cultures. In D. Jordan & M. Swartz (Eds.), *Personality and the cultural construction of society.* Tuscaloosa: University of Alabama Press.

Author Index

Subject Index